Words that Must Somehow Be Said

Edited and with an Introduction by Elizabeth S. Bell

North Point Press   San Francisco   1985

The editor and author extend their thanks to the
original publishers of these essays.

To E.R. Hagemann

E.B.

Contents

Introduction

"Surely no greater reward is offered to a writer than the knowledge that other men are reading the words that he has, by some miracle, retrieved from the depths of his own silence; the knowledge that other men are actually listening for the sound of his voice to call out from the page to them, and, above all, the knowledge that they believe the words they hear." The words belong to Kay Boyle, written almost two decades ago about the Italian poet Emanuel Carnevali. Yet these words explain a great deal about Kay Boyle herself and her extraordinary conscience as a writer who has, in many ways, recorded for us the entire twentieth century. Appropriately the essays in this collection reflect both literary and political matters, for she has been in the forefront of this century's major cultural and political movements almost since her birth in St. Paul, Minnesota, in 1902.

Her involvement, she has always maintained, is due mainly

to the influence of two rather extraordinary women: her grandmother who at sixteen became a schoolteacher in frontier Kansas, and her mother who encouraged the young Kay to exper-
iment with ideas by such enlightened means as taking the
child to the 1913 Armory Art Show in New York City where
a jeering, mocking, less sophisticated American public received its first introduction to Cubism and other forms of
modern art. Kay's mother also read to her and her sister the
avant-garde writers such as Gertrude Stein and the early
James Joyce. From childhood on, then, she became accustomed to new concepts and to new ways of seeing the old ones.

During the 1920s Kay Boyle herself became a member of
the movement of protest against conventional art and thought,
first in America and later in Europe. She worked first as an
assistant to Lola Ridge on Harold Loeb's New York magazine *Broom*, which published then-unheard-of young writers
such as Glenway Wescott, Waldo Frank, and Matthew Jo-
sephson, and here she developed friendships—for example
with William Carlos Williams—that would last a lifetime.
A few years later she would become one of the first reviewers
to recognize the full significance of Williams's classic prose
study of America, *In the American Grain* (1925). Her review
of this work praised his search for authenticity in the "chastity
of fact" from the American past. Williams's own experience
as a doctor led to his occasional outrage at those facts, for
example at the countless women dying in childbirth in the
pioneer days, "shooting children against the wilderness like
cannon balls." Yet he called also for recognition of the vitality
and grandeur of the American national heritage. It was a
message Boyle found stirring.

Kay Boyle, too, called for renewal and spirit in both language and message, as her writing from these earliest days
illustrates. She brought life to her works by drawing on her
own experiences in her fiction, and in so doing, brought a

very personal viewpoint to her characters and plots. The early evidence of this can be found in *Plagued by the Nightingale* (New York, 1931), her first novel. In somewhat fictionalized form she chronicles her life in France with the traditional French Catholic family of her first husband. She also wrote poetry, and one of her earliest poems, "Harbor Song," was published by *Poetry* in February 1925. Prose and poetry of hers were published in Ernest Walsh's *This Quarter*, and by the late 1920s she was involved with the convention-shattering "Revolution of the Word," an esthetic movement founded by Eugene Jolas, editor of the predominantly English language "little magazine" *transition* in which many of the French, as well as American, writers who were living in Europe were published during the 1920s and 1930s. She completed several other novels, among them *Year Before Last* (New York, 1932), *Gentlemen, I Address You Privately* (New York, 1933), and *My Next Bride* (New York, 1934), both of which are based in part on her life with the avant-garde in Europe, for even in these early years she displayed what would become one of her enduring trademarks as a writer— an unswerving dedication to reflecting in her work life as she perceived it. The actual events on which these novels are based are recorded in *Being Geniuses Together: 1920–1930*, by Robert McAlmon and Kay Boyle ([1968], 1984) which remains one of the best accounts of life in Paris during the glittering decade of the 1920s.

She never thought of herself as an expatriate, for at that time an American woman had to take the nationality of the man she married, and she had traveled to France on her first husband's French passport. Thus Kay Boyle remained at home in Europe during the 1930s when most other American writers returned to the United States. During that decade she wrote most of her novels and gathered prestigious American awards for her short stories. In addition to the O. Henry

Award for the year's best short story, which she won twice—for "The White Horses of Vienna" in 1935 and "Defeat" in 1941—she also appeared regularly in E. J. O'Brien's annual Roll of Honor for best short stories to appear in American publications. Her reputation as a stylist who had mastered the demands of the short story established her as a major literary voice. While her primary interests at this time remained fiction and poetry, the events of World War II and the years immediately following it prompted her to develop her commitment to the essay form.

In June 1941, when it was obvious that the European war would be of unbelievable proportions, Kay Boyle and her family traveled by train to Lisbon, where after a wait of six weeks they were able to book passage on the *Clipper* for the United States. After the war she returned to Europe, this time not as a freelance writer but as a correspondent for the *New Yorker*. Her stories reflected the changes she found in France and Germany and the problems postwar Europe had to overcome. She wrote at times with a sense of outrage at the lingering Nazi sympathy among segments of the people in both France and Germany; at other times, as in the part-story, part-essay "Frankfurt in Our Blood," she wrote with compassion about the suffering that remained in the aftermath of war. As an American who had lived for years on the European continent, she brought her unique insight to her evaluations; as a richly evocative writer, she enabled her readers to empathize with the subjects of her essays.

In the 1950s Kay Boyle's focus again changed. She was a target of McCarthyism and found that most of the journals that had previously begged for her work now avoided publishing her. *The Nation*, however, continued to print her articles, and those pieces, including "Farewell to Europe" and "No Time to Listen," record with vividness and sensitivity the plight of victims of prejudice and inhumanity.

By this time her involvement with political issues was well established. Although she continued to produce novels, short stories, and poetry, her nonfiction gained a stature and a maturity that could not be ignored. She became extremely active in the Civil Rights movement of the 1960s and in the protest against United States involvement in Vietnam; her experiences as protester became the basis for "Report from Lockup" and a novel, *The Underground Woman* (New York, 1975). More recently, she has been an organizer and active supporter of Amnesty International in San Francisco for over a decade. She writes of injustice in many of its settings, from Attica prison to the Indian encampment on Alcatraz Island, where several American Indian tribes laid claim to the abandoned prison in order to protest governmental violations of their land and culture.

Kay Boyle continues to be an active and vocal advocate of human rights and human dignity, as she has been, consistently, in her long and productive career. Her concern has always been with people, and her work—in both fiction and nonfiction—constitutes an impressive document on the dignity and resilience of the human being. From the beginning of her literary career, she has used her voice to make known the cries of the socially, emotionally, and politically voiceless. The essays in this collection show the development of her extraordinary consciousness: "I felt an obligation to speak (as Camus put it) for those 'throughout the world who have need that all those who can speak should give voice to their silence.'"

In the essays of this collection, whether they discuss literary topics or political ones, Kay Boyle combines the imagery and phrasemaking of her poetry with the character and scene-making of her prose fiction. The synthesis produces an amazing array of styles and forms, from the mock-epic "Battle of the Sequins," to the poignant narrative of "Frankfurt in Our Blood" with its "half-bottles of wine that made them speak."

She engraves sharp, clear scenes on the reader's mind: the frail young pregnant woman with whom she shared a jail cell, the Spaniard telling of his dead friends whose faces mysteriously appeared on brand-new identity photographs, Dylan Thomas struggling with himself and his talent. She transports us there, wherever "there" happens to be, and makes us see, almost as if literally, what she has witnessed. For example, in "Report from Lock-up" we meet her cellmates and join their imaginary escapes to Alaska, their letter writing, and their bouts of fear and anger. In "The Jew Is a Myth" we share another prison, the Vélodrome d'Hiver in Paris, crowded with eleven thousand Jews en route to concentration camps. The date is July 16, 1942, and the scene—"the ring of misery"—suggests a landscape from Dante's *Inferno*. Kay Boyle carries us to places most of us have been spared, but her words make us see even the familiar from new perspectives.

Sometimes she is almost strident, as in "The Crime of Attica"; sometimes she is ironic, as in the self-mocking "No Time to Listen." Always, however, her concern is for her message, contained in "words [that] make an oasis, richly green and deep with shadows in the parched wasteland of daily life." As a writer she has always recognized her responsibility to the human community: to convey the realities of human existence, even when those realities shatter our carefully constructed illusions. She wants her readers to care, as deeply as she does, about our relationships as human beings. As she tells us in "The Teaching of Writing," "If we as writers . . . can communicate that quite simple truth to others, then we shall have fulfilled our roles."

I. ON THE BEGINNINGS

*"Look into Memory's Dreamy,
  Evasive Eyes"*

The Family

"The retrieval of childhood experience," Janet Malcolm wrote recently in the *New York Review of Books*, "is one of the most mysteriously unpropitious of human endeavors. . . . Neither of the two 'I's' through which the story of a childhood is told is trustworthy: the testimony of the child, who was there, is lacking in understanding; the testimony of the adult, who is omniscient, is lacking in authenticity. At best, an uneasy truce between the child (memory) and the man (understanding) is achieved."

Yet writer after writer, century after century, at the risk of further troubling that precarious truce, feels compelled to set down a record of half-truths and elusive images, giving it a deceptive life on the printed page. The justification for the adult's scrutiny of the childhood years may be that it is a search for the reasons for the success or failure of the adult's life. But in that search may intrude the quite innocent, quite unconscious shifting of the blame for failure on others, while success may be at least in part attributed to the flawed recollections of one's own discriminating will. Nabokov called out almost in desperation for memory to speak, but how accurately is overburdened memory able to respond? Sean O'Casey, in recounting his life, avoided the unabashed first person singular and told the story of Sean as if it were the life of another man—a man, moreover, whom he did not know very well. There is no way for even the most honest among us to look into memory's dreamy, evasive eyes and know she can be persuaded not to lie, not to betray.

There are also autobiographical diaries, such as Cosima Wagner's and Anaïs Nin's, in which memory fails time and again to speak with accuracy; and there are memoirs such as Frank Harris's, banned and censored in their time, that are written out of the need to embellish the sexual potency of the vain and continuously rejected lover. The role Harris sought to play—and there are countless others who have played it in any number of languages in their literary confessions— was that of the insatiable and depraved sensualist who found no perversion too unspeakable to gratify his lust, which he claimed to have gratified with a proficiency it is doubtful he possessed. (Mrs. Harris once confided to me that her husband had confessed to her that not a word of the memoirs of his past life was true.) Yeats wrote in his *Autobiography* (1926) that at least a portion of his childhood misery was due to fear of his grandfather, although he could not recall his grandfather ever speaking harshly to him. "There was no reason for my unhappiness," Yeats wrote (as quoted in Daniel T. O'Hara's *Tragic Knowledge*, 1981), and then proceeded to offer a reason or two to justify his childhood's "morbid broodings."

With all of this very much in mind, I wish to say that I look on my childhood as an exceptionally valuable one. Both memory and unfaltering conviction tell me that this was because my mother gave me definitions that were miraculously free of dogma. I say "miraculously" because they were definitions of such grace that I could consider them in peace and quiet, alone, and find reassurance in their lack of contentiousness, their lack of implied authority. In Robert McAlmon's and my book, *Being Geniuses Together* ([1968], 1984), I wrote that because of her I knew from the beginning what my commitments were to be in life, and because my father and grandfather offered statements instead of revelations, I at least learned what I did not wish to be.

My remembrance of a childhood without ennui, without tears, and without the morbid brooding of which Yeats wrote, may be an illusion. I remember well the various illnesses which appeared to single me out for punishment, but I remember with a joy that has never diminished that very early in my life my mother, small, delicate-boned, witty, and articulate, who spoke of the stars as if they were acquaintances, turned out to be exactly my age. Because of continuous bad health as she grew up on the Kansas prairies, she had had barely any education, and so her spirit (I wrote in *Being Geniuses Together*) "remained fervent and pure."

There seemed to me no reason why I should ever go to school as she had rarely done so, and as a child she had had the time to reflect on many things as she hung, suspended in a brace intended to correct the curvature of her spine. As if collecting persuasive evidence why I should stay at home, I had a long siege with whooping cough when I was three, after which I had to learn to walk again; and it was a year later that I lost all my hair after typhoid fever and for a long while had to wear a tan silk cap; and then came the terrifying experience at the kindergarten across the road from us in Germantown, Pennsylvania, an experience which was the final argument in my case against my ever having to go to school. It was my first day there, and five minutes after I had entered that alien environment two little boys, sophisticated members of the preschool set, closed me in the total darkness of the cloak-room closet which I had submissively entered to hang up my coat. I was not found by the teacher until what seemed to me hours later but was probably five minutes, paralyzed with fright. The darkness of the cloakroom increased in impene-trability until it became in time symbol for the threat of all situations, all locations, that were not home.

The kindergarten crisis, reinforced by the frequent ill-nesses, had its effect upon the family. Mother gently ex-pressed the view that there would always be time in the years ahead for education. After all, my sister, two years older than I, promised to do brilliantly in everything she undertook: piano and drawing, swimming and dancing school; and, as time progressed, she earned straight A's in every subject; and she was to keep that promise throughout her life. Mother's untroubled and intuitive knowledge about books and paint-ing, theatre and music, people and politics, was my entire education. The bits and pieces of formal schooling I was later subjected to came to nothing at all. I can think of nothing and no one that Mother excluded from her awareness, and all that enchanted her, all that stirred her deeply, she poured out to me, explaining, gossiping, laughing, like one child con-fiding in another. The names were never to be forgotten. Ger-trude Stein, George Moore, Dreiser, Shaw, Isadora Duncan, Caruso, Romain Rolland, George Santayana, Oswald Gar-rison Villard, Mary Garden, James Joyce, John Cowper Powys, Alice Paul, Alfred Stieglitz, Norman Angell, Susan B. Anthony, Mozart, Upton Sinclair, Margaret Anderson, Jane Heap, Bach, Eugene Debs, Jules Massenet, Cézanne, Manet, Picasso, some in my childhood, some later, were among the many her enchantment with them brought to life for me. She could make even the dead live, for she knew that in the scheme of things there really were no dead.

It was not for a moment that she was awed by these names, nor did she ever seek to make the acquaintance of the women and men who stood behind them. Her friendship with Alice Paul and Alfred Stieglitz came about in quite simple and natural ways, and her acquaintance with Mary Garden and Powys was brought about by her wish to help a beautiful and talented young woman and a shy professor of literature in their separate careers.* Mother transformed the legendary names into familiar people whose dedication to their work set them apart. I do not know how, among countless other divinations, she realized it was important to take me to the Ar-

---

*Marie Lawall, who had studied singing in France and Italy, was a guest at the Meadowside Inn one winter, and Mother was impressed by the quality of her voice as she heard her practicing arias from *Louise* and *Thaïs* and *Pelléas et Mélisande* hour after hour every day. A note written to Mary Garden in care of the Chicago Opera Company brought a quick reply, and Mary Garden invited Mother and Marie to lunch in her New York hotel apartment. Several times as Marie sang, Mary Garden struck with one finger the key of high C on the piano, and exclaimed with delight. Marie Lawall became one of her protégées.

The sad, shy young professor was quite another matter. He longed to meet Powys in the wild hope of persuading him to speak informally to one of his classes, and he hoped that if Mother, after attending one of Powys's public lectures, invited the great man to dinner, this might be done. So Mother went to an afternoon lecture in Philadelphia, and Powys graciously agreed to dine at our house a week from that day. The young professor's wish was granted during cocktails before dinner, but then an unfortunate thing took place. In future years, Mother would tell friends about it and even laugh, but on that evening it was close to tragedy. Mother had planned the dinner with special care: there would be cream of artichoke soup, followed by a great, broiled salmon surrounded by miniature snowballs of new potatoes sprinkled with bright parsley—this is the way Mother would tell it—and when the white wine had been poured by our little maid into the long-stemmed glasses, and the beautiful salmon passed first to Mother and then to the guest of honor, Powys said: "I think I'll wait for the meat course."

mory Show in New York in 1913 to see Marcel Duchamp's "Nude Descending a Staircase" and Brancusi's "Mlle. Pogany" and his "Bird in Space." (But what Mother did not and could not have divined then was that exactly thirty years later Duchamp would be godfather to my son. Nor could she know that in Paris in the twenties, when Brancusi went off to other cities where his sculptures were being shown, he would leave his snow-white Samoyed with me to care for.) Isolated as Mother was from the literary scene, I also cannot explain her understanding of the urgent need to send word of support to Margaret Anderson, who was threatened with arrest for publishing in the *Little Review* chapters of Joyce's banned *Ulysses*. In a family that kept silent about many things, it was Mother alone who sent Margaret Anderson a telegram when she learned of the action the authorities might take.

In that far time of my childhood, there was no way for it to occur to me that it was perhaps out of an unending loneliness that Mother allied herself with the books written, paintings painted, music composed by men and women she would never know. It was difficult to speak at the dinner table at night of the acts of moral courage achieved by total strangers, inasmuch as the men of the family spoke of more familiar things. It was because of instances such as these that Mother and I became part of a conspiracy of silence and discretion, one that involved a great many people, some of whom lived in other countries, a conspiracy to bring to life another reality in which one could put one's faith and it would never be betrayed. Mother did not insist that I be a part of this clandestine deal she had made with strangers. She did no more than indicate milestones to measure the distance of my understanding, and those milestones are still there.

There was another complicity in her life, and that was her covert alliance with the underprivileged, the lost, the poor. She herself had no power, no money, not even an allowance from her father-in-law, my grandfather Boyle, whom my sister and I had nicknamed Puss. He gave his daughter so generous an allowance that she was able to travel to Europe every summer and he financed my father in all his hapless enterprises, but I think the exception he made with Mother was shrewdly planned. Wherever we lived he loved to take Mother shopping in all the finest stores; he would sit and chat wittily with the elegant and obsequious salesladies as he waited for Mother to come out of the various fitting-rooms to ask his opinion on every dress, and coat, and shoe that she tried on.

Our light-skinned, middle-aged, little maid, Fanny, who was active in an organization that worked for the ballot for women, was about the same size as Mother, and she would say to me as she stood in the laundry room ironing or polishing silver, "Your mother would give the clothes off her back to anyone who needed them," and that is what Mother did. So that the Boyle family wouldn't see, it was only on Sundays and on her days off, that Fanny would wear the dresses and coats and the fine shoes that Mother had given her. In Germantown, it was the Irish postman who walked seven miles a day and had trouble with his feet. He liked to sit in the kitchen and have a cup of coffee with Mother and talk to her about his fallen arches. With five children and a wife to support, the salary he was paid was barely enough to keep body and soul together, he said. And Mother would tell him that postmen should organize as women were now organizing all over America. There was her sister, for instance, a government employee in Washington, she would tell him, who after her work would go from door to door in the evenings, ringing doorbells and asking for signatures supporting the right of women to vote. One night her sister had rung the doorbell of a minister, and he refused to sign the petition, saying that woman's place was in the home. And she had asked the minister whose home he would suggest she go to, asking this logical question very quietly, and the minister had shut the door in her face. "I don't think a priest would have done that," the postman said, and he asked what my aunt in Washington, walking like that every evening, had done about her feet.

And there was also the shabby skeleton of the blind man in Philadelphia who stood motionless, day after day, with his head bowed and his back pressed against the wall of the telephone company's building. He was like a dead hawk hung up as a caution to all the others hurrying by, a warning not to grow old and never to be poor. He didn't seem to have any teeth, so his mouth was tightly closed like a leather purse and from a strap around the neck of his long, dark overcoat, which the mist of time was turning gray, hung a little tray of pencils, and beside them a tin cup to drop your money into. Only for Mother would he open the purse of his mouth, and say a few words about God blessing the kind and generous rich. In winter she brought him a pair of Puss's fur-lined gloves and put them on his stiff, red hands, and wiped his cheeks with her handkerchief when he began to cry.

Whether we lived in Philadelphia, or Germantown, or Bryn Mawr, or Washington, or Atlantic City, in the evenings Mother would read aloud to my sister and me. (My father and grandfather would also read to us, but not with any regularity, for they had the responsibility of work to do.) Mother read us *The Wind in the Willows*, and Lewis Carroll, and Francis Hodgson Burnett's *The Secret Garden* and *Little Lord Fauntleroy*; and later it was Carl Sandburg and Walt Whitman, and *Pride and Prejudice*, and *Emma*, and *Sense and Sensibility*, while she sat in an armchair between our two four-poster beds, her small feet in silver mules ready to run to the telephone ringing in the hall. If it was her mother who called, it would be a long conversation. Grandma Evans had worked for the Department of the Interior in Washington since 1881, so she was not able to be with us often, and Mother loved her better than anyone else in the world. If it was Mother's un-happy, older sister, Mother's voice became solicitous at once, for before we were born Aunt Nina had had a great tragedy in her life, and it was feared at times that old man suicide might be slouching around.

While Mother talked and listened, listened and talked, my sister and I, sitting up in bed in our nightgowns, went on with the drawings we always made to illustrate the stories Mother read. We felt in some way guilty if we put our pencils down for even a moment in order to stretch our fingers and relax our hands. If we weren't drawing with care and con-cern, we knew we should be trying to write stories and poems of our own, or at least letters to Mother's friends who had such fascinating names as Aunt Grassy, and Martine Ritten-house, and Mrs. Carrie Chapman Catt. If Jane Austen had not died nearly a hundred years before, Mother surely would have written to her to tell her of our responses to her books, as she had written to Kenneth Grahame concerning our feel-ings about Mr. Toad. Kenneth Grahame answered her letter very promptly, mentioning in it that he was a bank teller in London, and that he had written *The Wind in the Willows* between his working hours. (Years later we learned that he deeply deplored the Industrial Revolution and that he was actually Secretary of the Bank of England.) He wrote to Mother with great warmth and said that he seriously doubted Mr. Toad would ever be permanently reformed, so he dared not risk a sequel to the book, as my sister had suggested. Mother pasted the letter on the title page of our copy, and it remained there among the things we valued until all we owned was sold at auction (including the mahogany four-poster beds we had always slept in, my sister and I, and my gilded altar to the Buddha, and the Persian rugs, and Puss's rolltop desk, and the section bookcases we had, as children, transformed into art galleries and museums for our dolls, and the teakwood tea wagon, carved with oriental landscapes and figures, trees, and waterfalls of the greatest delicacy, that I wheeled into the sitting room every afternoon at five). Oh, I tell you, it was like a royal family going into exile and penury when the Boyle dynasty came to an end.

But that was some years ahead, and meanwhile when my father undertook to read to us at night it was Robert Louis Stevenson and Sir Walter Scott, and their dullness made me restless. Our grandfather Puss read us Conrad and Kipling (instead of the Irish poets, which it was surely his responsibility to do) and the lack of imagination in the minds of these two authors has depressed me ever since. The man we never found a nickname for, who was merely called Dad, read to us usually on weekends, for it was necessary for him to salvage what was left of his pride by making a great deal, in his muted, almost apologetic way, of the demands of his occupation during the week. When we lived in the Burlington Apartments in Philadelphia, Dad had been a partner in a bookshop Puss had put up the capital for which came to nothing in the end. It was not that he did not know enough about books, or that he was not a polite, if rather ill at ease, salesman. It was quite simply and quite tragically that he knew he would fail in whatever he undertook to do. He had dropped out of the University of Pennsylvania in his junior year, having persuaded himself that he would not be able to make it through his final exams. And the illusion of that fourth year, which he had feared to give reality to, must have stood immovable there for the rest of his life, impeding the way, arms folded, staring him down. It may all have been because Puss wanted no male rivalry in the family he presided over with such charm, such winning, gracious tyranny that he had come close to effacing my father from the scene; or that almost total obliteration may have come about because of something Grandma Boyle had done to her son a long, long time before.

She had died when my sister and I were still quite young, so she did not play a part of any immediacy in our lives. But I can still remember her beauty, even in old age, a beauty marred only by her wrinkled, ruby lips (which had never been debased by lip-rouge or by the depravity of wine). They were as stringent as if the taste of acid were always on her tongue, and her words themselves were warped and twisted by that acidity. Once, because of some minor infringement of decorum, she made my sister sit for three hours without moving a muscle in a dark, leather-seated chair whose elaborately carved arms seemed to hold her prisoner. And because Grandma Boyle's telling of still another tale was like a warning given us, I remember the story of her violent confrontation with her son when he was three or four years old. "As the twig is bent, so the tree will grow," she would say in bitter satisfaction, and with this in mind, she had told him one day to go upstairs and pick up his jumble of railway tracks and tunnels and other toys so that the chambermaid could clean his room. For the first time in his life (and also the last, it so happened) he had flown into a rage, and she had picked up a bucket of cold water ("It was winter," she would add, "and the water was really cold") that the stable boy was taking out to the horses, and she threw it over her son. "And that fixed that!" she would end in acrimonious triumph, her lips twisted by venom and outrage because of having to put up with such creatures as the rest of us.

And one other thing: the Evans side of the family never addressed Grandma Boyle as Jenny, although she called them by their first names, Eva, and Nina, and Kate. But to them she was always "Mother Boyle," as if the single word "mother" might recall to her the less severe aspects of parenthood. But

is all autobiography, including the inquiry into one's childhood, no more than a passing of judgment on others? The
evidence given here may not justify the sentences I have
passed on father, grandfather, and grandmother; but because
they are dead they cannot file an appeal, and there is no one
left to speak in their defense. Had I known Roland Sampson's
still unwritten books in that far past, and had I learned at
long last how to read, I would have sat on Grandma Evans's
lap, and she would have helped me when I stumbled on the
words. And slowly and fearfully I would have read aloud:

> The moral law rests on the fact that it is possible for every human
> being to develop in greater or lesser degree in one direction or
> another. He may seek to order his life and his relations with
> others on the basis of love or on the basis of power. The two
> forces are antithetical, but are directly related to each other, in
> so far as it is impossible to develop in both directions at the same
> time. To the extent that we develop our capacity for power we
> weaken our capacity for love; and conversely, to the extent that
> we grow in our ability to love we disqualify ourselves for success
> in the competition for power. To the extent that the forces of love
> in men triumph over the forces of power, equality among men
> prevails. . . . To the extent that the forces of power prevail over
> the forces of love, domination and subjection characterize hu-
> man relations. . . . The struggle between these dialectical
> forces is always the same. No one may contract out of it, however
> much he may wish to do so.
>
> (Ronald V. Sampson, *The Psychology of Power*, 1968)

If it was not the matter of the bucket of cold water, it may
possibly have been the trip to England which Dad had taken
with his sister, Madge, that had broken his heart in two. She
was perhaps eighteen or nineteen then, and he in his early
twenties, and Puss had sent them off for the summer on a
handsome tandem bicycle. He wanted them to see with their

own eyes where he had been in boarding school when he was a boy and where he had lived as a young man when he studied for the priesthood. (It was there, in the cottage they visited, that he had met for the first time his cousin Jenny, who was traveling with her mother in Europe that summer. The beautiful Jenny was eight years his senior, but that didn't matter at all to him. He had abandoned his calling, followed her back to America, and they were married in Philadelphia the following year.)

But the bicycle trip that my father and his sister had set out on had been a very distressing one for him. Aunt Madge rode in front, guiding them up the hills and through the glades and down the dales of the English countryside, while he pumped doggedly at the rear; for it so happens that the hardest work is done by the rider on the back seat, and on steep hills it is his energy alone that makes the wheels go around. But the inhabitants of the boroughs and hamlets they rode through were apparently ignorant of this and they jeered and called out insults at him as the two Yanks on the tandem bicycle sped by. It was not easy for him to bear the false accusations that were shouted out, the unjust charges that he was letting a lady do the hard work up there in front, while he took things at his ease behind. Once he had thought seriously of getting off the tandem and explaining the true reason for his riding in the rear, but he noticed one of the villagers had a pitchfork raised menacingly in his hand, he told us, and the last thing he wanted to do was to cause an international incident, so he and Aunt Madge pretended they had noticed nothing and pedalled on.

As far back as I can remember there was verbal violence at home as well. Inexplicable outbursts of rage and vituperation would occur between Puss and Aunt Madge, his daughter, startling everyone in the house. Aunt Madge was the attacked and Puss the attacker, but her spirit was somehow never broken. From the top floor of the Atlantic City house down to Nettie's and Fanny's remote quarters off the laundry room, their raised voices could be heard, Aunt Madge's at times muted by her tears. I would go quickly to the haven of my little workroom and close the door with trembling hands, and kneel down before the statue of Buddha on his gilded altar, and plead with him and the pure white, china Goddess of Mercy to intervene. And Mother would close her own door quietly, for this was not the kind of passing of judgment that one could share with others. It would have been some kind of disloyalty if we had done so, so each of us faced it in silence, quite alone. Dad, his shoulders always a little stooped and his hair beginning to go grey at the temples in the Atlantic City days, would slip out the front door and walk quickly down the street, as if he had an urgent appointment somewhere else, and he didn't want to be late getting there.

What caused these hideous scenes I cannot remember, and probably never knew. It may have been something as serious as Aunt Madge forgetting to give Puss a telephone message from his Wall Street broker, or her beginning to go to the Methodist Church every Sunday, or as trivial as her having told Nettie to serve creamed chipped beef on toast for lunch instead of liver and bacon and hashed brown potatoes, or because his immaculate white shirts had not been properly starched and ironed by Fanny, whom he believed had too many political issues on her mind.

(My sister and I had never been taken to any church, nor had we been baptized, because the family could not agree to which place of worship we should go. Puss had studied for the priesthood, we knew, and Grandma Boyle had been a Presbyterian, while Grandma Evans was a Christian Scientist. It was so involved, this question of what should be done for us spiritually, that we dismissed it from our minds, and the family apparently did likewise. And after I had gone with

Mother to Philadelphia to hear Mary Garden sing in Massenet's *Le Jongleur de Notre Dame*, I was reassured. If the young, wandering juggler could give homage to the Virgin by playing his violin and juggling the carved silver spheres of his trade before the altar, then I too could express my reverence by dancing and singing before my Buddha's gold and lacquer temple, and writing the life of the real Buddha in blank verse to run as a serial in our magazine. The poem never got beyond a description of the four signs the young Buddha had seen one day that had immediately given him the knowledge of what his concerns in life should be. These signs were as terrifying to me as they must have been to him when he saw them outside the palace walls: a man bent almost double with age, a sick man, a corpse, and a wandering beggar, but my blank verse was very blank indeed.)

As for Puss's apoplectic rages, it occurred to me in later years that Aunt Madge's lack of graciousness and charm compared to Mother, with whom he genially disagreed on every subject on earth, but with whom I believe he was very much in love, was at the heart of his fury. Once, after Mother had persuaded him to have lunch with her and Alice Paul, he complained that Alice did not have "a kissable mouth," the gauge, he often said, by which he judged every woman he met. Aunt Madge had also apparently failed this test. Before dinner on the days the ferocious diatribes had been exchanged on the third floor, Puss would ask Nettie to have a bottle of iced champagne and three chilled glasses brought into the living room; and then he, who never touched alcohol, would dance his little Irish jig and sing his little Scottish song: "For the heart of O'Hara was good as gold / And the life of O'Hara was bright and bold / And his smile was precious to young and old!"

On those evenings, he could call out in a merry voice to the family sitting in silence there, "What are you all in the doldrums about? What's happened to all of you?" and no one would answer him. Mother would ask to be excused and go quietly upstairs, past the marble bust of Beatrice on one side of the landing and the plaster bust of Dante on the other. (God knows which member of the family was responsible for their presence there, but it was Mother who told us the story of their love.) Aunt Madge's tears were ready to fall again, and her hand trembled as she lifted the soaked ball of her handkerchief to her nose. Dad poured the champagne into two of the long-stemmed glasses, as Puss had directed him to do, and Aunt Madge quickly took a swallow, and my father did the same, while my sister and I sat silently waiting for Nettie, tall as a giant in her long white apron, to come in and, as was her custom, curtsy to Puss as she said in a voice like a lullaby that dinner was served.

The winter spent in Bryn Mawr was perhaps the year 1914, and we lived through the slush of snow and darkness in John Singer Sargent's house. It was the first winter of the war in Europe, and, at Puss's urging, Dad had volunteered to serve on the advisory board of the Children's Homeopathic Hospital in Philadelphia. Like a regular businessman, he commuted back and forth by train every day. At times he would bring home medical colleagues to dinner, and as demi-tasses and liqueurs were served in the living room, Mother would read to the guests from Gertrude Stein's *Tender Buttons*, which had just been published. She believed quite simply that men advanced in the practice of medicine would natu-rally be interested in evidence of the parallel literary advances of our time. As she never in her life had been known to bore anyone, these evenings in John Sargent's house, which I was allowed to attend, had a salutary effect on both the humble and the proud.

Mother also liked to read to others a story of mine which dealt with the protocol of the Brandenburg Tor in Berlin, where we had spent a month two years before. I had just completed the final draft of the imaginary incident describing the daily ride Kaiser Wilhelm II took down Unter den Linden. His uniformed and bemedalled bodyguard rode behind him, the brightly colored plumes on his helmet streaming on the wind, his sword held high in his right hand, his withered left arm hanging forgotten by his side. He was a fine figure of a man until one day a shocking thing took place. To the horror of the assembled crowds lining the sidewalks and to his mounted bodyguard, his prancing horse took the bit in its teeth and raced through one of the lesser arches of the Tor instead of through the middle arch, the one reserved for royalty. The difference between Gertrude Stein's work and mine, Mother would say after the readings, was that Miss Stein's was intended to be true and not humorous, while mine, as original as hers, was humorous as well as allegorical. In Mother's eyes, Stein and I were of equal importance as writers of the modern school.

During the Bryn Mawr winter, another attempt was made to give me a formal education, this time at Miss Shipley's School, where my sister was a brilliant student. But, like my father's repetition of fiascoes, I too failed again. I can remember the depths of my despair over multiplication tables, an anguish as devastating as the early years of trying to learn to read. And I can remember one harrowing morning at recess time for the lower grades when, out of fear of having to romp with the other children and out of an overwhelming longing for home, I climbed onto an upturned, large clay flowerpot which stood in the shade against the school's ivy-covered back wall. I wanted to see into the classroom where my sister and her fellow students were diligently at work at their desks, and not until I stepped down in despair from the flowerpot did I see that I had been standing as well on an enormous velvet-winged night moth who had taken refuge in the shade. The furry worm of its body lay crushed under the sole of my left shoe, and from the torn span of turquoise and gold a ruby orb at the center of each wing looked up at me in accusation like a weeping eye. This was the first thing I had ever knowingly killed, and I knew I would not forget it until I myself would die.

It was through Mother's sister, Nina Allender, that Charles Sheeler and Morton Schamberg (and later Alfred Stieglitz) came into Mother's life. They were the first living artists we had ever known, and because we had seen their studios and their dedication to work, we painted and drew with increased care. Aunt Nina, whom we called Tante, was a strangely troubling woman, so unlike her mother and her sister that we were never quite at ease with her. Tante made friends with great difficulty, Mother had told us; but Morton and Charles and Tante had met before the turn of the century when they were students together on one of Robert Henri's summer painting tours to Italy. It was their respect for Henri as one of the group of revolutionary painters known as the Eight that had brought them together, as well as their perplexity about him as a man.

There was one story they told about him which shocked me more deeply every time I heard it, and yet I always wanted to hear it told again. It had happened in Venice during the summer when Henri and his students were staying at the same pensione as Whistler. The balcony of Henri's room, as fate would have it, was directly over the older, more famous painter's balcony. Whistler had purchased some rare goldfish, fantailed and with unusual black markings, and had set them in a bowl on the wide, stone balustrade of his balcony. One afternoon when the Master was out Henri let down a baited hook, and one by one fished the three handsome goldfish out. He then fried them to a crisp on the alcohol-burning ring he carried with him when he traveled, and lowered them back down again, one by one, into the fishbowl below.* "Isn't that what our British cousins would call a practical joke?" Puss asked in the affable manner he used when addressing someone he thought might be a potential enemy. And after a long moment of reflection, Morton would say: "It was a matter of two schools of painting. It wasn't a joke at all."

But it was Puss who had paid for Aunt Nina's trip to Italy with the painting class, and it was he who stood by her when her great tragedy occurred. She was living in Washington with her mother, Grandma Evans, painting and studying and seeking a job as an art teacher, when she met and married a young Englishman who, from all reports, was a marvel to listen to and to behold. His name was Charlie Allender, and Puss gave them the most elaborate of wedding receptions, having already, through his business connections, obtained a job for Allender in a leading Washington bank. The young man's family in England could not afford to come to the wedding, but they sent the bride a fine selection of the Allender family silver. However, they failed to mention that they had shipped young Charlie out of the country five years before to spare him from serving a sentence for embezzlement and forgery. But all this came to light a year or so after his marriage to Tante when he flew the coop one day taking another lady along with him, as well as an untold sum of money from the bank, and was never heard of again.

But Mother need not have worried about the possibility of Tante committing suicide, for she insisted on keeping his name. The reason for this was quite simply that she wanted to make the name Allender a respected name in Washington again. And in this she succeeded, for not only did she become

*It could well be that I have, after so many years, remembered the story incorrectly, and that it was not Henri who was the fryer of the fish, but Whistler, a man said to be of irascible ways, who fried his younger colleague's *Carassius auratus*.

an Honorary Co-Chairperson of the World Woman's Party but as well the official cartoonist of the National Woman's Party's publication, *The Suffragist*, before women were given the vote. During all those years she remained a government employee, and, following the franchise, she continued her work as cartoonist for the *Equal Rights* magazine.*

I was too young to be proud of Tante then or of the fact that my great-great-grandfather on the Evans side of the family had served on George Washington's staff. But even as a child I was impressed by Grandma Evans's office in the Land Grant Division of the federal government. The year we lived in Washington she showed me the large map of the western states that hung on one wall, and on that map there were differently colored thumbtacks which Grandma, standing on a stepladder, placed there to mark the various settlers' claims. They were known as "squatters," she explained to me, but she preferred to call them pioneers who had set out to open up the West. She showed me the drawings they had made staking out their claims, diagrams so simple that even I could understand them, showing how the trees were placed on the land where they had built their cabins, or how a creek wound through their land, or where a hill curved up, or the deep decline of a valley. They sent in these claims on any paper they could manage to find, and some who did not have paper would mark the boundaries of their territory on the inside of birch bark, and roll the bark into a scroll, and knot a string around it, and place a postage stamp on it where a postage stamp should go.

Whenever Grandma Evans came from Washington to stay with us during her vacation times and holidays, I would stand

*Nina E. Allender's cartoons are now in the art archives of the Library of Congress. Her drawing of Susan B. Anthony mounting the steps of the Capitol with a petition of 20,000 names (asking for the vote for women) to present to Congress was made into a postage stamp in 1936, in commemoration of the thirtieth anniversary of her death.

pressed against her chair while she sewed extraordinarily beautiful clothes for our Paris dolls, which were made of fragile china and were as slender as fashion models. She would always be amazed by their jointed wrists and ankles and knees and by the silk stockings and high-heeled shoes they wore. I would listen as fervently to her as I did to Mother as her needle went in and out of the silk of a doll's dress or the wool of a winter coat trimmed with feathers so that the dolls would think they were back in Paris again. She would tell me how she began teaching school when she was sixteen, in Kansas prairie towns where you could see the Indian fires at night burning along the far horizon. And she would tell me how the family had crossed almost the length of America when she was still a little girl, and how she had liked to run, singing aloud in the early morning, just ahead of the horses who pulled the covered wagon through the wilderness. They were usually the first wagon in a caravan of a dozen or more, and they would set out just before dawn, and when she looked back she could see her own footsteps in the dew on the grass. I knew she ran, and danced, and sang before the horses in the beginning of the day because she wasn't afraid of the Indians or of anything else in life. When she was seventeen, Mother had told me, Grandma had married the superintendent of schools, a man a good deal older than she was. Mother, her second daughter, was born in Topeka, Kansas.

I would listen and listen and never ask a question, not even the question that no one is left to answer: where Grandma Evans had found the courage to leave Kansas and a grandfather I was never to see and to move with her two young daughters to Washington, D.C.—probably known as Foggy Bottom then—and twenty years before the close of that century find a government job that paid enough to support the three of them, the salary being, at least for a woman, $720 a year.

II. ON WRITERS AND WRITING

"Interpreters of This Deep Concern"

In the American Grain

In *In the American Grain* William Carlos Williams appraises only secondarily, "in the name of beauty," another tradition in America. It is not one concerned with the tenacity of the pilgrim or the Indian polished to bronze, but the "Pocahuntus, a wellfeatured, but wanton yong girle . . . of the age of eleven or twelve years, get the boyes forth with her into the market place, and make them wheele, falling on their hands, turning their heels upwards, whome she would followe, and wheele so her self naked, as she was, all the fort over." A tradition of four dimensions, and, in incident, dimensions of an unfixed value that leaves them free to adaptation to the manner of life which existed at the time each incident functioned.

Chronology has been a matter of national moralities and geographical differences and it has excluded too much. The only qualities that could authenticate historical fact have gone unrecognized: the contemporaneous sense of place; the feel of cloth as it must have been, for instance, to fingers which knew it from their own loom. It is this that is of importance to Williams: the disassociation of fact from a prepared and prejudiced conception of it. He and D. H. Lawrence are the first to attempt a revaluation of experience which borrowed interpretations have confused.

In the national American mind there has been no doubt nor division of supremacy. The approach to America has always been an approach to the moralist, to the upright, to the "typically good man." But Williams examines the past in the records in town halls, in actual correspondence, in printed fact. Whatever has been written since is of little value to him, for in America there has been accepted only what Lawrence calls "the perfect citizen as a pattern to America." However the "perfect citizen" affected the wilderness is clearer and more truly known in what Franklin has written of it than in *post obitum*. And D. H. Lawrence has quoted Franklin writing this of the Indians:

> "We found that they have made a great bonfire in the middle of the square; they were all drunk, men and women quarreling and fighting. Their dark-colored bodies, half naked, seen only by the gloomy light of the firebrands, accompanied by their horrid yellings, formed a scene the most resembling our ideas of hell that could be imagined. There was no appeasing the tumult, and we retired to our lodging. At midnight a number of them came thundering at our door, demanding more rum, of which we took no notice.
>
> "The next day, sensible they have misbehaved in giving us that disturbance, they sent three of their counsellors to make their apology. The orator acknowledged the fault, but laid it upon the rum, and then endeavored to excuse the rum by saying: 'The Great Spirit, who made all things, made everything for some use; and whatever he designed anything for, that use it should

always be put to. Now, when he had made rum, he said: "Let this be for the Indians to get drunk with." And it must be so!'

"And indeed, if it be the design of Providence to extirpate these savages in order to make room for the cultivators of the earth, it seems not improbable that rum may be the appointed means. It has already annihilated all the tribes who formerly inhabited all the seacoast."

I speak first of the way in which Williams comes to his subject because in any métier an approach so single and detached is of rare purity. He has, as a critic, curiosity and doubt in opposition to whatever potential America's cultural approach might create. And as a poet and a critic he stands with those few who are unconfused by the value of inheritance. The intelligent are all aware of the gestures required of the great. Williams is in doubt. He is never quite convinced of the impeccability of his weapon, nor quite focused on the center of his despise.

He is convinced of contoured beauty and of the chastity of fact. With these he does not compromise. He does not write about the "wilderness" with affection, and few writers have avoided that. Even Gertrude Stein, in writing of her feminine forebears that "some looked very weak and little women, but even these, so weak and little, were strong always to bear many children," bends the facts themselves to a moral conception of them. While Williams writes: "Do you know that the old town records in Massachusetts show few men without two and many with as many as seven wives? Not at all uncommon to have had five. How? The first ones died shooting children against the wilderness like cannon balls." His forebears are not polished monuments seen in a clipped green square, but are strong enough to have withstood an actual wilderness, a "dark and bloody ground," and to retain sound and color and smell.

In Williams there is what he calls, in writing of Poe, "the strong sense of a beginning." There is nothing left over from another age. And this concentration of emotion in immediate contacts has produced a rich and violent prose which turns as tenderly to beauty as to the lifting of "dead Indians from their graves," to steal from them—as if it must be clinging to their corpses—some authenticity.

Mr. Crane
and His Grandmother

In his foreword to *White Buildings* (1926), a thin, artistic volume, Mr. Allen Tate writes that the poetry of Mr. Hart Crane "tends toward the formation of a state of mind, the critical equivalent of which would be in effect an exposure of the confusion and irrelevance of the current journalism in poetry, and of how far behind the creative impulse the critical intelligence, for the moment, lags." It is also suggested by Mr. Tate that the faults in Mr. Crane's poetry are those which one finds as well in the poetry of Mr. Baudelaire and of Mr. William Blake. And Mr. Arthur Rimbaud is once more on a title page saying "ce ne peut être que la fin du monde, en avançant." All of which places Mr. Hart Crane very nicely in the literary scene. We have Mr. Baudelaire, and Mr. William Blake, and Mr. Arthur Rimbaud. (And sotto voce Mr. Tate suggests Miss Sitwell, Mr. Wallace Stevens, Mr. T. S. Eliot. And Mr. Walt Whitman.) And ever so slightly Mr.

Marlowe and the Elizabethans, and then of course Mr. Hart
Crane's "avowed masters," Mr. Herman Melville and Mr.
E. A. Poe. So here we all are, and we know a great deal, and
we've just been ever and ever so intellectual, and now we can
get on to the poetry of Mr. Hart Crane.

Words, words, words, there are a lot of them. Mr. Crane
takes them very seriously. Here is a part of a poem of Mr.
Crane's:

> The siren of the spring of guilty song—
> Let us take her on the incandescent waves
> Striated with nuances, nervosities
> That we are heir to:

Mr. Jolas too has a lot of words, but not words that lisp,
or that follow a rhythm of the mind. Mr. Crane's mind is
neatly spaced. (Mr. Tate assures us that Mr. Crane's French
is better than Mr. Whitman's.) His emotions are reasonable
and just. And Mr. Crane is America's pride. The stalwart
modern son of Ohio. The pride of the moderns, I suppose,
because he is done with life and with civilization, presumably, with human emotions, with human ambition. He's got
himself onto another plane. He's doing what Schneider did
in *Dr. Transit*. And it's all doomed to failure because it is false;
it is dull and humorless; it's like Wells writing about men like
gods; it's a lot of words hiding a human fear. Words are shallow troughs for the deep water of the mind and it is only the
fierce, the living, the simple, the clear, the angry mind which
can overflow the troughs and go out over the mud, and over
the grass, bearing the light of the sun on it like an angry
shield.

There is no use getting up onto another plane and putting
words together in another way, words that insist upon a new
way of being heard, unless there is behind these words a

power and beauty hot enough to melt away the words on the tongue. It is this heat which makes Mr. Jolas write poetry. But Mr. Crane's fervour is Baptist, is Presbyterian; he is as phlegmatic as a Rotarian, as entertaining as the American Legion. He treats his lady friends like Trilbys. He patronizes his grandmother with "gently pitying laughter." And she was probably a better bet than he; a hardworking old woman maybe, with no time for foolishness; time for loveletters, yes, and time for life, but no time for the grand old manner, for acquired dignities, for cultured reminiscences.

Marianne Moore has written "difficult" poetry, difficult only because one's mind was less simple and less clear than her own, and the emotion, or the lack of it, has never been obscured by her words getting out of hand. You may say it is not poetry; or say, as do people who announce great stupidities with ease and authority, that it is no more than clever prose broken up into short lines. But besides its beauty it has humor which admits the falsity of its own humility. Or Robert McAlmon, who wrote this about a boar:

I began to shoot as he came at me,
And emptied the magazine of my rifle into him.
The bullets streamed like hot water spurting from a nozzle.
He came on.
Only as he made the leap to clear the hedge
Something within him snapped. In mid-air he poised and fell—
                                                        limp.
His teeth were chewing his tongue.
Torn to red shreds.
He grunted and mumbled.   ·
I watched his eyes glazing, changing from scarlet embers
To wax-covered glass—dull—
I was proud of his savagery.
He died.
He never was tamed to serve men's purposes.

This is what I mean by grandeur. It is not the painting on lamp-shades, it is in the light itself, steady as major scales played firmly across the keys. In these lines of McAlmon's there is no poetical prejudice, no false conception of emotion, there is no subterfuge for truth. And even if truth be relative, read Mr. Crane:

Compass, quadrant and sextant contrive
No farther tides . . . High in the azure steeps
Monody shall not wake the mariner.
This fabulous shadow only the sea keeps.

Preface to
The Autobiography of
Emanuel Carnevali

"They were just two kids, she a girl who happened to live across the corridor some place where he was staying," William Carlos Williams has written in his *Autobiography* (1967) of Emanuel Carnevali and the young wife he so quickly set aside. "She was not literary. He was straight, slim, with a beautiful young man's head, keenly intelligent—an obviously lost soul. Before him she was in obvious adoration. She was a peasant from the high mountains of northwestern Italy, he from one of the cities of the northern plain: here they were in New York, headed out but not toward money. This was New York at its best, the highest potential which you saw there with a catch in your throat, knowing it was almost certainly doomed to destruction . . . the first time he read in public somewhere, he had made her sit on the platform beside him, scared, not knowing much what it was all about—but he insisted on it, that those who heard might know *who* the writer was, not just he, but the two of them."

The marriage, the career as a poet, the young Italian poet's life itself, were indeed doomed to destruction. And yet Carnevali's autobiography should not be read as a tragedy. Surely no greater reward is offered to a writer than the knowledge that other men are reading the words that he has, by some miracle, retrieved from the depths of his own silence; the knowledge that other men are actually listening for the sound of his voice to call out from the page to them, and, above all, the knowledge that they believe the words they hear. This reward Carnevali was given, and if it was given for only a little while, this does not diminish the value of that high tribute he was paid.

I was nineteen when I first heard Carnevali's name: I had come East from the Middle West, and the editor in the New York office of *Broom* magazine (a handsome art and literary review published in Europe by Americans) took me on as typist and bookkeeper of sorts. The editor was Lola Ridge, an Australian poet of savage talent and fervent dedication to the arts. The day I began to work for her in the basement of 3 East Ninth Street she gave me some poetry of Carnevali's to read. She had known him in Chicago and New York, and now he had gone back, young, alone, and very ill, she told me, to Italy. The way Lola spoke of him was as eloquent as the poems themselves. I did not know then that it was only with unabashed eloquence and a kind of furious heedless courage that one could hope to seize in one's bare hands the blazing meaning of his name. I was young then and I had no way of knowing that Carnevali's radiant vision, unextinguished by the misery of his defeat, was already metaphor to the poets of America for all that daily circumstances demanded they endure.

Perhaps the disinherited of every generation ask quite reasonably, quite humbly, that they be allowed to hear one living man, just one, actually shout aloud their disputed tongue, and that they may be permitted to set eye on the actual substance of their own poetic logic. However it is, it is a lucky time that has its true poet, its Rimbaud, and in the 1920s Carnevali suddenly and almost inexplicably took on this role. He was the rebel, the man on the run, the stranger beating his head against the stars, that the others had been writing and waiting for. As was to be true of Dylan Thomas in a later decade, the syllables of Carnevali's name had the power to ignite the minds and hearts of those who did not fear to burn in the hottest, brightest fires of man's creative hell. William Carlos Williams was one of these. As early as 1919 he wrote of Carnevali: "We older can compose, we seek the seclusion of a style, of a technique, we make replicas of the world we live in and we live in them and not in the world. It is for you we went out, old men in the dark. It is for you that the rubbish stirred and a rat crawled from the garbage, alive! . . . The reason for our having been alive is here!" But in the same breath that he celebrated Carnevali's arrival and survival, Williams grieved over the inevitable departure and defeat. "Jesus, Jesus, save Carnevali for me," he besought America, or the history of the lost, or something as blind and deaf as life itself. "He is only beginning to disintegrate. . . . But he is slipping into the afternoon at twenty-one. . . . Rimbaud, Laforgue, Corbière, they offer him solace. They prove to him that he is fore-doomed. . . . Carnevali, perhaps you will do as they did. . . . We salute you" (*Others*, 1919).

Every resistance fighter in the underground literary movement of the 1920s came at one time or another to the basement office that Lola kept functioning on practically no funds at all. Williams, Marianne Moore, Bodenheim, Louis Ginzberg, John Dos Passos, Kenneth Burke, Jean Toomer, Slater Brown, and Waldo Frank were among those who came down the outside steps to the basement door. In the late afternoon, you could see their legs through the window, coming in from the rain or the snow. The resistance was against the established English language, and the fight was for the recognition of a new American tongue. Carnevali had at the age of sixteen fled the war in Europe and had acquired that new language, and in the brief eight years that he was in America he had turned it into revolutionary poetry and prose. A French critic, Regis Michaud, wrote that Carnevali was "one of the two American poets whose work attained an international standard." (The other, it is to be presumed, was William Carlos Williams, who used old words with an astonishing freshness, saying, for instance, "the fates of ideas living against the grain in a nondescript world have always held me breathless.") An American writer, Dorothy Dudley Harvey, to whom Carnevali dedicated his long poem describing his return to Italy, was to write of him that once he had abandoned the Tuscan tongue, our "limber, informal, changing slang became a part of him." Of his years in America, she wrote:

He came without money, lived as he could, sometimes through jobs, sometimes through friends, but meagrely; his friends quite naturally, in the fashion of the country, saying among themselves, "He is young, he ought to be able to keep a job, we all of us manage to keep jobs."

He worked first in restaurants, in Grand Central station, in the Yale Club, among others in New York. . . . And he told how once, without work for days or a real meal, he had picked up a piece of bread in Washington Square, and had thrown it down with tears. . . . At length he published—first in the magazine of *Poetry*, then in other magazines, *The Little Review*, *Others* . . . *Vogue*. . . . He was a hurried man, as in his tales he calls himself, until sickness overtook him. Among doctors who disagreed as to what the matter was, one called it by a Latin name which means intolerance of the spirit. In health he had that too.

Sights and sounds were not enough for their color, their tone, their wavelengths. They must be presage of amazing days, heroic vision. . . . He fought the drabness of this country he had given himself to. How much longer he would have fought . . . not as some men do for a change of government, but for a change of temper, who can say? . . . He is the new modern, one of the first rebels against the ugliness of revolution. A marvelous poem of his by that name sees revolution dispassionately—its grandeur and its stupidity. And another, "Making a Fool of God," belongs to us especially for a kind of shrewdness. (Parts of this are taken from Dorothy Dudley Harvey's foreword to *A Hurried Man*, by Emanuel Carnevali, 1925, and parts from a revised foreword, written some years later.)

Actually, Carnevali's illness had been diagnosed, Lola told me, as encephalitis lethargica, a form of sleeping sickness which seizes its victim by the hair of his head and shakes and shakes him endlessly until death intervenes. Carnevali's bold black eyes and his strong white teeth were shaken like dice in his head, Lola told me, shaken night and day, day and night, without respite. At times even tears were shaken from his eyes, she said, although he had no wish to cry. He was absolute in his refusal of this illness, and adamant in his will not to go under. Among the poems written after his return to Italy there are these lines that are like a fist shaken in death's face:

I know
that for having slept much
the dead have grown strong.

On days as these
they kick open their graves
and skip elegantly out.

They whisper horrible secrets
to each other and to me.

They carry their shrouds and
shake them valiantly.

O Goddess of dismay and melancholy
come to my help!
I still have withered kisses for you
kisses I don't want to throw away for I'm very poor.
Cleave me from my memories!

They bother me so that sleep flirts and flees,
flirts and flees.

Carnevali had not yet had a book out when I went to work
in the office of *Broom*. That was to come later, after Robert
McAlmon had founded his publishing house, Contact Editions, in Paris. In 1923, McAlmon published Hemingway's
first book, *Three Stories and Ten Poems*, and then, among other
distinguished books, had come the first publication of a canto
of Ezra Pound's, illustrated, and Gertrude Stein's *The Making of Americans*, and William Carlos Williams's *The Great
American Novel*. Carnevali's collection, *A Hurried Man*, became renowned in this literature of underground resistance.
It was one of the most exceptional in the list of thirty or more
exceptional volumes to appear in that decade under the imprint of McAlmon's Contact Editions or William Bird's
Three Mountains Press. "One of the best examples of—
what?" Williams wrote of it in his *Autobiography*. "A book,
a book that is all of a man, a young man, superbly alive.
Doomed. When I think of what gets published and what gets
read and praised and rewarded regularly with prizes, when
such a book as that gets shoved under the heap of corpses, I
swear never to be successful, I am disgusted, the old lusts
revive. What else can a book do for a man?"

Of Carnevali's work McAlmon remarked that its violence
was the violence of adolescence, but violence given another

dimension by his Latin irony and wit. Being purely Italian, McAlmon wrote in his own autobiography (*Being Geniuses Together*), Carnevali had the Italian lack of cant about "morals" and "soul" and "conscience." The two men had exchanged letters over a period of a year while McAlmon was in college and Carnevali was in Chicago on the staff of *Poetry* magazine. "I concluded that it was because he was a foreigner that he so passionately loved Whitman, and, later, Sherwood Anderson and Carl Sandburg." McAlmon wrote in true amazement. "Carnevali was to me more interesting than his American heroes." (Robert McAlmon has been called the forgotten man of the Paris literary scene of the twenties; but by those who knew and valued him he is not forgotten. Year by year, his work, and his positive presence on that scene are being given new definitions. Neither as writer nor as publisher does he deserve oblivion.) Then, in that decade, it was not a rarity when strong tentacles of faith reached out from poet to poet. It was in no way remarkable that Robert McAlmon should be publishing in Paris the book of a man lying ill in Bazzano, and that Bill Williams should write from Rutherford, New Jersey, that the book was one of the best possible examples of what a book should be.

When Lola first spoke to me of Carnevali, a few of my own poems had been printed in magazines, as well as small critical pieces on Rémy de Gourmont and other contemporary French writers, and a few unsigned book reviews in the old *Dial*. Because of the apparent parallels in our published writing careers, and because I was poor in New York on the same streets, perhaps even in the same rooming houses, where Carnevali had been poor, I felt an immediate commitment to him, a deep and unequivocal affinity. But it was not until 1923, when my French husband and I went to France to live, that I began writing to Carnevali in Italy. Out of my poverty into the depths of his, I sent books, magazines, and whatever bounty others sent my way; and letters, endless letters. And out of his poverty and desperate illness, he sent me poems, letters, and sections of the book he was trying to write in the public ward of the hospital in Bazzano. Everything he sent was typed—even his signature—on the thinnest, shiniest paper that was truly like an onion's skin. Ten pages or more of his writing, when folded over and then folded again, could be carried in one's pocket, as bulkless and weightless as a silk handkerchief. The letters, the poems, the sections of the book are now lost, but I remember that each word always had a reddish halo above it, as if the typewriter ribbon was stretched taut between black and red in its furious striving to get the sentences down.

Sometimes it would take Carnevali a day to do a sentence, a week to do a paragraph, for while he shook with the terrible ague of his illness, he would have to hold his right hand in the grip of his left in order to be able to strike the keys. And there would be long intervals when he would be too ill to set so much as a sentence down. He wanted the book to be called *The First God* or *Religious Stammering*. It was ten years later that I began to compile this story of his life for him, to piece it together from his letters to me through that decade, to trace it through the pages of *A Hurried Man*, and assemble it with the chapters of the novel, as he called it, that he was never able to finish. With every word he wrote me, Carnevali sent that simple gift that men take away from themselves to give so grudgingly, so sparingly, with such caution, to others; and that was the gift of tireless love.

In 1925, before bringing out the first number of their new quarterly, *This Quarter*, Ethel Moorhead and Ernest Walsh, himself ill with tuberculosis, journeyed from Paris to Bazzano to see Carnevali. In the first issue of *This Quarter* and in the numbers that followed they published Carnevali's work. After that visit to Bazzano, Ernest Walsh wrote in *This*

Quarter (1927): "His [Carnevali's] illness would kill most men. I felt he had become ill not because he was weak but because he was too strong. I never felt death in him. I tell you he had the power to entertain and buoy me although he was suffering much at the moment. I had the feeling that a god or a devil had exploded within him and fought for escape. But this prisoner made me laugh with him so I knew it was a god that had exploded. . . . There is no death in Carnevali. He is a live warm laughing and fighting man."

There were others who made the long pilgrimage to see Carnevali, among them Dorothy Dudley Harvey and her sister, Caroline, the wife of Joseph Delteil; Harriet Monroe; Robert McAlmon (who had him removed to a private sanatorium, and paid for a year's treatment there); Edward Dahlberg, who has written of his visit to him; and once Ezra Pound went from Rapallo to take Carnevali a radio which my husband and I had collected the money to buy for him. Finally, in 1933, as we drove our children through Italy on our way to Austria, where living would be cheap, we were able to get to Bazzano. On the eighteenth of July of that year I wrote a long letter from Cavalese to my beloved friend, Caresse Crosby. It reads in part:

I have been to see Carnevali, and I write you the first moment I can after. . . . We went on a blazing day, in the middle of the day, driving across the Italian plain which is certainly the hottest place this side of hell—and we got to the worst town of all, stopped in a dead white square with dust three inches thick on it, and went to the little café where he lives. I expected to find him downstairs, or sitting somewhere, but after a quarter of an hour the woman took us up to his room. The room faces on that blazing square, and the room is big enough just to hold a narrow iron bed, a cupboard with his piles of books, and a tin wash table on which his old typewriter sits. The gramophone Ernest Walsh gave him is on the floor. . . . The thing one feels when one walks into that cell and sees the figure on the bed can never be explained. On that bed there is the most beautiful man, shaking completely, all over, like a pinned butterfly. The whole bed seems in motion with his shaking—as if waves of water were breaking over and over and over and would never stop. But such a face on the pillow—a strong, big face, with black eyes, and the skin as pure and clean as ivory, and black locks of hair. A great strong well-made man with a great chest that lies bare—and with such beauty in his face that your breath is taken away. I don't know why it is, you do not feel illness. You feel this endless agitation which *will* stop—you feel it has to stop. But he says it never stops—neither in the night. Never, never. It never stops at all. And you don't feel weakness or sorrow—except the kind of sorrow no words can ever say. He is gay—he is the gayest person alive—the way Harry and Ernest Walsh were gay. He has a laugh that fills your heart—he says wonderful simple things. And we sat there and laughed and talked (how can I tell you that he made me feel gayer and bolder and more courageous than I have felt in years?), and drank two bottles of sickening sweet champagne in that ghastly filthy room which is his life.

I was writing this letter so quickly to Caresse that I did not mention two things which are still as clear as sunlight in my mind: first, that Carnevali held fiercely onto the bars of the bed behind his head as he talked, trying to still his shaking, and that his bare arms had been made strong as a prizefighter's by the endless vibrations that passed through them; and secondly, that small white moths flew in and out of his poor clothing that hung, grey with dust, on a hat tree in one corner of the room.

And in a little while [the letter goes on], but only for a second, I was crying in his arms as I never cry with anyone except you. No, there is no way to find the words to tell you. He is so tender, and he is so filled with love. It runs down his arms and out his fingertips. And he asks for nothing, nothing, for it is he himself who has everything to give.

One thing: when they brought the champagne, he made them set the glasses one on top of the other to make a tower so that the champagne brimmed over from the first, into the second, and so on, down, in a yellow torrent.

. . . The sight of him haunts me. I see him all the time waking or sleeping—quivering and quivering and quivering as if his whole soul were in revulsion from the filth and heat of the terrific place . . . the thing is so clear to me, my Caresse, that I should be with him always, for he is to me the last, the almost shattered remains of courage and beauty that are left. I don't know what to do—for I know that every day I live will be a rebuke to me, for I should be with him, and I have not the courage to say that everything else is a distortion except being with him. It is not as easy as explaining this as love—it is a necessity, for if the thing he is did not exist and had never existed, there would be no reason to live at all.

We are going back to see him. . . . I promised to go back in three weeks, and he said: "Three weeks is twenty-one days for you, it is three hundred years for me."

(From the Caresse Crosby Papers, Morris Library, Southern Illinois University at Carbondale)

Once I had seen Carnevali, the compiling of this book became an obsession with me. The words of it were now the only speech left to him to exchange with the men of his time and kind, and their responses to the questions he asked would be like a wild chorale of hope soaring above the blazing heat of that small café room. I typed and retyped the bits and pieces he sent to me, wrote to Bill Williams in Rutherford to send me all the writing that Carnevali had ever sent to him. In August 1933, I wrote again to Caresse, this time from Vienna, saying: "It must be placed, this book, or I will never write again."

In the end, all I had written to Caresse was little better than a lie. I did not find a publisher for Carnevali's autobiography in his lifetime, and I was never able to go back to Italy. (How weak this sounds now, so weak that the words fairly totter on the page, to say that I was never "able" to go back: I believe one is always "able" to do what one requires of oneself, and between my return to Bazzano and my own life stood obstacles that I, quite unconsciously, did not choose to set aside.) I spoke of Carnevali to every writer I met, and those who could emptied their pocketbooks for him (Caresse Crosby, Ira Morris, Eugene and Maria Jolas were among those who did so generously).

Until the fall of France in 1940, Carnevali in Bazzano and I in Megève, in the Haute-Savoie, wrote every week to each other. I was still fitting the sentences and paragraphs of the book together when the dark curtain came down between France and Italy. Since then there has been silence, and it can only be concluded that Carnevali died during the course of the war. There is no record of his death, no trace of his name or of the few poor things he owned. "That single book published by Contact Editions is as far as I know his sole testament," Williams writes in his autobiography. But now there is this book to add to the earlier testament of a man of whom Carl Sandburg said in the foreword to *A Hurried Man*: "He is of the sun treader tribe, also a walker in dark shadows. He seemed sometimes to be throwing himself at the sun. . . . He had a dream in Chicago of publishing a magazine to redeem perhaps some of the redeemables of America and Europe, even Russia and China, perhaps even Mars and Betelgeuse. . . . His writings are the record of a personality that burned with twentieth century flames, and that was marvelously alive to the intensities and the contrasts of American life."

Elizabeth Bowen

There is at least one bitter fight that the sensitive and distinguished writer is foredoomed to make, and to make alone,
and that is the fight to escape from those limits of sensitivity
and distinction that his own nature and the nature of his work
impose. He cannot—as does a richer writer—absorb virility
from the class whose problems he defines, for he is not writing of any class. He cannot borrow the language of his own
people in which to tell his story, for, properly speaking,
he has no people. This was the tragedy of Emily Brontë,
who of necessity created an imaginary kingdom in which her
imaginary people might survive, and who achieved but one
good book during her life's despairing search for her own
people and that people's cause. It was the tragedy of Henry
James, who sought in England (as T. S. Eliot has since) not
only the vocabulary but the very spirit to animate communication. It was the damnation of Poe, of Rimbaud, of Em-

ily Dickinson that there was not—or that they failed to recognize the features of—a functioning world to which they
could belong. There is an endless list of lesser writers whose
names might be added to these, and Katherine Mansfield's is
among them; but for the moment it is Elizabeth Bowen's minor tragedy which is our concern.

Five of Miss Bowen's books are before me—*To the North*,
The House in Paris, *The Death of the Heart*, *Look at All Those
Roses*, and *Bowen's Court*. In the first four the theme does not
vary, the symbol does not alter. The Child—be it child, or
artist, or woman—is the pallid and introverted figure who
sets out on that futile search for comprehension in an antag-
onistic and monstrously vicious world. The Child is, in essence, pure; but it has been outraged from the outset through
the mere fact of being given life. No amount of personal
dignity, of withdrawal from action, or willful self-efface-
ment succeeds in defending its soul. It must learn Miss Bow-
en's proud, bitter lesson—that only the unrecorded, unut-
tered, wholly clandestine communion with one's own ego is
the answer offered by the years. With an appalling lack not
only of humor but of true perception, this monotonous Child
moves through *The House in Paris*, through *The Death of the
Heart*, continues as young woman in *To the North*, persists as
Nancy, as Miss Fox, as Myra Wing, as Penny and Claudia
and the interchangeable others in *Look at All Those Roses*—a
journey which for a writer of Miss Bowen's sophisticated
gifts is a singularly immature and ungrateful theme. Yet,
recognizing in this record of martyrdom the martyrdom of
one more sensitive and distinguished artist on that tragic and
fruitless search for a people and its tongue, one is tempted to
withhold judgment for a little while.

The appearance of *Bowen's Court* at this moment of Miss
Bowen's search is of particular interest and significance.

There is the quality of change in it; it is unlike, for instance, *The Death of the Heart*, a book which perhaps serves best as pattern of her earlier work. In *Death of the Heart* we have the innocent heroine, the archvillain and the ruthless older woman (the exact equivalent of the Wicked Queen in Disney's *Snow White*). This is Miss Bowen's customary cast—lacking the always slightly déclassé hero—and it is indication of how far from humanity and reality Miss Bowen instinctively goes. Like her earlier ones, this book has neither vitality of spirit, nor beauty, nor continuity of style; *Bowen's Court* possesses the three. Her previous books have proved interesting because of a certain taut self-consciousness, a neurotic uneasiness which one hoped might lead in time to something richer. But only in *Death of the Heart* is there to be found a hint of what we have been seeking. Here Major Brutt, returned to England from the colonies, blurts out:

> "Yes, I've stuck out there abroad too long, it rather seems. I'd rather like, now, to be in touch for a bit. . . ."
> "But in touch with what?" said Thomas. "What do you think there is, then?"
> . . . "Well," he said, "there must be something going on. You know—in a general way, I mean. You know, something you all—"
> "We all? We who?"
> "Well, you, for instance," Major Brutt said. "There must be something—that's why I feel out of touch. I know there must be something all you people get together about."
> "There may be," said Thomas, "but I don't think there is. . . ."

But then Major Brutt plays the role of outsider in the piece. He is merely excellent character, and Miss Bowen has no respect for him at all.

Twelve years ago Miss Bowen inherited her family's home

in County Cork—"the property on which it stands having been in the family ever since a Captain Bowen from Wales received it in return for services to Cromwell during the Irish campaign." Miss Bowen herself was born in Dublin and has spent her summers at least in Ireland, and it was there she sought, in the early summer of 1939, in a country rife with human controversy, to retreat two centuries or more on that eternal quest to find her people—this time, perhaps in desperation, seeking out those people whose name she bears. In *Bowen's Court*, in a truly heroic effort to connect with reality at last, she writes:

> The urgency of the present, its relentless daily challenge, seems to communicate itself to one's view of the past, until, to the most private act or decision, there attaches one's sense of its part in some campaign. . . . I have written (as though it were everlasting) about a home at a time when all homes are threatened and hundreds of thousands of them are being destroyed. I have taken the attachment of people to place as being generic to human life, at a time when the attachment is to be dreaded, as a possible source of too much pain. . . . All this disparity or contrast between the time and my subject has only so acted upon my subject as to make it more important to me. I have tried to make it my means to approach a truth about life.

Here, in these words, has the nature of the search been formulated. She sought in this book—on the brink of all that was to come—to establish a past, almost any past, in order to feel the land firm beneath her feet. Perhaps through the expression of it, Miss Bowen has effected her own escape from the individual's dread of being implicated in what he will not be able to deal with or understand, from the fear of being impinged upon by the demands of human responsibility. She has given us her family's past much as the boy in *The House in Paris* gives the girl the little replica of the Eiffel

Tower—putting it in some kind of despairing pride and trust into our keeping as if to preserve this much, at least, of the paraphernalia of past action and vanished reality. And it is perhaps in this gesture, accomplished at last, that Miss Bowen's future as a writer lies.

Katherine Mansfield:
A Reconsideration

The Short Stories of Katherine Mansfield (1937) contains eighty-eight short stories: "all of Katherine Mansfield's short stories," the jacket states. The first ones were written in 1908 and 1910; the last, presumably, in 1922 in the months preceding her death. These dates are significant because they belong strangely to an old world, to another time, almost to another century, and these eighty-eight stories are irretrievably a part of that time.

It is first of all essential to isolate the two Katherine Mansfields if one is to come to any honest estimation of her work; it is necessary to set ruthlessly aside that lovely, proud, appealing woman who, with the aid of her best stories, has for a long time been a literary tradition to us. To respond to that figure's austerity, its pride and melancholy, and its heartbreaking loneliness brings one no closer to her talent but rather serves to exclude one utterly from any scrupulous appraisement of the work. This, to an extent, is true of many minor artists, but because of the circumstances of Katherine Mansfield's life and death it seems to me peculiarly true of her. (It is true as well of Rupert Brooke, whose work was enhanced by the appearance of his photograph in the frontispiece of his volume, by a perusal of his gallant letters home. While, contrarily, the work of such a poet as Hart Crane has a vitality eloquently and passionately its own, so independent of the poet's personality and life that one can scarcely reconcile the elements.) In this day of sterner issues and of a tougher literary appetite, the work of Katherine Mansfield must be considered as complete or incomplete within itself, shorn of the devoted enthusiasm of a Middleton Murray, deprived too of the day-to-day record which she kept and which revealed the sensitive, fastidious, the wholly neurotic and antisocial mind from which these stories came.

The other Katherine Mansfield is here in these six-hundred-odd pages—work, by the effort of the will, detached from the woman one was drawn to because one found facsimile of one's own weaknesses in her journal and from the woman one pitied because one knew her to be ill and lonely and afraid. These pages, delicately, tenderly, and carefully composed, are animated by situations so futile that it is difficult to believe they were ever not of importance but even of interest; stories terminating compactly on infinitesimal disappointments or with ladylike surprises, sketches of county types or foreign types or landscapes not so very different in technique from the sympathetic aquarelles that English ladies on the Continent sit down and do. There are blue skies with soft puffs of cloud in them, quaint houses, shimmering seas in pastel colors, Frenchmen invariably with big moustaches, dolls' tea sets, incredibly cute children, pretty names such as Pearl Button, pretty places, and not enough, for what the intent must have been, not love and comprehension for the persecuted young or old, or satire bitter enough for those she would condemn.

It is perhaps unfair to judge a writer's work by what he failed to write rather than by what is there. But had Katherine Mansfield succeeded in doing what she obviously *knew* could and had been done she might have been as enduring as Jane Austen and as invaluable to the history of her time. For there is in these unhappy little stories a thing that makes them different, that saves them, oddly, from being exactly what they are. It is there on every page, cried out in trembling and desperation, the awful, the speechless confession of her own inadequacy. Not the inadequacy of herself as a human being (although if one did not sternly separate the two it might revert to that in the end), nor her inadequacy as a critic, but the hopeless, the miserable inadequacy to see in any other and wider terms the things she sensed so acutely, the griefs or joys she witnessed or experienced. In line after line, and even in her omissions, one finds those unmistakable signs of panic as time passed and she knew. Even in the closing stories the cognizant despairing voice repeats its teeny-weeny words, restates its irritable and irritating themes, beseeches help, and, through knowing what the best is, knows how cruelly it has failed. Since the middle years of her writing it is evident that Katherine Mansfield saw clearly and recognized the savage, confusing wilderness beyond her world, a wilderness where only the tough and fearless can survive.

In some of her unfinished stories—and with the word *unfinished* one returns, in spite of oneself, to her personal tragedy—she asks, "Why is it so difficult to write simply—and not only simply but sotto voce, if you know what I mean?" But even in that day of less violent and less violently disputed issues, Katherine Mansfield herself knew the answer and all that it implied.

Tattered Banners

There are two Faulkners—at least to me there are two: the one who stayed down South and the one who went to war in France and mixed with foreigners and aviators; that is, the Faulkner of the Sartoris saga (and the countless other savagely and tenderly chronicled documents of the South) and the Faulkner who wrote "Turn About," for instance, and "All the Dead Pilots" and *Pylon* with no perceptible cooling of that hot devotion to man's courage although the speech, the history, the conflict were no longer his strict heritage. I believe these two separate Faulkners (separated more by a native shyness of the foreigner than any variance in ideology or technique) possess between them the strength and the vulnerability which belong only to the greatest artists: the incalculable emotional wealth, the racy comic sense, the fury to reproduce exactly not the recognizable picture but the unmistakable experience, the thirst for articulation as well as the curiosity and the vocabulary—that rarity—to quench it. The weaknesses there are, the errors, the occasionally strained effects, are accomplished by the same fearless, gifted hand.

It is not difficult to reconcile the two Faulkners, perhaps as simple as recognizing that a man is a good host or a good guest, but rarely both. On his own ground Faulkner is explicit, easy, sure; on someone else's he is a little awed, a little awkward, provincially aware of the chances he is taking. But I believe it is in the willingness to take these risks that Faulkner's whole future lies. That *The Unvanquished* (1938) happens to be one more chapter in the Sartoris saga is no valid description of it, nor that it is a book about the Civil War—a Civil War in which the issue of black and white is lost in the wider issue, not of justice and tyranny, subjection and freedom, or even sin and virtue, but merely of life and death. For one who loves Faulkner's work and has followed it closely and impatiently, the difficulty lies in isolating this book or any book from the others and trying to say this or that of it; his genius is not this book or perhaps any given book but resides in that entire determined collection of volumes which reveal him to be the most absorbing writer of our time.

On the face of it, this book is the story of an old lady whose home has been razed by Yankees and who sets out across the country, first driving two mules and then, when these are confiscated, two horses, wearing a borrowed hat on her head and holding over it a borrowed parasol. It is told in the words of her grandson, at the outset a boy of twelve who goes with her on that imperiously reckless adventure which leads toward Jordan, toward her career of racketeering and, like any Chicago gangster's, toward atrocious death; a boy who in the twelve years covered by the story matures first in emotion, then in conviction, and finally in act. "Ringo and I had been born in the same month," he says of the Negro boy who is their sole companion on the drive toward retribution, "and had both been fed at the same breast and had slept together and eaten together for so long that Ringo called Granny 'Granny' just like I did until maybe he wasn't a nigger any more or maybe I wasn't a white boy any more, the two of us neither, not even people any longer. . . ." And toward the end of the book when they are both twenty-four, he says of Ringo in a man's language: "He was sitting quietly in a chair beside the cold stove, spent-looking too who had ridden forty miles (at one time, either in Jefferson or when he was alone at last on the road somewhere, he had cried; dust was now caked and dried in the tear-channels on his face) and would ride forty more yet would not eat, looking up at me a little red-eyed with weariness (or maybe it was more than just weariness and so I would never catch up with him). . . ." The process of development, subtly, heedfully, skillfully accomplished through the seemingly inevitable metamorphosis of speech makes the book a record not only of an individual's but a nation's, possibly a civilization's, progression from violence to a passive and still undefinable bewilderment.

Elsewhere, the movement of that other group, the march of the liberated Negroes toward Jordan, starts like a whisper in the book, becomes "a kind of panting murmur" as they pass in the night, and swells to "women and children singing and chanting and trying to get to that unfinished bridge or even down into the water itself, and the cavalry beating them back with sword scabbards. . . . They just pass here without food or anything, exactly as they rose up from whatever they were doing when the spirit or the voice . . . told them to go, . . . going to cross Jordan. . . ."

It is, then, the sentimental and glamorous story of one old lady who sets out to find and ask a Yankee colonel to return to her "a chest of family silver tied with hemp rope, two darkies, Loosh and Philadelphy, and the two confiscated mules, Old Hundred and Tinney"; and like a single and undaunted

fife still playing, it is as well the essence of that war, a thing
as intrinsically and nationally and gallantly the South's as the
revolution is France's and the rebellion Ireland's: become
now a legend, almost a fable of tattered banners, makeshift
uniforms, incredible courage and inhuman ferocity. It has
those weaknesses which can be found throughout Faulkner's
work: the full-length portraits which abruptly become cari-
catures not likenesses of the living, the "ladies" without face
or substance, the repetitions, the maudlin lapses, the shame-
less voice of the evangelist declaiming in solemn, flowery
passages. But it has that fabulous, that wondrous, fluxing
power which nothing Faulkner touches is ever without. The
word for it may be glamour, or may be sentiment, but both
these words are mutable and I have used them here without
contempt, applying them in their best sense as attributes to
fact. They can confuse, they can disguise, but they can also
bring to the familiar a heightened, an isolated, and a therefore truer legibility. They were elements in that electric atmosphere and mystic climate in which Poe's men and women
lived and have survived and they are a vital part of Faulkner's
quicker, more comprehensive world. Faulkner and Poe, set
far enough apart in time, are strangely kin: unique in our
history in their immunity to literary fashion, alike in their
fanatical obsession with the unutterable depths of mankind's
vice and even more with his divinity.

If writing remains one of the Arts—with a capital A and
be damned to the current mode of splitting it two ways in a
poem or a fresco on a wall—if its sensitive execution still
demands the heart and the endurance that have kept artists
lying prone on scaffoldings painting year in and year out, and
if its success depends on its acceptance as convincing tragedy
or comedy, then it can quite simply be said of Faulkner that
he is the rare, the curious, the almost ludicrously authentic

thing. In this book, as in his others, he writes with that "fierce desire of perfection" which contemporaries said Michelangelo evidenced when "flinging himself on the material of marble" vehemently seeking expression for "the human elements of fervor and tenderness."

A Declaration for 1955

It must be twenty years ago that I was in London one bleak winter night, going toward closing time through the icy fog into the warmth—comparative, that is—and the uproar of a public house. Its name was the Fitzroy Pub, my husband told me, and it was a place, he said, where those who struggled with the arts, and struggled with poverty as well, came in the evenings to talk and drink. Even now I can see those fierce-eyed old women, not artists or writers but scrubwomen by day, who huddled and cackled inside the door, those toothless witches, with wool scarves bound like winding-cloths around their heads, who sat on the chairs along the wall, or slipped from them, rattling with alcoholic laughter, and slept, like ancient mummies, on the floor. And I remember one other figure in the smoke of the place, a young man in a blue-green suit and an open-neck shirt, with a lightish shock of hair on his head, a stocky young man, with eyes that burned so eloquently that once you had looked at him you could not turn away.

At this moment I feel him standing before me as he stood that night, his mouth wide open in something intended to be singing but was not, and I feel still the quality of tenderness that was behind the savage impact of his gaze. I have never forgotten the salute, or embrace, or whatever it was, that was in his eyes. He gave it to every human being he turned to, and he sang out so lustily in celebration that he was told by the men and women around that he was disturbing the so-called peace of the Fitzroy Pub. He would climb up on the bar and tell the press of people what the hills and the sky were like where he came from, and how far away he was from the place he wanted to be. But nobody there wanted to hear a word of it; in fact, some of them wanted to knock him down, and others wanted to smash his face in once they had succeeded in dragging him down from his height. Feeling was running so high against him that my husband and I started through the people to where he was being shouldered from pillar to post.

I thought he was an Irishman, and I wanted to save him from British violence because of that as much as I wanted to save him as an individual from mob brutality. But my husband had recognized the accent as he sang and said, "He's Welsh." I thought of him as a coal miner's son, connected by blood and birth with D. H. Lawrence, a young miner, I thought, come to the city and attacked for his gusto and his simplicity. So we pushed the men and women aside, and my husband shouted the worst of them down, and I can still see the Welshman's face, so young, so ruddy, and his eyes on us in that blind and tender salute as we got him clear of their hands. He said he had come out without a coat, so we got his muffler around his neck, and we took him out past the witches asleep in the filth and rot of their ragged shrouds. We went other places from there, the three of us, and we talked about different countries, and about high mountains, and the sea, and sometime toward the end of the night he said, "What's your name?" I told him mine, and I asked him his. By that time it didn't seem strange that I'd known his poetry for a year and could say lines of it to him, or that he'd read a story or two I'd written and remembered the endings of them, although where he'd read them he couldn't say. His name was Dylan Thomas, and I never saw him again after that, but I've always remembered how we fought for him, with something like dedication to someone who was more than a young man out of his country in that alien place where he was.

Perhaps because he was so often out of place among men, we take him now as symbol. Perhaps because we who write in America are in grave difficulties now, we cherish Dylan Thomas as if he were our own ego, our own wild soul freed of the flesh. An American critic, writing of the American literary scene, points out that thinking Americans, in this period of our nation's development, are deeply troubled because "the demands for national security and for individual freedom" are in conflict. But he speaks with confidence of a new trend in the work of young American novelists: a trend toward brotherly communion is the name it has. A number of new novels, this critic says, express man's longing to be identified with other men. Carson McCullers's *The Member of the Wedding*, James Jones's *From Here to Eternity*, Capote's *The Grass Harp*, and Salinger's *The Catcher in the Rye* are offered as evidence that a handful of writers at least has found that "comradely identification" is perhaps as dependable as anything else in this time when moral values are in flux. In these books, it is pointed out, the protagonists seek identification with others in an attempt to find security. The lost Frankie Addams of McCullers's book becomes one with Private Prewett of *From Here to Eternity*, and the merger continues with Cohn of *The Grass Harp*, and Holden Caulfield of *The Catcher in the Rye*. This composite figure of the critic's mind seeks "to belong," to be a part of our immediate world, as the writer, the artist, the individual of our time, seeks to make contact with what Santayana described in his last book as a world that "has turned its back on the attempt and even on the desire to live reasonably."

Is this theory of "self-definition or self-preservation through love," as the critic conceives it, good enough in itself to offer compensation to the writer in America? Or are the books that have been cited merely the last words to be spoken on the subject of the writer's defeat, gauged by standards that are not his own? I see them as essentially tragic books, heart-breaking in the stories of loneliness they tell but tragically illuminating, too, because the protagonists in them are Americans who strive not to be considered outcasts on their own soil. We know how persistently the American scene demands that one take part in it. It is good to join a group, a club, a society and not to try to stand alone; and if one cannot find that club, that group, the heart splits wide or shrivels like a leaf in loneliness. Is this, in the last analysis, what the books cited have to say? If Carson McCullers and Salinger and the others have written with agonizing truth not only of the individual but also of the writer's, the artist's situation in America, then that situation is even more desperate than was Dylan Thomas's on a winter night in the Fitzroy Pub twenty years ago.

Thomas Mann, among other writers of our time, has said that it is the writers, the intellectuals, of a country who bear the full weight of moral responsibility. It was the German intellectuals, Thomas Mann said, who allowed a dictator to come to power in Germany. Had they, through their works and by their vision, made richer promises than those he made, the man called Hitler would have been forced into exile instead of the writers of a country that he brought finally to defeat. Here in America we are politically aware. But although we rid ourselves of our demagogues by political action, we have not yet learned how to impeach an educational system the goal of which is to produce high-powered specialists instead of that perfectly balanced mind Henry Adams has written of, that mind which can produce an "absence of self-assertion or self-consciousness—the faculty of standing apart without seeming aware that one was alone." We allow our children to grow up in the belief that knowledge exists to serve a practical end. We accept the education media of television and radio, as presently exploited in America, as evils we cannot remedy and therefore must endure. We know that the majority of television and radio programs are a death sentence passed hourly on the creative impulse of our young, and yet we do not ask that this death sentence be reprieved for it permits us freedom as it wipes out the activity and the invention of our children. We do not cry aloud our protest as we see our children stricken by this disease for which no dimes are collected in prevention, no iron lungs designed, no wheelchairs pushed down the corridors of hospitals, bearing the victims of poliomyelitis of the will. (It might be said loudly that the Library Association of Great Britain has found that "Britons are reading more library books than ever—270,600,000 in the year ending last March—" because television shows have "increased interest in such subjects as archaeology, ballet, social problems," etc., creating an unprecedented demand for books about them. But however loudly it may be said, we will not hear.)

It has long been established that the writer, the artist, must partake of the world he finds about him if his work is to come alive and stay alive. But in an epoch such as this, when the collective material manifestations have outdone those of the individual spirit, then the artist, the writer, the believer, is unsure. Escape, exile, becoming the member of a group, whatever its nature, is not the answer; nor is that inner exile, that complete detachment of the spirit from the impingement of reality, which the intellectuals of totalitarian states have learned to endure. Now, in our time, it is clear that it is not the artist, the writer, the individual, who must seek to be accepted by the world he sees, but the scene itself that must be transformed to acceptability by the higher standards of the individual. The artist must know from the beginning that he does not belong, for the artist's deeper concern has always been not with what is taking place, but with the dimension of what might, within the imagination and the infinite capacity of man, take place. His concern must be with that belief which seeks, in Toynbee's phrase, "a higher level of conduct" both in act and in art.

The transforming of the contemporary scene is what I now ask of all American writers. I urge them to be the individual interpreters of this deep concern which can never find a place upon the air until a purer wavelength has been found for it. I would remind them that the voice of the artist, that voice which speaks with such superb authority in France, in England, in Italy, can, if they wish it, become the voice of authority here. "In France, more than in any other country," writes Marcel Arland, "it is the writers who today, as formerly, shape the language." This, in America, is heresy.

As a beginning, I ask that Maxwell Anderson write a play that refuses to compete with our corrupted popular media, a play that will not cause Bill March, that lonely, gentle, uncorrupted artist, to stir in anguish in his grave. I ask Truman Capote to condemn the scent of the rose if it serve the end of perfuming theater tickets. I ask Salinger to write maturely of maturity. I suggest that those who plan ninety-eight percent of the television and radio programs reconsider, for in this new era when the American writer recreates the scene, all that darkens the illumination of man's mind will have to

turn quietly and go. I warn the sponsors of television programs that the salesman with glassy eye and voice rising in
hysteria, who, his back to the wall, offers foam-rubber pil-
lows free, absolutely free, presages the end. I would ask the
lonely protagonists of novels still unwritten to reject communion and refuse identification, recognizing that writers
are men and women who have accepted a moral responsibility
and who must bear it, each isolated in his own conviction,
quite alone.

And now, because it is late of a bleak winter night, I would
send a message to Dylan Thomas, telling him again that when
the histories are written it is only the poets, and those who
read them, who remain.

A Man
in the Wilderness

In a letter written in 1958 from Mallorca, Spain, to William Carlos Williams in Rutherford, New Jersey, Edward Dahlberg cries out in despair: "As soon as you have architecture anywhere today you have foolish opinionated buildings, dogmatic functionalism, and all the depravity of the up-to-date, inhuman city. Nobody is educated enough any more to build a simple, unaffected home which is good, and has as much feeling, as an ancient proverb. When I look at a motorcycle or a taxi there are tears in my heart. For all the earth is ours, our habitation and sepulcher, and every country that falls under the infamy of money is a terrible wound to every other people."

Writing to Lewis Mumford from Berkeley, California, in 1953, Dahlberg reproaches Mumford for his worship of the machine and cautions him that to see "beauty in machinery is a great perversity" unworthy of his nature. In New York in

1951, Dahlberg writes his friend, Sir Herbert Read, that he does not approve of his way of living. "Do you think it is good to go to the foes of art to heal the artist? I don't care what money you get for whom, what you are doing is at the bottom a sin." He warns Read that he lives too shrewdly and that this is "the worst error of a poet. . . . For man must thirst, and must remain in the company of those who are athirst," he writes; and even if solitude is "a great pain in the heart," still "a man must remain in the wilderness."

To read Dahlberg's two present collections (*The Edward Dahlberg Reader* and *The Leafless American*, both 1967) is to enter the wilderness and to be all but overwhelmed by his passionate chronicling of the unremitting affront to the spirit which makes alienation the greatest peril to contemporary, sensitive man. The loneliness and the separateness which result from this affront are apt to engender a climate favorable to art. Kafka wrote of the consequences of disesteem obliquely, his language German, his vehicle allegory, and startled the lost to a deeper recognition of how forsaken they were. Dahlberg, whose work may be compared to Kafka's in its intensity of discernment and foreboding, writes of that merciless assault on the spirit in cadenced, occasionally archaic, and consistently splendid English. His language is classic, his metaphor frequently myth, but both language and myth are his alone.

Kafka was, in his time, not only Germany's most disturbing but also its most reliable prophet. As an artist he foretold with the maddest courage all the horror that was to come. Dahlberg, whose more than a dozen remarkable books have established a unique reputation for him in Europe as well as in America, deserves our recognition not only as stylist, as critic, as poet, but also as eloquent and unflinching prophet. He declaims against the outrage to every sensibility that faces us at this moment whichever way we turn upon our native soil, and he grieves for the disaster that lies, still undefined, beyond the perilous rim of contemporary American violence. What modern man calls progress, Dahlberg recognizes (with Yeats) as the dying of men's hearts. He sees the degradation of love and learning everywhere.

The ambiguous self in relation to history, to country, to sex, and to eternity, is furiously alive in all of Dahlberg's work, but it is in his letters that that self emerges in all its restless continuity. The letters are pages torn from the annals of his nights and days, his hopes and griefs, and transmuted into the actual substance of compassion, understanding, and yearning for those who are for the moment beyond the reach of his hand. "Bill Williams, you know, had another small stroke. I tremble for him, and also weep for him," Dahlberg writes to Josephine Herbst in 1958. "He has done so many things of which I disapprove, but how little I want to go on rebuking him. Poor, poor Bill, he is much too close to Nature. I would kill Nature could I save him."

But despite the sincere passion of his declared love, there is all too often a wariness in his approach to those whom he addresses, a lurking overzealousness that leaves one with the feeling that every human relationship Dahlberg has had was, without exception, a heartbreak to him in the end. At the very moment that he declares himself, he appears to tremble at the prospect of another devastating experience, still another emotional catastrophe from which he will never quite recover. "What the two of you cannot know," he writes to the Allen Tates in 1965, "is that I fear going to other people's homes, and when I do, I leave as fast as I can, without seeming to be rude. It is not that I do not care deeply for my friends, or that I prefer to be with the aristocratic intellects of our world. I dread unknowable disaster."

Lawrence Durrell once wrote a number of letters to Henry Miller on the subject of the artist's fear of accepting

his own identity. He cited to Miller "Cezanne's fear that society would get the grappins on him . . . Gauguin's insistence
on what a hell of a fine billiards player he was . . . and D. H.
Lawrence fervently knitting, knitting, and trying to forget
Sons and Lovers"—and there was Miller himself eating like
mad to establish a reputation for himself as a gourmet. "Here
are numberless types," Durrell wrote, "of the same ambiguous desire on the part of the artist to renounce his destiny.
To spit on it." This was not for the moment Dahlberg's desire
or dilemma. He knew from the beginning who he was and
that he was destined, both as man and writer, to be an exile in
the land of his birth, "first in the wanton streets of Kansas
City," he writes to William Carlos Williams in 1957, "then
in an orphanage, and then a waif of letters in New York."
His dilemma, rather, was how to be a writer, and he studied
the works of others avidly, seeking to find the way.

From the time of the appearance of his first novel, *Bottom
Dogs*, published in 1929, there could be no question but that
he had found his own exceptional speech. The Job of American letters, one critic has called him; others have termed his
autobiography, *Because I Was Flesh*, a masterpiece, and "one
of the few important American books published in our day."
"The truth is," this outsized figure of American literature
writes almost in panic to his friend Allen Tate (from Mallorca
in 1962), "that I am a great coward before I dare venture one
sentence. No man goes to the guillotine with greater appre-
hension than I sit down at my desk, no longer with a quill or
a pen, but with a fell machine. . . ." For to Dahlberg, a book
is "a battle of the soul and not a war of words."

Leon Edel recently took Joyce to task for calling out in his
letters for help, love, and money. Dahlberg's letters appeal
for these same solaces. Is the artist to be reproached for artic-
ulating the constant cry of all living men; is he not rather to
be cherished for having spoken it so eloquently? And is not

the attempt to answer that despairing cry the reason for all teaching, all learning, all writing, from the Greeks to Abélard, from the Old Testament to Joyce?

The voices of Camus and Sartre, Faulkner and Hemingway, no longer reach the young in the far journey they are taking; and Salinger, who was once their spokesman, is now more silent than the tomb. This wayfaring generation, hair long on the shoulders and wounded faces stanched by beards, murmurs of Allen Ginsberg, Timothy Leary, and Bob Dylan, uncertain as to whether these saviors (or even William Burroughs and John Rechy) are saying fearlessly and honestly enough the words that must somehow be said. Born in 1900, Dahlberg offers a philosophy of rebellion, but of dignity and discipline as well, to the young who have the insight to look his way. That philosophy, strong and undismayed, is stated in almost every page he writes. It is there in *The Tragedy of American Love* and in *Heart Speaketh to Heart*, both of which are included in *The Edward Dahlberg Reader*. It is there in his uncompromising letters, and strikingly there in the essay "Thoreau vs. Contemporary America," in which he extends his hand to the uneasy, saying:

> We are fatalists only when we cease telling the truth, but, so long as we communicate the truth, we move ourselves, life, history, men. There is no other way. This is the simple epitome of the wisdom of nonresistance to evil. It is what Confucius, Thoreau, and Tolstoi taught. It is the incredible, the visionary way, and it announces treason and betrayal more boldly than firearms or airplanes.

Farewell to New York

Ever since the beginning I have kept clear of Longchamps
in whatever street it lay, so that when the Spaniard—to whom
I shall never cease paying homage—said it would be simpler
to meet at the one which lay halfway between our two direc-
tions, I believed I could not bring myself to go. But I knew
it could never be entirely Longchamps as long as the Spaniard, who carried his pride and his history with him, was in
the place, so at six o'clock I crossed with the green light at the
corner. There was winter darkness on the avenue outside, but
as soon as you went through the revolving doors the gilt and
glitter leaped to meet you like the blaze of a jewelry counter
in a ten-cent store. Just inside stood the imitation fruit-and-
vegetable cart trying to give the genteel commotion the air
of a musical-comedy market square—with the bounty and
gaiety that should entail—and not succeeding. The Spaniard

was waiting on the other side of the vegetable wagon, and in spite of the crowd he found a table nearly at once, and the waiter who mourned on the outskirts was stricken with an even deeper grief that we had pushed our way far into the corner to it and sat down.

"We would like tea with lemon, and some pastry," the Spaniard said. It was clear right away that we asked for something far too simple. It would be too easy, too agreeable a thing to bring tea and pastry at this time of day. *This time next week*, I believe the Spaniard went on to say, *you will be in France. I have some letters to friends for you in my pocket—poets, writers, political exiles*, he said, *I wish I could be with you, but tell them I will be there certainly by spring. In the spring*, he said, as if the intentions of men would change with the season, *the last act will be played in Spain, and the ending will be a good one*.

"You can't just order pastry," said the waiter who stood beside the table. He was young, but his voice was as testy as that of an old woman, "You have to look at the menu and order the kind of cake you want."

"Stop," said the Spaniard gently, for I had already got up from my chair in my impatience. He laid one hand on my arm and drew me down into my seat again, and he looked up into the waiter's face, "Young man, be polite. Let us be polite to each other," he said.

The instant the words were spoken the waiter's face altered. In the short time he had been in this brilliant palace he had forgotten so much, he had forgotten his entire youth perhaps, and the Spaniard's words recalled his memories to him.

"Yes, of course, you are right," the waiter said. He stood looking in amazement and happiness at the Spaniard. He had absolutely forgotten that people had ever spoken to each other that way.

But the Spaniard, being accustomed to saying the words which recalled men to themselves, had forgotten the waiter almost at once, and now he was thinking of France again.

"This time next week in France," said the Spaniard, "remember the French know better than any other nation of men that in political exiles there exists a special devotion. An artist suffers guilt and loneliness when he is alienated from his country, but the artist has a spiritual terrain of silence which is native to him, and which he can turn to in any country where he is. But if a political man no longer stands on his own country's soil he is maimed and mute, and he must be a great believer in a great faith in order to survive."

The waiter, with exceptional gentleness, put the tea and the cake down before us, and we began to eat at once, and while we ate, the Spaniard told me the story of the exiles in Paris who went to have their identity photographs taken in the rue du Palais.

"There is a little photograph shop where they do it there," he said. "They have a sign hanging out saying: 'Six minutes to wait and thirty francs to pay.' So you go in through a contraption like a subway stile, one foreigner after another, an endless string of outcasts paying thirty francs each as they go. It was a cold December day when we went, a dozen or so of us who had survived Franco and Vichy, and so still had a name and an identity. But some of us didn't have overcoats, and we walked with our jacket collars turned up around our ears, and our hands in our pockets, knocking our feet together to keep the blood from stopping in the cold.

"Have some pastry," said the Spaniard quickly. "My God, I can feel the cold now. Have some tea. Even after two years I can feel the cold." So they filed into the photograph place, he went on, and one by one, like a chain gang passing, they laid their money down on the counter and passed into the booths beyond. "There was our group of Spaniards, and there were men from other countries, too," he said. "Czechs, Poles, students who might have been Hungarians once, and men with dark skins from the colonies. Exiles," he said, "eternally seeking to persuade themselves and others by means of a likeness reproduced on paper that they still had the right to a name and a physiognomy."

Into the curtained booths they passed, one after another, and fixed their eyes on the spot the woman indicated, and faced the mirrors and the glare. And once the invisible camera had opened and closed, they moved on again, one by one, in single file, their shoulders hunched, their hands thrust in their pockets for warmth, to wait the six minutes huddled against the wall.

"And then the strange thing happened," the Spaniard said. "The finished photographs would come out of a slot in the photographic machine, strip after strip, and a girl with scissors in her hand would pick them up and glance through the crowd for the face as she quickly cut them apart. And the man to whom they belonged would push forward through the others, and take his photographs still damp and limp in his hand, and look at them curiously and uneasily, with a little display of the vanity he had left, and go out into the cold again. And then, suddenly a strip of photographs came out which belonged to no one in the place," said the Spaniard. He took a great swallow of his tea. "The girl with the scissors waved the little handful of photographs in the air, and no one went forward to claim them. 'He must be here. Where is he?' she said. 'Let him come through to get them. This is holding everybody up.' She raised the photographs up high so that we all could see him, a thin, tired-looking young man with long black hair that he hadn't had the time or money to get cut, with a foulard knotted around his neck. He was certainly not in the photography shop with us. None of us had seen him there. And then one of the Spaniards standing beside me in the crowd made a queer sound in his throat, and he called out: 'I knew him. We came from the same town, we went to school together. He was killed in Durango in 1936.' There was silence in the place," said the Spaniard, "and then the girl said, 'Are you trying to make a fool out of me?' But she did not say any more, and she put aside the photographs of the man who wasn't there. Then she picked up the next strip, and clipped it, and the one after that, and the men they belonged to pushed their way through the crowd and got them, and went out the door. But with the third strip the same thing happened—there was the photograph of a young man who wasn't in the room with us. He had a beard, and a scar down one side of his face, and another of the Spaniards called out, 'That's Amaro. That's my brother. He was shot in Guernica.' The girl did not say anything that time because the tears were running down his cheeks," said the Spaniard. "But the next strip and the strip after that, it was just the same, and at the sight of the unclaimed photographs the voices would call out from the crowd in the shop, 'That's José Casals. I was with him in Madrid before they got him.' Or, 'That is Ramón Rodriguez. They killed him at Almeria.' They were there," said the Spaniard, "in spite of death. When we go out now, with our bellies full, we will find them in the dark, for they are always there."

The Spaniard gave me the letters he had written to his friends, and we went out and we said good-by at the top of the subway steps in the rain. "Write," he said. And his eyes were sad and bright in the city darkness.

So I write you now, Spaniard, that if I feel guilt it is not because I am a writer alienated from the soil of my own country for a little, but because there are writers and poets to whom the invitation to speak was given, a long time ago, and they gave their answers.

"You are all mad," wrote Ezra Pound in 1937. "Spain is

an emotional luxury to a gang of sap-headed dilettantes." "If I were a Spaniard I should be fighting for Franco," wrote Evelyn Waugh in the same year. "As an Englishman I am not in the predicament of choosing between two evils. I am not a fascist nor shall I become one unless it were the only alternative to Marxism." And T. S. Eliot opened the door a little way and whispered, "While I am naturally sympathetic, I still feel convinced that it is best that at least a few men of letters should remain isolated, and take no part in those collective activities."

Excerpt from
"The Long Walk
at San Francisco State"

One night in May 1968, when I was having dinner in the home of a colleague from the English Department of San Francisco State, he received an urgent telephone call to go to the college. It was after nine, but other teachers were there, attempting to get to the Vice-President for Academic Affairs in the hope of dissuading him from inviting the police on campus. Several hundred students were sitting in the main entrance of the Administration Building, the sit-in being the culmination of a week-long crisis that had erupted between Dr. Summerskill's resignation as President and Dr. Smith's appointment to the post. "I'm going up at once," my colleague said when he came back to the table, and I said I was going with him. "Look, it's going to rain," he said—as if this would keep me from climbing Mount Blanc or crossing the Rubicon. "It's my college as much as yours," I said, which was not entirely true. He had been there several years longer, and indeed it was he who had hired me in 1963. But he finally took me along.

All the way up Nineteenth Avenue I kept asking myself what I was doing feeling committed to a college. I had lived on mountaintops, carried my babies in a rucksack on my back when I skied, believed in poets more than any other men, honored French Resistance fighters and Italian partisans, crossed into Spain with letters from the exiled to the brave and the defiant and the imprisoned there, and brought their illicit messages out. And now, through force of circumstance, I was, of all unlikely and unsuitable things, a college professor. I was a professor, moreover, who spoke of her institution as if it were a possession of the heart. "That's because of the students," I said to myself. "That's because they're the great and vital thing."

But that wasn't entirely true either. There were other things that made State all it was. One of them was that down the hall of the Administration Building that night came Alberto Moravia, just in from Italy, choosing to arrive when one of the great social dramas of our time was being played. We had met in Rome in the last months of World War II when Moravia had come down from the mountains to his liberated city. That we should both have been at San Francisco State that night seemed to affirm that the dissension then under way was a continuation of something that had begun a long time before, a process we had both borne witness to in another time and place and had taken our part in as well.

Moravia was bemused by the mildness of the students' demands, which were that Air Force ROTC be removed from the campus, that several hundred disadvantaged black and Third World students be admitted to the college in the Fall 1968 term, and that faculty with the same ethnic background as the students be hired to teach special courses. Young men and women all over the world were asking for far more, and asking it with greater fervor; and twenty-five years earlier Moravia had seen Italian partisans ask for an entire country, an entire people, and get a good portion of what they asked. He showed a bleak interest in the report that a troika composed of the Vice-President for Academic Affairs, the Vice-President for Business Affairs, and the Dean of Students had been locked in an office that afternoon by the students. Once liberated, the three men were in no frame of mind to listen to faculty recommendations that they walk down the hall and discuss the students' grievances. The teachers who urged this solution were certain that if the students had been asked to go home and send a delegation the following day, they would have cheered. A monsoonlike rain was beating down outside, and although they sang that they would not be moved and that they would overcome, it had been a long week, and many of them were stupefied by lack of sleep, and their spirits were low.

Just before the first police units appeared, Moravia was whisked away by friends, for this was no place for a citizen of another country. And as four uniformed keepers of the peace advanced down the long empty hall to the scene of weariness and disjointed song, I walked toward them, feeling in that moment solitary and unfettered, as every individual alive has the right to feel at every instant of his life. When we had come face to face, I said to the four men: "Gentlemen, you may go no farther. This campus belongs to the faculty and students, not to the police." The sergeant, a short undistinguished man who carried a walkie-talkie that crackled with messages directly from God, barely glanced at me as he said, "Aw, lady, come off it"; and the four of them marched directly through me, as if I had as little substance as a cloud.

I could have pursued them and pounded my fists against their dark blue backs as they made for the closed door of the troika. Or I could have stopped them short by telling them a thing I had learned at a three-day conference on suicide I had taken part in six months before. The conference had drawn attention to statistics showing the high rate of nervous break-downs and subsequent suicides among members of police forces throughout America. There had been discussion as to whether the pressure of their work had brought so many to the point of taking their own lives, or if it was the particular combination of characteristics which had originally led them to choose the role that ultimately caused their self-inflicted deaths. Training in the violent punishment, and even extinc-tion, of others, it was suggested, might bring them more readily than other men to the act of drawing their service revolvers from their holsters and, often standing before a mirror, blowing out their own brains instead of those of fel-low citizens whose class or color they happened to dislike. I could have told the policemen about this. But I ended up doing nothing. I was on a year's probation, having served twenty-one days in Santa Rita Prison following my second arrest for sitting down in a doorway of the Oakland Induction Center, and that year was just beginning. I felt I didn't have any more time to give to that or any other interruption to the living of daily life. I did not know of the daily turmoil that lay ahead for everyone at State.

At midnight the patrol wagons began drawing up in the Holloway Avenue parking lot. Sixty persons were arrested, among them members of the American Federation of Teach-ers, Local 1352, who volunteered to be taken into custody in place of some of the students. What purpose these arrests served it is impossible to say. Did the police action prove the absurd futility of locking administrators in an office, or did it, on the contrary, call public and administrative attention to the students' demonstration and thus create a wider under-standing of the need for an open Economic Opportunity Pro-gram? Did the subsequent prison sentences and fines serve to break the spirit of students and faculty to such an extent that they would act with greater propriety in the future? But less than six months later, students would be demonstrating in increasing numbers, and faculty would be marching in support of their demands. What I did learn that night was that there is no chance at all if you try to do it alone. One AFT member was to say later that "the record of faculty action must cease to be a record of faculty impotence." The following day I joined the AFT.

That night in May marked the moment when San Francisco State ceased to be a place that I went to for the purpose of meeting with students, either in classes or in conference. Almost without warning, it became a concerned state of mind, much as a country, particularly in defeat, sheds its actual soil and takes on a richer meaning. All that followed was a part of the sequence of engagements in an unending battle for something one might as well call decency, a battle in which the ardent and powerless have little chance to win. This began almost without warning, I have said, but at least one warning had been given me. During the previous winter I had sought to sponsor the writing course of Sonia Sanchez, the black poet who had been teaching a course for no credit in the Experimental College at State (and this in a college where you can get credit for a course in bowling). Although the engagement fought to sponsor Sonia Sanchez was eventually won, I took no pride at all in the triumph, for in the process I had lost too much faith in the potential for forthright action of those in the college administration who obstructed the way.

The ways of academic procedure, being new to me, are deeply puzzling. I can still see no reason, for instance, for the vast amount of printed matter, largely from department heads, that day after day fills our mailboxes to overflowing. These communications keep us informed of absolutely everything except the truth of how things are. At no time was I given a Xeroxed directive telling me that I, or anyone else, was not permitted to sponsor a black teacher's course in the English Department, no matter how exceptional the qualifications of that teacher, and that I'd better forget about it. That was probably the one notice they forgot to put in my box.

Sonia Sanchez, a tiny, childlike figure with an enormous black aureole of hair around her small, tense face, was now in the second semester of teaching credit courses in the English Department at San Francisco State. I sat in on the night sessions and listened to her woo from the eight or ten black students in the class the everyday vocabulary of their lives. She asked them to set down on paper the things that were driving them nuts, and to get these things down in their own words, not in the language of some other writer whose books they had been asked to read sometime, somewhere. No white teacher had ever made them believe that the way they spoke, and what they thought, was worth writing about. All they had ever learned in other classrooms was what a problem they were to a troubled white society.

Sonia Sanchez was putting into practice the curriculum the Black Students Union was fighting for: an area of learning that was connected to black people's lives by a language that did not belittle or confuse them. In those night sessions her students wrote poetry that would have meaning to others in their community, and that is probably one of the things that good writing does. Like the others, I wrote poems in Sonia Sanchez's classroom, but the trees and mountains and winds and sand and sea I wrote of were scenic props. They had no more relevance to life and death than a lace handkerchief discreetly dropped into the bellowing anguish of a slaughterhouse. There were four-letter, and five-letter, and frequently twelve-letter words in the poems the students wrote and read aloud. It is quite possible none of them knew Sonia Sanchez's poem "malcolm" or her "Memorial—To Bobby Hutton." "Malcolm" was, of course, Malcolm X, and Bobby Hutton was a seventeen-year-old Black Panther who, one spring night in 1968, in his undershorts, with his hands held high above his head, was riddled with bullets as he obeyed the order to walk to a police car. But even if they did not know her poetry, they knew that Sonia was asking them to speak and write in a college classroom a language that they had always been reluctant to write, or to speak too loud, before.

The Teaching of Writing

Teenagers and students in their early twenties make teaching
an endlessly exciting experience for me. Young people have a
particular gift for reviving freshness of thought and language
and emotion. Last year, for instance, one of my sixteen-year-
old students began a composition with these words:

> All during dinner I was sitting in the Chablis wine bottle, obliv-
> ious to what my father was saying. The cool, clear liquid held
> me up buoyantly, like a turtle on a lake in spring. I saw myself
> swimming gently, easily, over to the side of the bottle nearest to
> my father, and I was treading wine. The green glass distorted
> his face horribly so that his moustache and lips were merged in
> a snarl which became grotesque every time he moved his mouth
> to chew.

The picture these sentences evoke is startling in its purity
and far more revealing than a long discourse on the lack of

communication between a father and his daughter. Words like these make an oasis, richly green and deep with shadows, in the parched wasteland of daily talk.

How to release reluctant students to speech is the first problem for the teacher of writing. At times the young find it as difficult to express their inner thoughts in words as do those whose minds have solidified into all but unbreakable moods. But why, after all, should this inability to speak with the heart as well as with the lips be blamed on "restrictive teaching"? Is it not more a case of restrictive thinking (induced by restrictive living) causing this muteness, which perhaps no teacher can cure? One can suggest reading to such students—great poetry, great novels—to help allay the fear of speaking. But one cannot be sure that the students will dare to understand the words that other men have said. It takes courage to say things differently: Caution and cowardice dictate the use of the cliché.

One can speak of Dylan Thomas crying out in fervor and eagerness, while still in his early teens, "If *Paradise Lost* had not already been written, I would have written it!" One can suggest to one's students that they forget for the moment the daily, insoluble problems of family conflicts, or creative writing courses, or difficulties in transportation, and write of the night mind, of their own night minds. But this does not mean that they will instantly begin to probe beneath their conscious thoughts for the great fortune that is lying there like hidden gold.

Once I quoted to a class of adults André Malraux's statement that to fulfill one's destiny one must never cease converting one's life to wider concepts and wider uses.

"Well, how would you suggest I do that here in this small town?" a gentle old lady student once asked.

"Perhaps each of us has to find the way himself," was the only answer I could give her. "In the Connecticut town where

I live, for instance," I added, "I entered into the lives of the men on skid row, tragic derelicts of men who stood all day in doorways, or leaned in huddled groups against a wall, where the sun would warm their blood for a little while. . . ."

And the little old lady asked me then, "Well, if I did that here, what kind of a dress do you think I should wear?"

Most adults, having somehow lost touch with the great simplicities, have forgotten that to write is to speak of one's beliefs. Turning out a typescript with the number of words neatly estimated in the upper right hand corner of the first page has nothing to do with writing. Neither have questions about the prices paid by *Harper's Magazine* or the *Atlantic Monthly* or the *Ladies' Home Journal* or *Esquire*. Writing is something else entirely, as the young instinctively know.

One of the last things Albert Camus averred before his untimely death was that "a man's work is nothing but a long journey to recover through the detours of art the two or three simple and great images which first gained access to his heart." At times I ask my students to write of nothing at all until they can define those images. Only when they have done so are they in some measure prepared for that long journey of which Camus spoke.

For the benefit of one of my students who actually believed that writers must be intellectuals, Robert Frost sat down with me and her and explained the vast difference between the two. "Intellectuals," he said, with a gesture of impatience at the thought of them, "deal in abstractions. It's much safer that way. Writers take risks. They deal in anecdotes and parables. The Bible is written in anecdotes and parables."

It is not always easy to convince students that what Frost said is true. To the recalcitrant who may, quite paradoxically, accept the miracle of Christianity while rejecting the inner world created by the mind of man, I tell the following anecdote:

My friend, a French painter and Resistance fighter, was put in a concentration camp by the Nazis. Every evening during his long incarceration, he and two or three of his fellow prisoners created a world to which their jailers had no access. Entirely by means of conversation and gestures, they dressed for dinner in immaculate white shirts that did not exist, and placed, at times with some difficulty because of the starched material that wasn't there, pearl or ruby studs and cuff links in those shirts. With the greatest gallantry and deference, they helped one another into jackets that were formal or informal, as befitted the restaurant in which they had chosen to dine.

Moreover, these imprisoned men took on different identities every evening, and the conversation therefore differed as they sat down at a table glittering with silver and crystal that their eyes only could perceive. With their varying identities, the menu and the wine also differed. If they were playing the role of distinguished diplomats, the conversation was of wooded alpine regions and the hunt, and they ordered wild boar and pheasant from the waiter who was not there. On occasion, they sent dishes back if the food was not done to their liking.

They drank Châteauneuf-du-Pape throughout the meal and Château d'Yquem with the dessert pastry. At times, after tasting the wine, they found it had not been properly corked and they had it taken away. There were certain restaurants they did not patronize a second time because the lobster had been overcooked or the after-dinner brandy had not been served in the traditional wide-bowled crystal that one could cradle in the hand.

On the evenings that they saw themselves as men of letters, they quoted from the great poets while they dined, reciting all the lines they could remember of Homer, Dante, Milton, and Shakespeare. If they were scientists, at least one among them would be a Nobel prize winner, and they would discuss da Vinci and Spengler and Einstein. The words they spoke were real, if nothing else was, and the lonely courage that other men had expressed gave them the courage to survive.

So to those students who have not found the way to write from inside the bottle of Chablis, one must never cease to offer bottles of even richer, finer wines. And one can ask them as well to listen to the words of a very great young writer of our time, James Baldwin, whose fervent essays put much of contemporary, so-called creative writing to everlasting shame. "Although we do not wholly believe it yet," Baldwin has said, "the interior life is a real life, and the intangible dreams of people have a tangible effect upon the world." If we as writers and as teachers can communicate that quite simple truth to others, then we shall have fulfilled our roles.

III. ON THE BODY POLITIC

"Shout Aloud Our Disputed Tongue"

Farewell to Europe

For over a quarter of a century I have lived in Europe, and, perhaps because of the physical distance between me and my country, when other aspects of American life were lost in vagueness, America's tradition of individual freedom remained singularly clear. During those years my forebears acquired a special stature, and perspective lent them a meaning possibly greater than was actually theirs. For instance, I have always believed that my great-great-grandfather on my mother's side, a General Bauer who served on George Washington's staff in the Revolution, was a man who felt so deeply about political freedom that he volunteered to give his life for it. I believe, moreover, that in making the choice he did, in the time he made it, he not only played a part in creating a nation but accepted as well the individual responsibility of establishing a tradition of social freedoms, and I am proud he made that choice.

There are others among my people who belong to America as well as to me, and through the years their lives have been part of my own. There was my great-grandfather Moore, a doctor, who after much thought and with some misgivings left Philadelphia with his family and settled in Kansas at a time when the Indian fires burned along the horizon at night. He was "almost overcome by the vastness" that confronted him, but he recognized it as a site for individual endeavor, and winter and summer he traveled by horse and buggy through that vastness to his scattered patients.

His favorite child, my mother's mother, was a school-teacher at sixteen and raised her own children on the Kansas prairies, and I think of her as a pioneer as fearless as any who broke new soil. I know that her eldest daughter, Nina E. Allender, the official cartoonist of the National Woman's Party and a staunch fighter for the franchise and rights before the law of all American women, belongs as well to a tradition to which I am committed by pride. I shall tell my grandchil-dren, as I have told my children, of the Children's Crusade that crossed America in the early twenties—a struggling cru-sade of children and their mothers who walked across the continent to Washington to petition the White House to set their fathers free. When the marching children, some ill, all weary, came through Cincinnati, my mother opened our doors to them, and she washed and fed them, and when they left she walked to the outskirts of the city with them, helping them carry their placards reading: "My father is in prison for expressing his opinion, " or "I have never seen my father. He is still in prison because he didn't believe in war."

I have spoken of these forebears of mine to Europeans, and their presence with me on foreign soil helped establish among us a common tongue. I have talked of my father's father, Jesse Peyton Boyle, whose people came from Ireland, and who was a man of passionate opinions, furiously expressed. He was a lawyer and the founder of the West Publishing Company in St. Paul, and his belief in the rights of the American male citizen brought him daily to the point of apoplexy. In the years I lived abroad my grandmother, my mother, and the others were somehow there with me in explanation and justification of the things I said about America. They were present when Europe looked to us for liberation from the Nazi armies, and they were there when that liberation came. They went with me, these ardent believers in the spirit of free inquiry, into the political prisons of Franco's Spain and into the processing centers of Western Germany, where refugees from the East waited for asylum. Indeed, it would perhaps be more accurate to say that I went to these places because my forebears were with me and that it was they who led me there.

But by 1949 a change had come into the faces of Europeans when they spoke of America, and my forebears seemed to feel uneasy in their revolutionary roles. In 1951 scattered editorials appeared in the foreign press, and Europeans asked curiously, incredulously, about the "democratic tension" in America. Which of the basic freedoms was the voice of one man condemning, they asked, and which did he honor, and—far graver—which of the freedoms could survive his daily abuse? In late 1952 and early 1953 the press of England, Germany, France—although never a single organ of the Communist Party—spoke bitterly of this man, an American, whose name was not Eisenhower or Dulles, but something quite different from either of these.

One German newspaper editor, a close friend for several years, and a tough, seasoned fighter for democracy, struck the table with his fist and said: "If there is another side in America as articulate as this one man's, then get more and more evidence of it to us over here. I don't want to fill my paper with the reports of his accusations, with accounts of the suicides of honest men. I want to give the German people another America, an America as dynamic and eloquent as his. If his voice doesn't speak for your countrymen, then let us hear other voices ringing out. Only Einstein, once a German like me, spoke loudly enough for us to catch the echo over here."

"Don't go back to America now," a Paris concierge I have known for fifteen years said to me in the spring. "It isn't your country anymore"; and because of the silence that fell suddenly around us, I believed for a moment that my ancestors had died. As she washed the tiles of the entrance hall or peeled the potatoes for the soup at night, the concierge spoke of one man only, and it was not Pinay or Laniel or even Mendes-France. It was an American, and his name was McCartair, and if he didn't like the look of your face, he'd subpoena you right in off the street, she told me. "Stay away from America the way the French who could manage it stayed away when fascism was in the saddle here. It doesn't last, fascism. It's a corpse that the ambitious try to pump the blood of life into every now and then. The French people will see it doesn't get any more transfusions in a hurry here," she said. When I spoke of other Americans to her, she shook her head, and poured us each a glass of wine in sympathy. "There is only Monsieur McCartair," she said. "There is no other side."

For over four years I taught in a women's prison in Germany, and the director of the prison stands, a clear, pure figure, as strong as stone, against the grimness of that place. She is calm and proud, wise and humble, eager, and open, and uncorruptible, and gracious as few Germans have ever sought to be. One of my last evenings in Europe was spent in her small house near the prison, spent in talk, as so many times before, with a group of students from the local university. She said to me then, "Write to us about the other America. It must be there."

And one bold young student of political economy said that this "other America" on which the common people of Europe had counted, and counted still, had no press even in America to speak for it. "The same kind of censorship through indecision is taking place in America now as once took place in Germany," the student said. "People can't risk losing their jobs by buying a paper that defends the freedom of the individual. So, one after another, these papers die. That's what happened in Germany twenty years ago, so the other side was never heard. That's what's happening in America today."

"Tell them when you get back," said the director of the prison, "that we had our demagogue too, and for a long time we laughed about him. We said that for the German people he was an impossibility. And tell them when a dictator came to power in Italy, we said—out of our national contempt for the Italian moral fiber—that we, a democratic people, with the history of democratic trade unions like a strong backbone to support our economic life, could never be swayed emotionally as they had been. But little by little, while we talked of our traditions, the demagogue talked louder, and our civil liberties narrowed, narrowed, narrowed, until one day they were no longer there."

"Stay in Germany where you can say and write what you please," said the youngest and brashest of the students as we sat in the little house near the prison that night, and nobody thought to laugh at the irony of history.

"*Don't go back to America until the tide has changed,*" were the words written in a letter from England that I carried in my bag. "*Don't go back to a state of mind that can justify a military treaty with Franco's Spain by that impoverished word 'expediency.'*" And a message from a Spaniard in exile in the south of France lay beside the Englishwoman's letter, and it said, "*Wait to return until the campaign promises have been kept by your President concerning the Taft-Hartley law and the*

McCarran Act. The air in America will then be easier to breathe." And the voice of a young Frenchman came across the frontier, saying to me, "*There are periods in the history of every country when there is no course left to the intelligent citizen but to stay away.*"

And then, as if they had been roused from sleep, my forebears stood up from their chairs. The women among them waited, their eyes fixed gravely on me, for me to speak, but the men walked back and forth in agitation, and the little house near the prison trembled with the vehemence of my Irish grandfather's ire.

"No, this is the time to return," I said to the German students seated in the room, and to the Frenchman, and the Spaniard, and the Englishwoman, who were not there. "This is one of the times in history when one must go back and speak out with those of the other America clearly and loudly enough so that even Europe will hear."

No Time to Listen

Mr. Samuel Dodson is the kind of man who might give you a lot of trouble if you didn't make things clear to him from the start. Unless I can make him understand about the responsibilities of a writer, he's going to keep right on interfering with my work, and I'm too busy to have interruptions. Working late at night every night of the week is wearing enough in itself without Mr. Samuel Dodson coming up the stairs into my room at any hour of the night or day and simply standing there.

The trouble is, Mr. Dodson has been around too much and seen too many other ways of living. I knew it at once when I had lunch with him in the school cafeteria that day. He's taken courses at integrated universities, and he's learned from firsthand observation, he said, that many white persons are intellectually dull, and he's learned in scientific studies that racial superiority is a white man's myth. He's sat down in theatres and restaurants in other states just like any other American, and he's traveled in Canada where people looked on him not as a Negro but as a cultivated, self-respecting man. He happens to be tall and distinguished-looking, with a light tan skin, and there's an air about him that might mark him for a minister. But the fervor of belief has turned to bitterness in him. You can tell this as soon as he begins to speak. He's been working-principal of the Negro elementary school in Frankford for sixteen years, and he ought to be used to things by this time. But instead he's filled with grief and acrimony. He says when he drives down from Canada and finally crosses the Delaware Memorial Bridge, it's not only the temperature that alters, but socially and psychologically it's as if he walked out of an air-conditioned room on the hottest day of summer onto the burning sidewalks of the South.

In the first place, Frankford, Delaware, doesn't mean anything at all to me. I came here for the first time ten days ago. It's a place you can hardly see on the map, downstate in Sussex County, with parched cornfields and chicken farms spread all around the town. The residential district is made up largely of frame houses, and the homes of the white people are white—some of them Georgian, with tall pillars soaring unblemished on either side of the front doors—while the Negro homes are weathered and grey. But the Negro elementary school is a modern building, set a little way out of the town where it won't bother anyone at all. There's a big playground at the back of it, and the desks and chairs and tables look new, and the floors are bright, and the whole place is as clean as wax. In the town of Easton, dynamite was found outside a Negro's home on September 13, after the opening of school, but that's over the state line in Maryland and has nothing to do with Frankford, Delaware. There hasn't been any trouble like that in Frankford because the schools haven't integrated here. But Mr. Dodson has lost his perspective on the situation. He says the lines of communication are closed like a fist. The white and the Negro school boards are separate, he says, and the teachers' institutes are separate, and the parent-teacher organizations, and all recreational and amusement activities, and all parades. The town council has no Negro representation, he tells you, and he makes it seem as perilous as if he were a captain seeking to bring a foundering ship to port in darkness through a stormy sea.

Perhaps if I told Mr. Dodson about the book I'm writing he'd stop getting in the way of the sentences I want to get set down. I'm writing a novel about Germany, and it has a certain importance because I hope it will make people understand about the things that have always happened there, and that are still happening now. I'm writing about the German school system, for instance, where the sons of workingmen are written off, and higher education is reserved for the sons of the socially elite. This is a fairer procedure, they will tell you, for then students without an adequate social background are spared the embarrassment of finding themselves out of their milieu. I'm bringing into the book the conspiracy of the German medical profession to keep the simplest kind of medical knowledge from the man in the street so as to safeguard the prestige and the tradition of the man with a degree. I want Americans to know what kind of injustices and inequalities are condoned by custom in other countries, but when Mr. Dodson comes into my room and stands there by my typewriter, I can't think of anything except the things he said to me at lunch that day.

He kept talking about communication as though that were the only thing that mattered in life—interracial communication and even communication between man and man. He was going down to a migrant labor camp next day to talk with people; but what language is there to speak, he asked, if there

is no word of hope to give men and women who live in abandoned chicken houses, or even above and adjacent to the
chickens, and who have no destination beyond the ending of
each day? They have only kerosene lamps, or low-voltage
electric lights, he said, to penetrate the darkness, and no designated part to play in either the Negro or the white community. He said that the required mile distance from home
to elementary school which entitles a child to bus transportation seems at times to be differently applied for Negro children, or else the distance must, at times, be measured differently. "The punishment involved in waiting along the high-
way for the often uncertain arrival of the bus, the trudging
to and from the bus stop in rain, hail or snow," he said, "is
one of the causes of children giving up school in discourage-
ment. And then they start helping their parents on the land,
and that's the end of potential individuals, potential citizens,"
he said, sitting there larger than life in the school cafeteria,
forgetting to eat the potato salad and the canned peaches on
his plate that day. "But, damn it, a mile isn't far, Mr. Dodson!" you might want to cry out, but then he'd answer, "It's
far when you're six or seven years old, it's far at the wrong
time of year. And it's farther than ever when you've missed
the bus, and started to walk, and a bus carrying white children who live only a couple of blocks away from you passes
you by. That makes the difference farther than any living
child should have to walk, no matter how long he lives," he
said.

I tell you I can't do anything about it, Mr. Dodson. I
haven't got the time. Today I'm supposed to be correcting
proof on my novelette about Spain which is going to be published in the spring, and it's essential that it be printed so that
people who haven't been there will know. In this story I tell
of the labyrinth of caves that the outcasts of the civil war in
Spain have excavated in the clay soil surrounding the city of

Madrid. Fifty thousand or more, when I was there, living like prairie dogs underground in the clay. There, children are sleeping on beds of rags while their fathers are on the run, twenty years later still in-and-out of political prisons and on the run, and their wives and their children living—if you call it that—and rotting and dying there. It's the contrasts that are so flagrant in Spain that I want to make clear to Mr. Dodson. There are women so elegantly dressed, so handsomely bejewelled, that you stop and look in wonder; and then, just beyond the reach of their gloved hands, those others who sell their ration cards to buy a shirt and live on refuse and market pilfering. That's the kind of thing I'm trying to say.

I haven't the time to listen to Mr. Dodson saying that when he stands up in assembly every morning, the words stick in his throat, and he can't get them out. "These children here haven't been given any part to play in life," he said that day. "They're born, and they accept the years of school the law has sentenced them to, and they feel they're doing time until the doors of their teenage years open and let them go free. All they want in the end is a little cash to jingle in their pockets, and maybe a hot rod, if they can hope that high. That's the fulfillment of their lives. There isn't anything beyond that for them, and I can't tell them any differently."

There must be a way of making Mr. Dodson understand that I have my own work to get on with and I can't listen to him. There must be some way of keeping him from crossing the Memorial Bridge and getting out of Delaware.

A Day on Alcatraz
with the Indians

I spent Christmas day on Alcatraz with the Native Americans because it seemed to me the most logical place to be. A friend of mine has a small motorboat, and we crossed the bay that windy morning with a cargo of propane gas. Butane and propane gas for cooking are among the great needs of the Indians there. Once the boat was moored on the windswept dock of Indian Land, we began the steep climb up the cold north side of the island toward the sun. Jeeps and trucks stood abandoned along the way, for the Indians need mechanics and gas and motor oil and batteries to get the mechanical hearts of these stubborn vehicles to beating once again. And there was a little pile of abandoned clothing, too, clothing that charitable members of the white middle class had sent over to the Indians on their bleak rock: blue-satin, spike-heeled slippers lay there, and tinsel dancing shoes, both pairs quite worn from somebody else's dancing, and a not-new apron embroidered with holly sprigs and the legend: "Now is the season to be jolly."

The road winds up between overhanging rock and crumbling balustrades; green moss and wild, thick vines on one side, and on the other, barges and boats below straining at their moorings. Beyond them, freighters were passing in the rough waters of the bay. We were not kings bearing gifts, nor had we followed any star. We were simply two white Americans stumbling up the narrow stairways that weave in and out of the old walls, carrying cooking gas to an almost annihilated people, our only virtue that it was not, for a change, either tear gas or napalm that we were using as currency. In this legal taking over of Alcatraz, in this stunning act of the imagination and the will, not the least of the triumphs is that the needs of the Indians are, as on the reservation, material ones. The essentials of the spirit, isolated from the mainstream of the country's life, have heroically survived.

At the top is the prison itself, and, having passed the ruined buildings that once housed the guards and their families, and the storerooms and offices, you come to this monument that has stood for a long time in monstrous celebration of man's implacable fury against man. No place in these United States could be more appropriate as symbol of the Indian's imprisonment on his own soil. I walked with a young North Dakota Indian through its long hallways, mounted the spiral iron stairs, knowing this was neither federal, nor even American, but a place constructed by men of every nation, every creed, every time, for the purpose of depriving humanity itself of whatever hope there might be left. Even though the cell doors hang open now, the memory of desperation speaks hollowly from every stone. The Indians have spread newspapers on the cement floors of these cells, and they sleep there. In the isolation row of the third tier, there are no bars, but blank doors, four inches thick, that served to close each prisoner off from life and light. In one of these cells, an endless row of small even lines moves from the door around the walls, scraped by the fingernail of a man who had perhaps endured in solitude there for twenty years. "Each mark is maybe for each month or year he spent in here," I said, and the young Indian who stood beside me, touching this record with his fingertips, cried out, "Not each month or year! Each century, each century!"

In the hall far below, the Christmas tree in Indian Land was a limb of driftwood, its forked branches ornamented with the tops of tin cans hung on thread. They moved in the cold air, catching the light, the names of tribes painted in color on them, and on some the single world "Genocide." In the office, where uniformed men had once sat, were stacked cartons of toys donated by the dozen by toy manufacturers. There is no heat in the prison, but the thought of the generosity of man for a moment warmed the blood. It was cold waiting in line for Santa to come, and when you held the children who got tired, they put their arms tight around your neck and looked closely, gravely, into your eyes, as if searching an unknown territory, uncertain what they might find. I remembered Bill Brandon saying that the Indian child approaches the outside world prepared for a joyous embrace, and gradually the outside world makes him understand that he is out of kilter with the people he had expected so to love.

That Christmas day, the white Santa did not arrive from the mainland; and what were the toys so lavishly donated but playthings that the outside world was not buying in such great quantities as before. There were machine guns, bazookas, and tanks with revolving turrets. "A couple of real tanks would be more useful," one young Indian said with uncharacteristic bitterness.

Since the last week of December (provided the generators

are functioning) "Radio Free Alcatraz" has been broadcasting at seven-fifteen every evening on the Pacifica network. The broadcasts are not appeals for assistance or for donations, but are interviews with the Indians who have come to this focal point from every state. The twenty-three-year-old Indian organizer of the program (who served four years in the navy) is John Truedell, and he speaks of the Indian civilization of wisdom which was submerged by the white man's civilization of knowledge. "It does not seem as if knowledge has done the best thing for humanity," he says. "In the time of wisdom, I respected my brother's dream and he respected mine."

The question of the ways and means of making a living on the reservation comes into the interviews. One girl described a government enterprise that had recently opened on her reservation, the manufacturing of army guns. Indian workers are paid $1.60 an hour for this work, but only one member of a family is permitted to apply. Another spoke of the Indian rodeos, where cash prizes are to be won in the competitions, but that is a seasonal source of revenue, as is the leasing out of grazing land. Another had turned down a scholarship at Brigham Young University because no courses in American Indian history or culture are available there. "We can learn more about our past and about our future right here on Alcatraz," they say. John Truedell has not at any time referred to the "My Lai Incident," and it was perhaps not his intention to draw a parallel when he said that the killing of Indian women and children was the customary practice of the territorial white man. "This was the best way to strike at the roots, at the reproduction, of a people they wanted to efface," he said.

If our government grants the Indians this piece of their own territory, it must be the beginning of restitution, not the end. To concede them nothing but another prison would be a tragic irony. More than once on Christmas day, when I spoke to them of the grimness of the conditions on The Rock, Indian women smiled and said: "It's no worse than on the reservation where we live." And others said: "We are learning how to work together, tribe with tribe. It hasn't happened before like this. This is where our new nation will begin."

The Crime of Attica

A Time to Die, a painfully and at times embarrassingly honest book, might more accurately be titled *The Education of Tom Wicker*. From the opening paragraphs, as Wicker describes a luncheon at the Bill Fay Club in Washington, where he can hold his own in conversation with "erudite men" who express their views on "everything from art to politics" while eating lamb chops and drinking good wine, one senses that the book will be primarily Wicker's story, the confession of his own real or imagined inadequacies.

The time is September 1971. On the ninth of that month (the day before the luncheon) 1281 inmates out of a prison population of 2243 rebelled against the inhuman conditions at the Attica Correctional Facility in upstate New York. The inmates seized fifty officers and civilian workers as hostages and took control of B and D Blocks, the exercise yards, and all connecting tunnels and catwalks. By afternoon, the pris-

oners issued their "immediate demands," addressing them to
President Nixon and New York Governor Nelson Rockefeller. Among these demands was the stipulation that observers,
particularly newsmen and reporters, should come to Attica
to be witness to and assist in the negotiations for a settlement.
Tom Wicker, associate editor of the *New York Times*, was
among the fourteen observers the rebelling inmates specifi-
cally invited, and when his secretary relayed the message to
him at the Bill Fay Club luncheon, although he knew little
or nothing as to what it was about, Wicker took the next flight
to Buffalo.

The rebelling inmates, seeking to stage a protest that
would be for once a wide-open book against injustice, a book
which the entire world could read, asked in addition for "*all
the people*" to come. Ultimately thirty-seven observers were
moving in and out of the stewards' room of the Attica administration building, sleeping little, eating little, alternately
hopeful and despairing as they played their parts in discussions in the safety of the stewards' room or at the negotiating
table in the potentially explosive atmosphere of D-Yard.

Among others the prisoners had called for by name were
William Kunstler, who became attorney for the rebelling inmates, U.S. Rep. Herman Badillo of New York, two members of the Young Lords party, and Bobby Seale of the Black
Panthers. In this company, Tom Wicker describes himself as
a man whom the world looked on as a success, but who saw
himself as "overweight, affluent beyond his sense of decency,
a writer who feared he had written nothing that would last"
(does one really have that on one's mind?)—in short, "a dis-
appointed man" of forty-five who believed he "had fallen
short," and who saw the Attica story as one "that might make
him think better of his work, even of his life." For "the stuff
of immortality" that is his concern he knows is lacking from

the *New York Times* thrice-weekly editorial column that he writes.

In telling this story of his life Wicker does not use the pronoun, *I*. As did Norman Mailer in *Fire on the Moon*, he refers to himself in the third person, and that person still bears the heavy burden of guilt of his upbringing in a small Southern town (Hamlet, North Carolina) where "backyard help was handed a generous plate at the back door and [where] it was only natural that the plate later was scalded against whatever might be 'catching.'" There, growing up, "he could hear black feet scuffling overhead at the movies, but it never entered his mind that the sound was ominous, that if he could hear the colored people, he might someday have to see them." Not until Wicker is forty-five, and not until his involvement in Attica, it would seem, does he come to the realization that "there is some evidence to suggest that the more people imprisoned, the more criminals are made; and that the longer the term, the likelier the inmate is to re-cidivate." Yet he notes that shortly before the Attica uprising, he "had written sympathetically about the death of George Jackson at San Quentin," and that, "unknown to him, the Jackson articles had been given wide circulation in the black press and on the prison grapevine." The predominantly black rebelling inmates at Attica had apparently overlooked Wick-er's choice of the word "death" in place of "murder," and in their hour of crisis called on him to come.

Although the blow-by-blow account of the events during those four tense September days has been as scrupulously and as emotionally documented in earlier publications (among them, Herman Badillo's *Attica*, Representative Claude Pep-per's *Prisons in Turmoil*, and *The Official Report of the New York State Special Commission on Attica*), Wicker's book has the value and virtue of being one more voice confirming that the carnage of the final solution need not have taken place. Wicker's contribution to an understanding of the tragedy of Attica does not lie in his Faulkneresque excesses of rhetoric (such as, "No American would ever be free, he thought in his exhaustion and despair. That was the inescapable truth of it, harsh as the story of Lucifer's fall. They who had sought to be masters would be forever slaves. Having loosed in the traffic of souls the darkness within themselves, they had loosed as well the black living image of that darkness, and the fear of darkness made flesh, darkness rising in savage triumph, not only had haunted their world and their children's world but would haunt the world of their children's children. Because what was feared so much had to be hated—relentlessly, implacably, ruinously hated. But hate only begets hate."). It does not lie in such irrelevancies as references to his impending divorce, or that, having neglected to bring along a suitcase, he could not don a clean shirt and underwear after a shower in a Buffalo motel, or that once, "in a fierce dinner-table debate with James Baldwin" he (Wicker) had declared "a willingness to trade his white skin for Baldwin's literary talent." (It is to be assumed that Baldwin did not take him up on this.)

Wicker's contribution lies in his depictions of the various prison officials, as well as of Rockefeller's representatives, and also in his credible (if at times uncharitable) analyses of his fellow members on the observers' committee as they seek for compromise on the rebelling inmates' twenty-eight points, which superseded the earlier demands. "At a meaner level of calculation," Wicker wonders "if his own association in the public mind with radical figures (i.e., Kunstler and Seale) might not damage him. It was a normal if not uplifting thought of a kind he had had frequently in his years of ascent. Sometimes he had responded with contempt for such hesitations; at other times he had acted upon them ignobly or timidly." Unforgettable as well are his descriptions of the bonfire-illuminated and moonlit security-team scenes in D-Yard when " 'the inmate security team'—a long curving human chain" with locked arms protected the observers from any violence that might threaten from the hundreds of prisoners on the other side of this human barricade. And Wicker's contribution lies as well in the sound of his voice asking Governor Rockefeller to come to Attica, not to enter D-Yard, and not to meet with the inmates, but to sit in the safety of the stewards' room and talk with the observers there.

The day before the September 13 massacre in D-Yard (when ten hostages and twenty-nine inmates lay dead or dying, all killed by troopers' and officers' fire), Tom Wicker and two other reporters, one from the *Amsterdam News* and the other from the *New York Daily News*, interviewed five of the hostages on radio and before television cameras. Wicker reports that each hostage was asked if he had a direct message to send the governor, and each replied that he had. The first hostage to speak said: "I want the Governor to get his ass here now." Hostage Captain Wald, the senior officer at Attica, said in part: "Governor, we are here in the yard with quite a group of people and anything you can do I am highly in support of. We lived for four days under the same conditions they [i.e., the inmates] are living in, and we are thirty-eight men who understand exactly what they are trying to get for themselves. . . . It would seem a shame to waste a group of educated men like this."

Hostage Sergeant Cunningham answered Wicker's question as follows: "One of the recommendations: if he says no I'm dead. He must give them clemency, he must give them clemency from criminal prosecution. . . ." Eighteen hours later, Cunningham was shot dead by ten pellets from a state police shotgun. "On September 14," writes Wicker, "Dr. John Edland, the Monroe County Medical Examiner, found the bodies of eight hostages and nineteen inmates awaiting his examination . . . that afternoon, Dr. Edland—after what he later called 'the worst day of my life'—made public his findings. Not a single hostage had been killed by knife wounds. None had been castrated or mutilated. All had died on Monday morning, September 13. All had been killed by bullets or buckshot—some hit as many as 'five, ten, twelve times.' "

Those on the side of life had believed there were still a number of possible solutions to be explored, and it was in this hope that a public statement issued by the entire observers' committee had urged Rockefeller to come. When this appeal failed, Wicker had telephoned from the stewards' room to Rockefeller in his Pocantico Hills home. It was hoped that if Rockefeller came he would, in Wicker's words, "pick up the same vibrations, the same sensations we had about the buildup of frustration, hostility, and anger on the part of these heavily armed men [i.e., the assault forces] and the fact that there was bound to be a considerable amount of violence once an attack was carried out." The telephone call to Rockefeller, as described by Wicker, as well as in *The Official Report of the New York State Special Commission on Attica*, lasted over an hour. Wicker, Clarence Jones, publisher of the *Amsterdam News*, Herman Badillo, and State Senator John Dunne of Nassau County, New York, all spoke, and "each crossfirmed what the others had said to the Governor—that a massacre was about to take place."

Jones and Dunne told Rockefeller that his presence would give the observers "greater credibility with the inmates," and might even provide "that additional ingredient that could tip the scales toward the possibility of a peaceful solution." Dunne later testified that "We didn't ask the Governor, we pleaded. We pleaded in the name of humanity to please come up to Attica to meet with us." To Wicker, Rockefeller said:

". . . and I just want you to know how grateful I am and how much I really admire what you and the others are doing up there. I know you've all worked hard and taken great risks and I appreciate it, I really do. It's just great . . . just great." And Rockefeller did not come.

Rockefeller, Wicker points out, "was not a man of many doubts" (perhaps "any" would have been the more accurate word), and as he talked with Wicker his voice soon lost its cordial tone. He expressed his understanding that when men had worked hard and risked a lot on a given issue they were ready to grasp at any straw. He told Wicker "quite candidly" that the idea of his coming to Attica was clearly "just one of those straws." He reiterated that the real issue was amnesty, and that his legal people had looked into the question, and he did not have the constitutional authority to grant amnesty. Even if he did have the power, he added, he wouldn't grant it because he was convinced that "holding hostages was the wrong way to get redress to grievances," and that such amnesty "would violate the principle of the equal application of the laws." Wicker is rightfully astounded by the irony of this. "In a country where so many wealthy or well-represented lawbreakers go free," he reflects, "where the killers at Kent State and Jackson State were not even prosecuted, where minorities . . . suffered from openly prejudiced law in whole regions, where the poor and disadvantaged of all races usually felt the weight of police, courts, and prisons," by what concept of justice could "the equal application of the laws" be upheld in the case of the Attica brothers?

Wicker's book, as well as all other reports I have seen, makes clear that because of the extensive media coverage of the rebellion and the openness of the negotiations, the inmates never for a moment believed that the state would move in on them with guns. Tear gas, yes; clubs, of course; but not gunfire. In his 1972 statement to the New York State Special

Commission, Rockefeller described his telephone conversation with the observers.

> I felt [he testified] that they did not want to admit defeat in this and see this thing go back to the Commissioner [i.e., Russell G. Oswald, commissioner of the NY State Department of Correctional Services]. So I said, "Well, what do you think would be accomplished by my presence?" And their answer was, "Well, we don't know, two things. One, something might happen and two, we could buy time."
>
> "Well," I said, "who do you want to buy time from? Are you worried that the prisoners are going to move and kill the hostages or are you worried the state is going to move?" And they said, "No, we're worried about the state."

On September 15, 1971, two days after the Attica massacre, Rockefeller is on record as stating that the attack had "come out" better than he had expected, and that he felt the state troopers and other officers had done "a superb job."

Twice during the 1974 Senate Judiciary Committee hearing on Rockefeller's nomination to the vice-presidency of the United States, I wired members of the committee, urging that Wicker's book (then unpublished) be subpoenaed as of vital relevance to the deliberations on Rockefeller's fitness for a government post. I, too, had read Wicker's pieces on George Jackson, and knew that he had participated with courage in the D-Yard negotiations. But after reading *A Time to Die*, I question whether Tom Wicker's burden of guilt is not too personal a burden to ask others to share. His conclusion that prisons have failed as places of rehabilitation, but instead make hardened criminals and desperate men out of small-time breakers of the law, is startling to those who have not traveled the long road he has come from Hamlet. "The facts and the judgments," *The Official Report of the New York State Special Commission* writes of Attica, "disclose only the tip of the fiery hell that lies below." Yet it is possible that a public not given to reading official reports, no matter how vivid and forceful the language, will be more likely to turn to the Book-of-the-Month Club's choice of Wicker's account and come to recognize the dimensions of the crime of Attica as seen through the troubled vision of one man's anxieties.

Report from Lock-up

I

It may be that none of us can ever get out of the solitary confinement we've condemned ourselves to (out of fear, out of pride, out of loneliness) until we find ourselves in actual prisons of iron and stone. We constructed these prisons, just as we did our own individual places of detention, building them on the ruins of other epochs, accepting as viable the oubliettes of other centuries, other continents. When everything else we have put our hands to is gone, the granite and iron cemented by our pitiless morality will remain as monument and gravestone to our time. The walls of Troy and Limerick were built to keep the invader out, but we have built walls to keep the lost and bewildered among us out of our line of vision, walls to seal our fellow citizens away. The interior decorations include the ancient wrist, ankle, and waist chains, and we have added the modern touch of bulletproof glass. What are we going to say to history about our fear of facing one another in a courtroom or in a taxicab except through this impregnable barrier which half of our countrymen make use of to outwit the other half? We can listen to Dylan singing his ballad of the cutting down of George Jackson, singing (and tears stand in my eyes every time I hear it) that "the whole world is one big prison yard" where "some of us are prisoners, the rest of us are guards" and not believe it until the moment that we too see the landscape through windows fitted with iron, and hear the doors locked behind us, and before us, and around us. That is the moment when you come out of your own solitary confinement once and for all, and if you're lucky there's no way for you ever to go back again.

William Carlos Williams, poet, doctor, essayist, is one of the gigantic figures we have to honor for escaping while still young from his own solitary cell. It was not through the experience of prison that he escaped, but through his coming to an understanding of the conditions of his patients' lives. "I lost myself in the very properties of their minds," he wrote in his *Autobiography* (1967), "for the moment at least I actually became *them*, whoever they should be, so that when I detached myself from them at the end of a half-hour of intense concentration over some illness which was affecting them it was as though I were reawakening from a sleep. For the moment I myself did not exist, nothing of myself affected me. As a consequence I came back to myself, as from any other sleep, rested."

II

There were two women in the room called lock-up which they put me in that evening in 1968, two white women sitting on their cots, talking to each other across the intervening space, who did not look in my direction as the deputy led me in. I

was handsomely fitted out (as were they) in a grey prison dress
that hung unevenly nearly to my ankles and on my bare feet
were tennis shoes, once white, and two sizes too large. Over
my left arm I carried two worn sheets, a pillowcase, a greyish
towel, and in my right hand I held a toothbrush and a small
cake of soap. Once the deputy in her smart uniform had gone
and locked the door behind her, I turned the mattress on the
third cot to find which side was the least stained, and then I
made my bed. I laid the folded khaki blanket under the flat
pillow, and I lay down on the flat, flat cot whose springs cried
out in pain. From then on I became the two women who were
supplying each other with the facts and figures of their dreams
as they sat on their cots in the narrow room.

They were not young women, and not beautiful women.
One was a fleshy, weary-eyed Canadian who talked of the
Yukon, and when she gestured the dimples came and went in
her plump elbows, the fat tied as if by strings to the invisible
bone. Her mouth was a small trapdoor between her sagging
cheeks, a door that snapped open and closed on the words she
spoke. The place they'd head for when they got out would be
Whitehorse, she said, but they would go even farther, the two
of them pushing always deeper into the wilderness until they
finally reached the mines.

"Silver, lead, zinc, even gold, you know," she was saying.

"I really like your accent. I really do," the other woman
said.

"Silver, tungsten, and coal, you know what I mean?" the
Canadian woman went on with it.

"What's tungsten?" asked the woman from maybe Brooklyn, maybe New York, who had wandered this far without a
compass to keep a rendezvous in lock-up with a woman she
had never laid eyes on before. "What's tungsten?" she repeated, and she began to laugh, the round little face between
the dry, yellow slabs of the pageboy bob framed by an inch
of grey. "Sounds kinda indecent to me."

"It's part sheelite, tungsten is," said the Canadian. The trapdoor of her small, trapped mouth hung open, black as the hole of Calcutta, and her flesh jerked with laughter.

"Oh, did I hear you right? Did you say you-know-what?" shrieked the other woman. "Did you say 'shee—' or am I hearing crazy?"

"Listen," said the Canadian, snapping the trapdoor abruptly closed. "We can't waste any time now. We got to keep pushing ahead. There's the Yukon Territory and beyond that there's the Klondike, where the gold is waiting. That's where the men are. That's where they've got to be," she said, and now her voice had taken on another dimension. Now she was speaking of the real, not the dream. I was no longer someone lying on a cot across the narrow room from them, face turned to the wall, lying there in a long grey dress with the hem ripped halfway out, and dirty tennis shoes on, nameless and without history, listening to what they said. I had become nothing more than a bunch of rags there hadn't been room to stuff onto the dogsled as they urged the huskies on through the driving snow, bent on getting to where the men were before night fell. "They've been mining silver and panning gold," the Canadian woman said, "and they're crazy for women, just crazy for them," and the other woman could be heard rubbing her palms together in glee.

And then the mood abruptly changed, as if the hypodermic of dreams had been suddenly snatched away, and the teeth of the lady from Brooklyn or New York began to chatter like castanets in her head.

"Do you think I'd get on up there in the cold and all?" she asked, plaintive as a child. "I'm American. Always have been. I love every state in the union, only some are better than others for professionals," she said.

"We can get our hair touched up at the roots before we go," said the Canadian in answer to the question that was asked.

"They'd have a choice—me light, real honey blond, or

was once anyway, and you the brunette type," the other woman said, trying to make it weightless as feathers so that the wound of desperation would go away. "I might have trouble with the language in a place like that."

"There won't be any trouble!" the Canadian woman shouted. She must have jumped up from the cot then, and standing erect on the runners of the sled she began cracking the long serpentine whip over the flanks and the muzzles of the harnessed dogs as they raced over the hard-packed snow. "We'd pick it all up and get out quick!"

"I'd rather do business with the gold miners than the ones come out of the coal mines," the other woman said. "I bet they're black all over, right down to their you-know-whats," and she gave a shriek of laughter, but there was the sound of something else in it now, sharp and jagged as broken glass.

"Gold's cleaner than coal, you're right about that," the Canadian woman said, her voice gone sweet with craftiness. "You can carry it easier, too," she said.

It was growing dark, but neither of the two women on their fierce ride toward freedom could stop long enough to switch on the single bulb that would tremble, faint with light, its twisted vein out of reach in the peeling ceiling overhead. Outside the barred window in the door, the hallway was as still as the grave, and if the sound of footsteps had come tripping down it, or the kindly face of a deputy brightened the grating, I would have sensed it there like a searchlight turned on us and sat bolt upright on my bed.

"Please, lady, dear lady, why am I in lock-up? How do I happen to be here?" I would have asked her.

But beyond the door there was silence, total silence. Only in this one room did the panting dogs run wilder and wilder through howling winds, the steam of their breathing hot as fire on the forty-below-zero air. Whitehorse must have been left a hundred miles behind by this time, but the Yukon and

Klondike and Indian Rivers were still to be crossed. One after another, the Canadian woman was naming them all, not forgetting Bonanza Creek, on whose banks there was more gold than gravel. She had the statistics, she said. Twenty-two million dollars in one year was what had been panned there, she was saying as the sled sped on, but she didn't mention which year or century. That was because she was too busy flailing the dogs in their desperate race against the falling night. Maybe in the middle of this room stood an outsized hourglass whose sifting sand measured time, and she kept one cautious eye on it as she talked, but I wasn't going to turn my head to see. She was speaking of the Porcupine, and the Chandalar, not to mention the Tanana, all navigable, she said, as if navigating them was what she and the other woman were going to do. All tributaries of the Yukon, she added knowingly.

"The way I do it, I get them to buy a six-pack," the woman from New York or Brooklyn was saying in the accumulating dark, "and then we go up to the room, and while we're lying on the bed we get rid of a can or two, and then I let him—"

"I never lie down with them until I've got the knockout potion into their drinks. Get it, knockout potion?" the Canadian woman chortled.

"I get a charge out of your vocabulary. I really do," the other woman said. But the Canadian woman's mind had turned to something else. She was trying to find a way now to cross the rivers lying ahead when there wasn't any moonlight available to put a shine on the ice and no way to see the foot path over the torrents of water that had been turned to marble by the cold.

"Then I go through the pockets of the pants they've got hanging over the back of a chair," she said, "and if the pants and the shoes are in good condition, I take them along." She was speaking briskly enough, but the edge of the precipice could be heard in her voice. It was lying just ahead. "I'll kill anybody if they're blocking my way to that window over there. I'll kill anyone standing between me and you and the Yukon," she said.

"I never took anything but their wallets. That's all I ever did, bar none," the American woman said piously, and she began to cry in a stifled, piercing, childlike way. "I got to have a shot of something, I tell you. I got to have it."

"I'd kill anyone I thought was hiding it under the pillow over there, maybe hiding it under her blanket," said the Canadian woman, and suddenly she struck the wall with her fist, as if it was a face she couldn't bear. "Ask for it, ask for it!" she shouted so loud that it must have been heard a mile away. "If they have any hearts under all that regalia, they'll give it to you! Yell loud enough and they have to give it! I read that, it's a medical fact!" In the vast reaches of the nordic night through which she battled her way, she was ready to strangle the huskies one by one if they didn't run until their hearts burst in the cages of their ribs, carrying her to where she wanted to go. Despite the bars, she was going to get through the window that looked out on the darkening courtyard, stamping the life out of the bundle of rags lying on the third cot as she went, blazing her escape through prison-yard and over prison wall with its fine barbed wire worn like a crown on its granite brow. Before rigor mortis set in she would throw the carcasses of the dogs, like sacks of bones, at anyone who tried to stop her, lifting them up by the taut curves of their bushy tails and flinging them at her pursuers in place of hand grenades, in place of tear-gas canisters, and the loud report of guns. "The facts and figures are on our side, and so are the statistics!" she shouted out of the fury of her advance across the black glass of the Klondike River. "They're thousands up there who'd stand by us, nearly twenty thousand!" she halloo-ed back to the woman from Brooklyn, or wherever it was, who had fallen and who now lay rigid, as if frozen, on the bare boards of the floor.

"Maybe up in the Yukon," the fallen woman whispered in what could have been her dying breath, "there might be men wanting to settle down. There might be some of them looking for women to make them good wives. Out of the lot of them up there, there might be some."

It was her own tears that stopped the sound of her voice, but the Canadian woman had no time or use for pity as she beat her savage tattoo on the impervious door. (Oh, lock-up, what a battleground of terror you are, and no stretcher-bearers to come and bear the mortally wounded away!) First she would slap the door with the flat of one hand, and then with the mighty fist of the other the steady, ominous rhythm would be hammered out.

"Two hundred and five thousand three hundred and forty-six square miles, that's the size of the Yukon!" she roared. "Water surface two hundred and seven thousand and seventy-six square miles! Mt. Logan is nineteen thousand eight hundred and fifty feet high!" she shouted, the thousands, the hundreds, the odd numbers, beaten out in fury on the door. "What have you got on this side of the border to compete with that?" she cried.

"I love every state in the union," the other woman whispered from the ice floe of the floor, and her teeth were chattering again.

"Let me tell you this," said the Canadian woman, and she struck the door an even fiercer blow. "Five months of the year, five months out of every year," she said, and suddenly the remembrance of it must have changed the air she breathed, for her hands fell quiet, and her voice turned almost gentle in the trapdoor of her mouth. "Five months out of every year the days are twenty hours long. I know every inch of it from the Arctic Ocean to Skagway and back again. Five months out of the year you can sit on a park bench and read, just like sitting under a neon light, you can read a newspaper at two o'clock in the morning," she said.

"Why do you want to do that?" the other woman asked through her chattering teeth. "Why read a newspaper in the park at that time of night?"

"Because nothing in this country can compete with that, that's why!" the Canadian woman shouted, and now it seemed that the door of lock-up would have to split apart under her blows. "Where in the United States can you sit on a park bench and read a newspaper in the middle of the night, every night for five months? You can't sit in Golden Gate Park in San Francisco and read a newspaper all night, or in Dolores Park, but in Yukon Territory you can, I'll tell you that!"

"Well, keep it down, keep your information to yourselves, ladies," the deputy said from the safety of the hall, and she switched on the searchlight that would show them up for what they were: prisoners, just hallucinating prisoners, held fast by lock and bolt and key. "Get into your beds. Don't let me hear another sound out of any of you," the deputy said, not in anger, but in hopelessness at speaking words, whether she knew it or not, that make a language wither and die.

III

The next three days and nights were as dull as ditchwater, because in the lock-up room I was transferred to, the two prisoners who shared it with me had straight stories to tell. Very early in the morning I had been escorted up the hall to more spacious quarters, with the added attraction of being adjacent to the dark stronghold of The Hole. This room had three barred windows that looked out on the prison-yard, while the other had had only one, and for an instant at the crack of day I thought this might be a promotion. As in the first, there were three cots in the room, and two women, one black, the other white, sat on those they could call their own. There were no chairs in lock-up, but the authorized night tables were smugly present, and into the drawer of mine went the prison-issue toothbrush that was fashioned to dissolve, lock, stock, and barrel, if you tried ramming it down your own or someone else's throat; and into my tidy drawer went my cake of pink soap, and the washrag and towel gone grey and weary in confinement. My sheets and pillowcase of the night before were purified still by the mercury-bright waters of the Klondike, and worn as they were, bleached by the stain-less drifts of Yukon Territory snow.

"Dear Deputy," I had asked the lady in her smart khaki as we journeyed up the hall together, "why have I been put in lock-up in the first place? In all my stays here, I was never considered dangerous before." But she had not answered. "Could I telephone my heroic attorney, Robert Treuhaft?" I had suggested in the instant before she click-a-locked us all in again, and she spoke her mind on that with an unswerving look at something else at the other end of the hall.

The girl sitting on the cot in the far corner was pregnant, and as I settled in in my domain she gave me a wan smile. She said it was seven months now, and that her husband was in prison on the men's side of our condominium. She had blue-veined temples and wrists, this girl, and long, light hair, and eyes the color of African violet petals, with the rings under them a lighter shade. When she said she was having trouble with the food that arrived on the metal truck that came creaking up the hall three times a day, you knew this was why there was little or no buoyancy left in her pastel-tinted flesh. Except for the grey prison dress and the split tennis shoes, she was a Marie Laurencin portrait painted like a mural there, perishable and frail, with the great windows of her eyes like delicately stained glass. Across the room from her, the large black prisoner, who had lain down now, dark and mountainous, on her narrow cot, sized me up in a minute and a half.

"I bet you could write me a good letter. I needs someone to write me a good letter," she said.

Possession is a mutable word, a word with a number of differently colored masks it puts on and then takes off at will. It can be blood red with rape, or brassy with wealth when domiciled in a safe-deposit box, or mad as a whirling fakir if you see it as witchcraft, and another time amorous as Venus in the embrace of love. Possession, black as a pit, black as The Hole outside our door, was what the Marie Laurencin girl and her husband were accused of, but she said, sitting there on her cot, that they'd never possessed anything at all. They'd never had very much money, and they'd been taking care of her sister's kids, she was telling me just before the cold globs of oatmeal and the sloshing cups of dark warm water that was breakfast came trundling up the hall. Her sister was off on a week's nursing job in Eureka, a graduate-trained nurse, divorced, she said, and a guy they didn't know dropped by the house one evening. He was the one who possessed, but the Marie Laurencin girl and her husband didn't know it until after it all took place.

"I guess he was a pusher," the girl said, a little uncertain about the word. "He used the phone out in the hall a couple of times, maybe making contacts. We didn't hear what he was saying because my husband, he's a carpenter, he was sawing wood to make the baby a cradle. That was three weeks ago." She said it was on account of the baby that she worried about the food she couldn't eat, and I said there had to be a doctor here, even here there had to be a doctor. "There is a doctor," she said softly, "but I think he likes men better than women. I heard there were two women sick here at different times, and they could have got well, but he didn't get help to them in time."

"I knows one thing. I knows you could write that letter for me that I got to get written," the black lady called out to me, sweet as honey, from across the room.

I wanted to tell the Marie Laurencin girl a lot of things. I wanted to tell her about Angel Island and Alcatraz, but it didn't seem the time to talk about it now. I wanted to tell her about Birdman's isolation cell on Alcatraz that he'd been in for seventeen years, as if this would make as light as thistle-down the burden of weeks that she and her husband would have to bear. There were straight little marks, each fine as a thread and maybe half an inch high, marching the length of his cell's walls, I wanted to tell her, and a few tiny horses, with their forelegs lifted, and a few birds with their wings spread, scratched there by his thumbnail. It was a Native American who had shown me that cell on Christmas day at the time of the Indian Occupation, and when I said that must have been the record Birdman kept of the months and the years he'd spent there, the young Indian ran his forefinger across the marks. "Not months, not years! They were centuries he was talking about. He was marking the centuries," was what he said. In the time when prisoners were in every cell on the island, instead of Indians spreading out newspapers and sleeping there with their children now, the young man said that they must have been like an audience in a movie theatre, sitting looking out of the dark through the bars at the bright movie screen across the bay. "Sometimes I see it like that," he said, "the prisoners watching the real life of America being played. And then sometimes I think of it as the other way round, and it was the men in the cells who were acting out the history of America, and the people over there in San Francisco were the audience, not applauding or booing or doing anything about it, but year after year just seeing it taking place."

And beyond Alcatraz, a little farther out in the bay, there

was Angel Island, and I wanted to tell the girl about the Chinese who had been imprisoned there, and whose ghosts wandered the beaches now, and knelt in suicide under the trees. (In his novel, *Good Luck, Happiness and Long Life*, Shawn Wong writes: "Everyone [on Angel Island] knows how to hang himself. There are no nails or hooks high enough to hang a piece of cloth from and leap from a stool to a quick death. There is only one way: tie your piece of cloth to one of those big nails about four and a half feet off the floor, lean against the wall to brace yourself, and bend your knees and hold them up off the floor. Then your bones will be collected and placed on the open seas.") But what help or solace would that have been to her? Once upon a time, I wanted to say to her as I rocked her and the unborn baby to sleep, lots and lots of Chinese men used to come to California, come looking for work because the grasshopper and caterpillar and hummingbird tongues they were used to eating for breakfast had run out where they lived in China. Aside from that, they liked the idea of working outside in the clean, sunny air of California, laying railway ties. But they didn't know immigration prisons were waiting for them on Angel Island; they didn't know because the way Frank Chin's Tam Lim explains it in *The Chickencoop Chinamen* (1973): "Chinese are made, not born . . . [made] out of junk-imports, lies, railroad scrap iron, dirty jokes, broken bottles, cigar smoke, Cosquilla Indian blood, wino spit, and lots of milk of magnesia."

And rocking, rocking, I wanted to say to the Marie Laurencin girl that there was really nothing serious to worry about here, nothing tragic, as there had been on Angel Island. "Do you know," I might start babbling to her, "that when the women and children finally managed to beg, borrow, or steal the money to join their men, they too were closed up year after year until the end of time, and the mothers stopped letting their kids go to the washroom to wash, because that was where the Chinese, made out of junk-imports and broken bottles as they were, had chosen to hang themselves? Well, that couldn't happen here."

Perhaps I ought to keep quiet about that, I thought, and also about Shawn Wong's great-grandfather saying to him in his dreams (in *Aiii-eeeee*, 1975): "I left for San Francisco one month before my brother. In those days, ships were bringing us in illegally. They would drop a lifeboat outside the Golden Gate (Bay) with the Chinese in it. Then the ship would steam in and at night the lifeboat would come in quietly and unload. If they were about to be caught, my people would be thrown overboard. But, you see, they couldn't swim because they were chained together in the hold of the ship. My brother died on that night and now his bones are chained to the bottom of the ocean. No burial ever." That was prison, too, prison of a worse kind, not like the place we were confined to, but still it was prison, wasn't it? I wouldn't put this question to the blue-veined baby still to be born, but I'd just rock its mother back and forth, back and forth, making up lullabies for it and not saying a word about the great-grandfather who had whispered down the years to Shawn: "Do not send my bones back to China. Bury me here beneath my tears."

Deeply embedded in the words of lullabies there is a shuddering sense of tragedy, it came to me then. I thought of Colin, *petit frère*, being promised a drink of water if he would stop crying and go to sleep while his mother was upstairs making cakes, and his father was having the time of his life sawing wood in isolation, far below. And there was the lullaby from somewhere in the South saying that way down yonder in the meadow a poor little lambie was lying with the bees and the butterflies picking out its eyes. "Hush-a-bye, baby, don't you cry," it seemed to me was how it went, but how could it have gone like that when the little lambie was bleating out "Mama, Mama," and Mama off nibbling clover somewhere? I remembered the bough breaking in still another instance, and down coming cradle, baby, and all, and it seemed to me for a brief moment that some of the poems the Chinese had written for their children and their children's children on the walls of their Angel Island prison rooms might be the cradle songs of solace I was looking for. It may even have been that the Chinese mothers sang those poems to the children they bathed in the tin basins of water carried so carefully from the row of sinks in the washroom to the dormitories so the children wouldn't have to see the dead kneeling temporarily there.

(But can you remember those poems carved in the wood by carpenter's nail or point of knife, or painted on by finger or brush dipped in melted tar? How do I know what I can remember? I answered myself. I only know that their knives, like their detention, would be solved if these immigrants plunged them into their own or one another's hearts. I can remember lines from their poems better than lines from Pound's *Cantos*, or from "Prufrock" or "The Wasteland." I can't recall the names of those who wrote them, and my versions will be garbled versions, such as:

> He traveled far across the ocean on a long voyage,
> Feeding on the wind, sleeping on the dew, and tasting hardship.
> Even though Su Wu was detained among the barbarians,
> There is hope that one day he will come home.
> When Han Yu encountered a snowstorm he sighed
> And thought of the years he was banished.
> From ancient times heroes often underwent ordeals.
>
> This poem is an expression of the distress
> That fills my belly. I leave this as a memento
> To encourage fellow-souls.

Or else:

> It has been several full moons since I left my native village.
> At home, the family stands at the door, eagerly looking for
> letters.
> Whom can I depend on to pass the word to them
> That I am well? Green waters surround the grassy hills
> Of this island. If I ascend to a high place
> And look far out, I still cannot see the shore.

The lines I was remembering might well fail to sound like
poetry in the little, porcelain ears of the Marie Laurencin
girl, and despite the cruel tradition of cradle songs, they perhaps did not even qualify as that. What baby, born or unborn, would want to hear a Chinese prisoner crying out: "My
stomach is full of grievances, but whom can I tell them to?"
Or another one murmuring scarcely aloud: "Staying on this
island, my sorrow increases with the nights and days"? And
even less would the newborn and still innocent wish to hear,
no matter how beautifully the words were sung:

> I can do nothing but frown
> And feel angry at heaven.
> When I am idle, I have a wild dream:
> That the consent was given me by the contemptible Westerner
> To land on the continent of America.

But there was a lighter moment one prisoner wrote of,
something about the waves beginning to laugh "ha-ha-ha" as
they broke on the beaches:

> From this moment I bid farewell to this building [he wrote],
> And my fellow villagers are rejoicing with me.

Even if it had been built of jade, oh, my countrymen,
This building would have turned into a cage!

No, none of this would do.)

What would be encouraging to tell the Marie Laurencin
girl about was all I had done in the times I was here before.
I had been free as the breeze, working in the Rehabilitation
Center garden, digging up iris plants, and cutting their
tough, green sabres off, and then splitting the earth-clotted
bulbs in two. Like preschool children, we had been allowed
blunt-nosed scissors to do our work, and trowels with rusted,
crumbling edges. They trusted us, as God had once trusted
Adam and Eve, and when we had replanted the multiplied
iris bulbs at a gracious distance from one another, we had
responded to that trust by returning the scissors and trowels
to the appointed authorities. It was here I had learned that
once every two years this must be done to iris plants so they
don't end up strangling one another in the crowded ghettoes
of their beds. And another time when I was here, I had even
been allowed to hear through a crack between the boards of
the garden fence Martin Luther King speaking outside the
prison-yard. He had come all the way to the hinterlands to
tell us we were doing the right thing. On other occasions I
had been allowed to do kitchen duty, and at five o'clock every
morning I would spring from my pallet and speed like a deer
to the kitchen area, proud of always being the first to clap the
mandatory canvas boudoir cap on my head. I had been authorized to boil dozens of eggs, turn over a hundred pieces
of toast on the grill, and stir the oatmeal while it was still
pulsing in the cauldron, and no questions asked. But this time
I had been hustled into lock-up, and I didn't know why I was
here.

"Maybe they thought someone might try to spring you,"
suggested the black woman from where she lay on her cot

across the room. "I heard two prisoners was sprung right out of this room last week."

"They sawed through the bars over there in the bathroom," the Marie Laurencin girl said quietly. "That's why there's plywood nailed across."

If I had spoken of Alexander Berkman then, perhaps the walls of lock-up would have opened wide and let in a presence that would have changed the look of what we were; but I couldn't bring myself to begin. If I had said he'd been sixteen years in prison, more than half of them in solitary, and he had come out not only sane, but compassionate and humorous, would that have been any help to the two women locked up with me here? I could tell them that Berkman's longing for liberty had so obsessed him night and day that it finally became, as he wrote in *Prison Memoirs of an Anarchist* (1912, 1970, 1975), "an exclusive passion, shaping every thought, molding every action"; but would that have any bearing on the fact that the black prisoner wanted me to write a letter for her, and that the Marie Laurencin girl wouldn't be able to eat the oatmeal when they brought it up the hall? "The underground tunnel masters my mind with the boldness of its concept, its tremendous possibilities," Berkman wrote, but even if we embraced that concept, where were the tools with which to start our tunneling? "The world of the living is dim and unreal," Berkman went on writing. "Escape is the sole salvation." And even though I believe every word Berkman has ever set down on paper or spoken aloud, I still didn't know whether escape from prison meant for him escape from the unreal world into the real, or from the stone and iron reality of prison into the world of fantasy which even Berkman made the error of calling liberty.

But the moment had come now when I must cross the room to the cot on which the black woman was reclining, and tell her I didn't have any paper, or pencil, or pen. When I stood beside her, she heaved her great weight up on one padded, black satin elbow, and the broken springs of the cot moaned in pain.

"My public defender, he got me my commissary privilege," she said. She reached out to pull open the drawer of her night table, and she brought out the ruled pad and the ballpoint pen. "I got to keep in touch with him," she said.

It wasn't a very long letter that she dictated to me, but it was important to her that the spelling and the punctuation be exactly right. "Legally right," was what she said. She had a singular confidence in me as she lay there, monumental and onyx-fleshed in her grey dress that many had worn before her, and I could have written anything at all. When I had it all down, I read it aloud to her, to the sound of the breakfast truck creaking up the hall.

> "Dear Sir," it went. "The gentleman who was stabbed to his death in the Flamingo Bar on Monday night, which I plead not guilty to by reason of self-defense, had thirty dollars of mine in his pants pocket, the left one. I don't see no reasons why his widow should get that money that was mine. The gentleman and I had been going steady for six months, and the widow had no accessory to it."

I thought maybe she didn't mean the word "accessory," but she said she did. When the letter was done, she folded the sheet of ruled paper over and put it in an envelope, and she gave me a long dark look.

"What you in for?" she asked, and because of the nebulous dimensions of my crime, I lowered my eyes before her gaze.

"For demonstrating," I said. "I'm serving thirty-one days on weekends and holidays. That's so I won't lose my job."

"Demonstrating about what?" the black woman asked.

"Well, a lot of us sat on the steps of the Induction Center

in Oakland," I said, explaining it almost in apology. "We just sat there, hoping the draftees wouldn't climb over us and go in. We were demonstrating against the war in Vietnam."

"Against the war in Vietnam!" she said, her voice gone high in incredulity. "Ain't you never heard of national honor?" she asked.

IV

I don't remember what I said or didn't say in the next three days and nights to the Marie Laurencin girl who couldn't eat and to the black woman whose cot springs sighed under her weight when she got up and when she lay down and when she turned over, before she was transferred out. There were things I wanted to tell them both about, but it isn't easy to say to people who have other things eating at their hearts that there is a history of women speaking out before judges and juries, so there is no reason to feel any loneliness when you stand up there to say your own small piece. There was a woman my aunt drew a picture of, and the drawing my aunt made became a postage stamp in time, so that letters mailed in that particular year had a picture on them of a little woman with a small, black bonnet on her head and a red shawl drawn around her shoulders, walking entirely alone up the steps of the Capitol building in Washington, D.C.; and although you can't see it in the picture my aunt drew, she is holding a scroll in her hand. Never were steps more cold and bare than those this woman mounted, and never were columns more forbidding than those standing massively on either side of the dark door. The scroll she carried bore the signatures of 20,000 Americans who were asking that women be allowed to vote (and in the end that petition wasn't considered valid because the 20,000 names were those of women and not of men). Maybe a few people here and there that year noticed the picture of Susan B. Anthony on the postage stamp printed long after she was dead; perhaps not only women noticed, but other painters, other artists, who in that instant felt like a blow the total courage of a woman so small to the eye that you had to take a magnifying glass to be able to make out her bones.

But instead of mentioning that, it might have been better if I'd just gone on telling the Marie Laurencin girl and the black woman about the times before when I'd worked in the prison annex with the others, all of us busy putting patches in the seats of the male prisoners' overalls, or buttons on their grey prison-issue shirts. It was there that the chorus of young, young voices kept on warbling: "I bin in an outta this place so many years, I don try countin em no more," or: "This time I took the rap for my kid sister, but none of us, we don go roun makin no announcements bout why we're here. At firs, a long time back, I use go roun askin who done what, but after a while you don bother askin no more cause everybody done just bout the same"; or saying: "It ain bad, not here it ain. You gotta bed with sheets, an you can quit hustlin whiles you in, and you gits three meals a day. I knows which deputies goin be like my momma to me and which ain. Here is jus somewheres you come back to res up fore you goes back outside and git busted again. Tha's been my life since way back, an I got no complaints"; or maybe saying: "There's two things I knows a lot about, an one's women an th'other's dope. When youse in here, you gets to likin women, an thas cool. You in here for you reasons like I'se in here for mine. We both believes in them, an soon as I gits out, I go back, do my thing, and you gits out an go back doin yours. . . ."

Somewhere, far away, Bob Dylan was perhaps still singing: "They were frightened of his pow'r, they were scared of his luv. So Lawd, Lawd, they cut George Jackson down," but I wasn't able to hear him, and no one else seemed to be listening, perhaps because it was never one of his smash hits. In the same way, down through the decades, scarcely anyone seems to have heard Susan B. Anthony saying in the court-room: "I shall earnestly and persistently continue to urge all women to the political recognition of the old Revolutionary maxim: 'Resistance to tyranny is obedience to God.'" And while I was thinking, or merely believing, these things, there was a cautious tapping on the barred windowpane set in the door, and I saw a girl's black face there, her dark eyes seeking us out. I quickly got up from my cot and went to where she was.

There was more than one face at the barred window now. There were two, then three, then four or five, girls coming back from breakfast, passing lock-up on their way to work in the annex, where I was no longer allowed to go. The eyes were fierce, or gentle, or else troubled with sorrow, and at times they darted quickly, warily away to see who might be coming up or down the hall.

"What the hell they put you in lock-up for?" came the hushed voices through the crack of the door, through the key-hole; or else the words took shape in silence behind the glass: "Wh-a-a-a"—with the mouth wide open—"th-h-"—with the rosy tongue curled behind the bright white upper teeth—"he-l-l-l"—in a scream no one could hear—"the-e-e-y"—with the mouth stretched in a grin, only it wasn't grinning—"d-o-o-o t-o-o-o-y-o-o-o-o?"—with the lips pursed for kiss-ing.

The eyes that kept skittering this way and that were the same that had seen to thread needles for me in the glorious freedom of the sewing room, but they were sharp now with a different, darker precision. In the instant before these pris-oners took flight, they pressed their mouths against their side of the barred glass, and on my side I put my lips against theirs, and the misty shapes of our embrace stayed a long time there, a long time after the two deputies had cleared the area of all human sight and sound.

I don't know what I actually said and what I only intended to say to the Marie Laurencin girl and the black woman before they took her away. It may have been that I mentioned Paul Goodman writing of Alexander Berkman that he was one of the beautiful human spirits that "the regimes of the world cannot put up with." It may have been this tribute by a man who had never known him that brought Berkman back into the room with us and started me talking about the birds he had lived with and loved. In one of his letters (one written on January 15th, 1900, and got out sub rosa from solitary), Berkman says: "I write in an agony of despair. . . . You remember my feathered friend, Dick. Last summer the Warden ordered him put out, but when the cold weather set in, Dick returned. Would you believe it? He came back to my old cell, and recognized me when I passed by. I kept him, and he grew as tame as before—he had become a bit wild in his life outside. On Christmas day, as Dick was playing near my cell, Bob Runyon—the stool, you know—came by and deliberately kicked the bird. When I saw Dick turn over on his side, his little eyes rolling in the throes of death, I rushed at Runyon and knocked him down." So Berkman was put in solitary again. And then in June of that year, a time when "unfledged birdies frequently fall from their nests," Berkman was able to procure two starlings. "Old Mitchell is in ecstasy over the intelligence and adaptability of my new feathered friends," Berkman wrote, "but the birds languish and waste in the close air of the block; they need sunshine and gravel, and the dusty street to bathe in. . . . One day the Warden strolls by and joins in admiration of the wonderful birds. . . . 'Who trained them?' he inquires." On that day Berkman pleads for and is granted permission to take the birds out for ten minutes every morning, provided he stays near the greenhouse, where there is sand for them to flutter and shower in. If he crosses the deadline of the sidewalk or exceeds his allotted time by a single minute, he will go back into The Hole again.

What is it about birds, I asked myself, that made such disparate prisoners as Berkman and Birdman turn to them in their confinement, one in the Western Penitentiary of Pennsylvania, the other on Alcatraz? Birdman, twice a murderer, Berkman, a man who had failed in his attempt at assassination, both found solace (if that is anything like the word) in the small, swiftly beating hearts and the clinging threads of the feet of these fragile living things. (Fragile, my eye, I thought, for weren't they powerful enough to spread their pinions and outwit any wall, and cover watery expanses which no man could hope to swim?) In his thirty-odd years in Leavenworth and other jails, Birdman wrote two books about birds and their diseases, "scholarly works" they have been called by those who ought to know. But on The Rock, no pets, no birds, not even a spider to tell your troubles to, and, anyway, total silence was the rule. Birdman couldn't exchange so much as the time of day with Al Capone who was working in the laundry there.

As for Berkman, it so happened that the tunnel his friends were excavating from their end, under a nearby house, was discovered, and he was returned to solitary. That fact wouldn't be of much comfort to the Marie Laurencin girl or the black prisoner; nor was there any point in speaking of Berkman's computation of his future, which went:

$$264 \times 30 = 7,920 \text{ days.}$$
$$7,920 \times 24 = 190,080 \text{ hours.}$$
$$190,080 \times 60 = 11,404,800 \text{ minutes.}$$
$$11,404,800 \times 60 = 684,288,000 \text{ seconds.}$$

That he came to the realization later that he had allowed only thirty days per month when the year consists of 365 days, and at times 366, wouldn't cheer them either. So he revised the multiplication and was aghast to find that he had closer to 700,000,000 seconds to pass in solitary. "This is from the hospital, sub rosa," Berkman wrote on July 10, 1901. "Just out of the strait-jacket after eight days. For over a year I was in the strictest solitary; for a long time mail and reading matter were denied me. I have no words to describe the horror of the last months." But it occurred to me that it would perhaps be better to tell my two cellmates not about men, but about other women, for that would come closer to touching their own lives. I would not complicate things by dwelling on what Martha Tranquilla had once said very quietly. It was after she had served her sentence at Terminal Island for refusing to pay income tax, inasmuch as she considered herself exempt from taxation, claiming all the children of Vietnam as her dependents. She was asked by a magazine to write on the subject of the treatment of women in prison, and she said she could not. In her experience, she said, women and men were treated with equal injustice in jail.

I could simply begin by saying that once upon a time there was a woman named Alice Paul, and when I was a little girl I saw her every now and then because my aunt drew the covers for the equal rights magazine called *The Suffragist*. Sometimes Alice Paul came to lunch at our house, and once my grandfather, a gracious-mannered descendant of the Donegal Boyles, a man with an astute, legal mind, was persuaded to come home for lunch one day in order to meet a "suffragette." That evening, my mother asked him what he thought of this young woman who had degrees from Swarthmore and the University of Pennsylvania, and who had done graduate studies in English universities, and gone to jail with the English suffragists.

"She wrote her doctor's thesis on the status of women," Mother told her father-in-law, speaking gently, so gently that you could scarcely hear her, yet everyone always heard what she had to say. "She wanted firsthand experience about the position of women in industry," Mother said, "so she became a factory worker in England."

"Very interesting," my Grandfather Boyle commented.

"And then," Mother went on, "she became involved in the women's militant movement in England. How I wish you'd been there as her lawyer to plead her case!"

My grandfather shook his head and smiled his gracious smile.

"You know that my judgment of a woman doesn't depend on what she thinks or what she does," he said, "but on whether or not she has a kissable mouth. Alice Paul does not have that attribute," he said.

But that wouldn't have been of much interest to the Marie Laurencin girl or the black prisoner, who was perhaps about to go to a sterner jail where her heart and her pride would finally have to break. It would make more sense to tell them about an American prison, I thought, and something about Alice Paul when she came back to Washington. I wanted to say to my cellmates, and to the deputies, and to the little black girls who had left the imprint of their lips between the bars on the glass pane of the door, that it was a part of our history, our own personal history. But I never found the way to say it, except by rocking the girl and her unborn baby to sleep, sometimes in the afternoon, and sometimes at night. Women had picketed the White House, went the chapter and verse and the rhyme and reason of the lullaby, and group after group of them were arrested, Alice Paul among them, and some were given three months, and others were given seven months, for obstructing traffic. "I'm seven months pregnant," murmured the blue-veined girl in her sleep, and I said, "Keep him in there as long as you can, because once he's out his troubles will begin."

In England, where Robin Hood could have been charged
with assault with a deadly weapon in Sherwood Forest, and
where women had burned mailboxes and torn down parts of
buildings, sentences like that weren't handed out, was all part
of the lullaby I warbled softly to her; but when I came to the
lyrics about the hunger strike and the forcible feeding in the
Washington, D.C., prison, I thought I had better forget the
rest. Suppose they got the idea of forcibly feeding the Marie
Laurencin girl because she couldn't eat the cold oatmeal and
the fried eggs that had turned to leather by the time they got
as far as lock-up? She was asleep now, so whether I sang or
not wouldn't make any difference, but I didn't get up from
the side of her cot because that might have startled her awake.
Instead, out of the file of my staggering memory, I took the
folder marked "Women," and I found the crumpled, hand-
written letter I wanted, and I smoothed the creases from it
with my hand.

> Alice Paul is in the psychopathic ward [it read]. She dreaded
> forcible feeding frightfully, and I hate to think how she must be
> feeling. I had a nervous time of it, gasping a long time after-
> ward, and my stomach rejecting during the process. I spent a
> bad, restless night, but otherwise I am all right. The poor soul
> who fed me got liberally besprinkled during the process. I heard
> myself making the most hideous sounds. . . . One feels so for-
> saken when one lies prone and people shove a pipe down one's
> stomach. . . . Don't let them tell you we take this well. Miss
> Paul vomits much. I do, too, except when I'm not nervous, as I
> have been every time against my will. . . . I don't imagine bath-
> ing one's food in tears very good for one. . . . We think of the
> coming feeding all day. It is horrible.
>
> (Doris Stevens, *Jailed for Freedom*, 1976)

Actually, it wasn't a letter at all. These words, and others
like them, were written by Rose Winslow on tiny scraps of

paper and smuggled out of the District jail to her husband and to the women who still picketed the White House gates.

Now the black prisoner was gone, and the shallow breath of the sleeping girl was soft as a moth's wing on my hands as I sat on the cot beside her. So I took another folder out of the file of our past history, this one from a legal subdivision labeled "Men," and the statement I wanted was instantly there. "Immediately after the police court judge had pronounced his sentence of sixty days in the Occoquan workhouse on the 'first offenders,' on the alleged charge of a traffic violation," Dudley Field Malone's voice (in *Jailed for Freedom*) said quietly, "I offered to act as attorney on the appeal of the case." He had then telephoned President Woodrow Wilson in the White House and asked that he be allowed to see him without delay. "I began by reminding the President," Malone said in the uncanny hush of lock-up, "that in the seven and a half years of our personal and political association we had never had a serious difference. He was good enough to say that my loyalty to him had been one of the happiest circumstances of his public career. But I told him I had come to place my resignation in his hands as I could not remain a member of any administration which dared to send women to prison for demanding national suffrage." The President had replied that the women had been unmolested at the White House gates for over five months, and he added that he had even gone so far as to instruct the head usher to invite the women in on cold days to warm themselves and have coffee.

"The manhandling of the women by the police was outrageous," Dudley Field Malone's words to the President continued, but now it was difficult to hear him because of the wild, sad keening that had begun to come from the black depths of The Hole, just a skip and a jump outside our door. It was either the crying of a woman who could bear no more, or else the anguish of a cat wailing for the love of her kind in the total imprisonment of night. Then almost at once a deputy's voice, that I didn't want the Marie Laurencin girl to hear, rang out in the hall, saying (as a college president of San Francisco State had once screamed out to students and faculty through the police bullhorn): "If it's tear gas you want, then keep right on and you'll get it! You'll get it, if that's what you're asking for!"

After that, there was silence again, and Dudley Field Malone said quietly to President Wilson that the entire trial of the imprisoned women, conducted before a judge of the President's appointing, had been a perversion of justice. And then the President spoke out in total incredulity. "Do you mean to tell me that you intend to resign, to repudiate me and my Administration, and sacrifice me for your views on this suffrage question?" It was growing dark in lock-up now, and in another minute the deputy on duty might rap on the barred glass and gesture from the hall for us to turn the light on, or might put her key in the lock and step in and herself switch on the ailing, overhead bulb. But I kept on listening to Malone, and now he was saying: "You ask if I am going to sacrifice you. You sacrifice nothing by my resignation. But I lose much. I quit a political career. I give up a powerful office in my own state. I, who have no money, sacrifice a lucrative salary, and go back to revive my law practice. . . . But I cannot and I will not remain in office and see women thrown into jail because they demand their political freedom."

Just before the deputy's key rapped sharply on the glass, Malone exhorted the President to comprehend the inevitable impatience and righteous indignation of the women of America who had, for over half a century, demonstrated peacefully for a political right. He was urging him to take action on the suffrage amendment when the deputy called out from the hall, "Lights on!" I got up carefully, carefully, from the cot, soft-footed as a cat in my outsized sneakers, so as not to waken the girl. And Malone, too, got to his feet and said quietly: "I left the executive offices, and never saw him again." After I had turned on the switch, and taken my towel and soap from the drawer of my night table, I went to the lock-up shower, where plywood nailed across the window took the place of sawed-through bars and broken glass. It was then, as I soaped myself up and down and back and forth under the strong, warm needles of water, that I felt the lump for the first time. It was very small. It was really nothing. When I dried myself, it was still there. By six-thirty in the morning, when the cart creaked up the hall with breakfast for one and all, it had not gone away.

That was the first morning the Marie Laurencin girl ate anything. Slowly, and with great delicacy, she swallowed two pieces of toast soaked lifeless in the liquid that was neither coffee nor tea.

"I had a good night's sleep," she said. "Maybe that's why. The baby likes the food all right. You ought to feel the way he's kicking!"

I said I was going to ask that the doctor come and have a look at both of us, saying this as briskly as if I only needed to walk across the wall-to-wall carpeting to where the princess courtesy phone was waiting for me to dial the seven digits with my elegantly varnished fingernail, and speak the syllables of his name.

"I'm really, once and for all, going to get everything straightened out for us," I said. Sometimes the pill nurse, with her little brown basket of aspirin and castor oil and a vitamin or two, came into lock-up, and sometimes she didn't, but as she walked up the hall that morning, I tapped on the window in the door, and she turned and came back, and took out her ring of keys. "We both really have to see the doctor," I said when she stood there in the room with us, her gingham smock purple and gold and fresh as a daisy, a charitable lady with a neat crown of greying braids worn high on her head. "It's urgent. It's quite urgent for both of us," I said, and she took two aspirin tablets from the vial of them in her basket, and handed me one, and then crossed the room and handed the other to the Marie Laurencin girl. "But we really want to see the doctor," I said, and she answered in a low voice, as she drew the white serviette over her basket again, that the doctor wouldn't be back that week. "Then my attorney. I want to call my attorney," I said, but she had already opened the door, her defense an aura of vagueness, a mild bewilderment, so that it seemed now she was not quite certain this was the way out. Once in the safety of the hall, she locked the door carefully again.

Then the last talk I was ever to have with the blue-veined girl took place. She asked me if I believed what some people said, that if you couldn't get on with your mother, then you would have trouble all your life getting on with other people. "I'm afraid of that happening between him and me," she was saying, speaking of the unborn baby, when the two deputies unlocked the door. It was perhaps a little after seven o'clock, and they had come to escort me to still another lock-up room. This one gave every promise of being the most interesting of them all. In the very center of it sat a bare white toilet, slightly spattered inside and out with excrement. It was clear that whatever you did, you did it with your sister-prisoners either looking on or turning their heads the other way. Five women were sitting on their cots, and a sixth cot stood there empty, its sagging mattress waiting invitingly for me. The five women, three black, two white, seemed very lively, and greeted me with something like delight.

"The ladies' room convenience don't flush from here," one of them called out to me, and they all burst into laughter. "You use it, and then you yell your lungs out for a deputy to flush it from the hall."

As I put my towel, and my piece of soap, and my suicide-proof toothbrush in the night table drawer, another of the women said:

"Welcome to the toughest lock-up on the premises. They done their very best out here, and they come up with this one. Sisters used to flood the place, holding down the handle of the john, so they changed the system. They just don't seem to have no faith in us."

It was a large black woman sitting on her cot who said to me: "You look likes you could write a letter for me, lady. I gotta write a letter to my public defender about a son of a bitch that had my thirty dollars in his pocket when he dropped down dead right before my eyes in the Flamingo Bar."

But there wasn't the time to discuss past, present, or future prison history in the brief interval before a deputy turned her key in the lock of the door, and motioned to me. Outside in the hall, she said:

"Your lawyer's here."

I wanted to make my appearance before Bob as a woman if not of great beauty, at least of dignity, but I didn't have a comb or any lipstick to aid and abet me. So with my grey dress hanging unevenly and my sneakers flapping, I followed the deputy humbly to where he waited in the visiting room. We put our arms tightly around each other, and I don't know whether I told him first that I had been in lock-up for five days and nights, or whether I mentioned the lump to him right away.

"You know, where ladies get lumps," I said, "the usual place."

"Lock-up?" Bob said eventually, and his quick, dark eyes went darker. "Let me see the lieutenant at once," he said to the deputy standing near the door, her key ring swinging in her hand. But the lieutenant wasn't on duty yet; she was maybe getting the auburn beehive of her hairdo into shape, I thought, but I stood there, humble and modest, and did not speak. "Get my client to the county hospital within an hour," Bob said. "I'll be back to check on that." And he said to me: "I'm going to court now to report this to the judge." I didn't cry out to him then, "What if I were black or yellow or penniless and forgotten, Bob? What if no one came at seven-thirty in the morning to speak his piece for me?" But before he left he answered with bitterness the words I hadn't said. "I know," he said. "I know."

V

One of the differences between a police car and a paddy wagon is that you can see out of a police car. When a police car skims quietly along a freeway, you can see the landscape of America on one side, and the passing traffic on the other. On the left, I could see settlements of rusticated motels, and gas stations, and supermarkets, and signs saying "Grub," or "Eats," or "Body Work," and swimming pools bright azure oblongs in the early morning sun. On the right, Greyhound buses swept past, the riders in them looking down, as an audience high in the gallery might look, at the spectacle of a woman in a grey dress traveling alone inside a wire-meshed cage. Once or twice I wanted to raise my hand and wave to the passersby, but rightly or wrongly I believed that every prisoner has a certain dignity to maintain, no matter how trifling the sentence the authorities may have chosen to mete out.

So I rode on with my dignity, a bulletproof plate of glass, strengthened with chicken wire, between me and the driver, thinking of freeways as the arteries of America. And if these were the arteries, I asked myself, then where was the heart from which these broad veins flowed? Recklessly, heedlessly, they poured from state to state, from prison to prison (as well as from picnic-ground to picnic-ground), wooing us, urging us on, all of us, with their passion and purpose, from the solitary confinements of our lives. But what the passion and the purpose were, and whether our escape was actually escape, I did not know.

At the desk of the county hospital, the deputy who had driven me told the clerk that she was from the Rehabilitation Center, and was bringing me in for examination for breast cancer, and it might have been a misdemeanor, or even a felony, of which she spoke.

"The patient's name?" asked the girl behind the counter, and the deputy said:

"You don't need a name. Just put down number 2362."

IV. ON THE HUMAN CONDITION

"A Quite Humble Pageant"

Battle of the Sequins

I did not know that sequins were being worn this year. I did not know until yesterday that garments stitched with sequins were being fought over on department store counters. I did not know that blouses seemingly entirely fashioned of sequins, hard and brilliant and metallic as hummingbirds, were coveted as gold, or beauty, or fame is coveted—especially if they come with little sequined caps to match. Apparently a great many people did know this, for the battle taking place for these things was a bitter battle. It was a battle among women—as terrific as any that is taking place in the rain or the snow or the jungle among men. For if one woman succeeds in getting the only size forty-two blouse in topaz sequins, there is still no assurance that she will be able to get the topaz-sequined cap to wear with it. It is quite possible that she may have to go home with the heartbreak of having got only the blouse, and not the little cap, or perhaps with the little cap in a different color.

Yesterday, in the department store, the women who had gone there to buy were surrounded by mirrors—mirrors on the counters, mirrors in the lifts, full-length mirrors in the panels of every door. So that everyone, if he paused for an instant, could see exactly and unequivocally how he looked. But the faces of these women were turned away, their eyes were fixed on something else; they were there to outwit one another, and they had no time to face themselves. In the mirrors there might have been the singular reflection of other women—women who skipped quickly back into a trench before the shellfire got them, dragging with them the body of a companion who had fought three winters with her feet bound in rags, as were the feet of the other women, and who now had been killed. Perhaps they are Russian women, perhaps English women, perhaps women of the French maquis. It is difficult to say whether they are beautiful or not, for their faces are masked with filth, with sweat, even with blood. Their skin is cracked, weathered; their nails are not varnished. The dead woman who had fought through three winters with them and whom they kick down into the bottom of the trench for safety has been dragged so far by her feet that her mouth and nostrils are stopped with dirt. But whatever has happened to her eyes, the vision is set as clear as glass in them. When this thing is finished, those of them who survive will sit down under a roof again and hold their children against them, and they will never be afraid, no matter how old they grow, to look at their own faces in the mirror.

Across the walls of the department store there were words written, written more violently and boldly—in spite of their absolute invisibility—than the legend which states that it is a legal offense to smoke in a retail store. "Caution," say these indiscernible words. "You are warned by the authorities against stopping to look at yourselves in the mirrors." Not because you will see your own shape or face reflected; not for an instant. But because the leaves of jungle trees still suddenly grow there, tough and strong as rubber, and bright green in the mirror. You will see the hair that grows on the bark of trees in that tropical place, and the blades of green on green, and then, without warning, you will come upon the man lying there on the jungle floor with the blood like an open fan, spread as thick as tar and as black, beneath his head. He is a young man in a khaki shirt, and his beard is a week old on his jaws, and by his eyes you know he is not dead. His eyes are watching the men who come and kneel, and who set down the stretcher beside him, and his eyes move in quick desperation from one face to the other, asking them not to let it happen. It is when they lift him that the black fan opens a little wider on the grass, and the look of ice moves over his face, and you know he is asking nothing of anyone anymore.

"Customers are cautioned not to look," says the sign of which no one can perceive the letters, for if you stop to look you will see something you do not wish to see. You will see the shallow water of the river flickering, and out of the muck of the river's bed you will see the other boy crawling on his knees. His shirt is ripped away, and his arm is hanging from the shoulder by two delicate threads of sinew or nerve or splintered bone, and the blood is not running from it, it is spouting from it the way water will spout from an open water hydrant and pour, foaming, into the gutter below. You are cautioned not to look, for you have come here to buy sequins, and if you look you will see that his lips are stiff and that his teeth are shaking in his head as if he were cold. But this is the tropics, and he is not cold, he is merely frightened. He is crying, with little shuddering gasps of terror shaking through his teeth. He is saying: "I am not going to die, am I? Tell me, I'm not going to die, am I?" and he comes crawling toward you, crawling like a beast through the mud. He has almost reached you, he has almost touched your skirt with his hand when you hear the woman's voice saying: "I've been waiting twenty minutes, and then this customer gets in ahead of me and gets the last 42 in topaz——"

"Listen," said the salesgirl, leaning forward. "You can't take them with you."

"Take what?" said the customer.

"Sequins," said the salesgirl. "You know, things that glitter."

"I didn't want to take them with me," said the woman. "I wanted them sent COD."

The Jew Is a Myth

Let us take Madison Square Garden as parallel. It will serve as proscenium, not for the pomp and tomfoolery of the circus, not for the streaming, stampeding panic of the rodeo, but for a quite humble pageant of incarceration. For within Madison Square Garden will be enclosed eleven thousand Polish and Russian Jews. These Jews will have been arrested at their homes in New York City, will have been rounded up by the New York police in their apartments, rooms, tenement dwellings, where they have been living for a number of years. Entire families—old people, some of them scarcely able to walk, babies carried in their parents' arms—will be brought to Madison Square Garden and they will be given the benches to sit on, but they will be forbidden to circulate in the empty arena below. There they will remain, seated, awaiting the performance which is never to take place, for they themselves are the performers as well as the spectators.

"The tide rose," writes an eyewitness of the scene. "The ring of misery widened hour by hour, invaded the amphitheater, reached to the roof, and came down to the row of boxes. Fresh files of people carrying suitcases surged through the dark entrances and were at once seized and devoured by the benches. . . . Everyone was seated and could sleep only seated. . . . Sleep thus lost its hours, its rights, its substance." As the hours passed no food was provided, there was no question of washing. "By the end of the first day," continues the report of the eyewitness, "the latrines were full and overflowing. . . .There were a large number of women among the prisoners. . . .They menstruated. Soiled, ashamed . . . they searched everywhere for newspapers . . . they stained with blood the already impossible latrines. . . . Sickening pools spread everywhere. An intolerable stench filled the vast amphitheater and dishonored it." The first intermission in the performance came on the fourth day, when certain of the spectator-performers, such as women in labor and persons actually too ill to be moved, were evacuated either to hospital or to concentration camp.

Such a performance did take place. The date of its opening night was July 16, 1942, and it was not staged at Madison Square Garden in New York but at the Vélodrome d'Hiver in Paris. During the first days and nights of its run news of these mass arrests spread through the city, and a number of doctors, "nearly all Jews," volunteered their services to care for the eleven thousand prisoners. Among this group of doctors was the eyewitness quoted above—Dr. Charles Odic, not a Jew, but a Catholic of Breton stock.

"Only the children remained something like children," Dr. Odic writes in his book, *Stepchildren of France* (1945). "They played, they ran about. If one looked closely, their games were not the usual kind. Invented as a necessity, they hid a deep distress of which I later had numerous proofs." They played, at least, until they succumbed to tuberculosis, to pneumonia, to starvation, or to the "furious epidemic of measles" which broke out in the Vélodrome d'Hiver. "As I leaf over the entry book, there is a TB mark against almost every name on every page," writes Dr. Odic when he follows some of these victims to Drancy. "When at last a doctor had an opportunity to listen, the child was lost. It could not be sent anywhere for a change of air. If Jews pay taxes even when the state has deprived them of all means of livelihood, they have no right to sanitariums. Vichy drove out all who were patients in such places. . . . Some day one coughs up a little patch of poppies, and then one arrives at the end of a journey so ill begun, a journey that might have ended so differently from in horror at the bottom of a pit of hate."

From this document, which deals with the despair of countless people, emerges an army of terribly living, unforgettable individuals. On these pages, which record the anguish of an entire race, is set down the shameful story of the Jews of France. "French to the core," writes Charles Odic, "Israel of France had the honor to bear our Cross when it was heaviest. What better patent of nobility!" There is Bertha Fraidrach, three years old, who must stand there naked in her bed forever, forever demanding that her mother be returned from her gas-chamber fate; there is Gaby Feld, who, "as she disappears under the arches of Death, becomes Gabrielle . . . a little Jewess, as humble as a violet in the woods, who Hitler had not foreseen would perfume her adopted country with the odor of her suffering"; there is Henri Krasnopolski, thirty months old, who explains to the doctor that the newborn babies crying nearby "are not crying about the cocoa, but because they want their mommies who have been taken away." And then one day, our eyewitness writes, a child does not leave its bed. "By evening it is delirious. It still breathes, it breathes too hard, its little carcass wriggles on the straw, but its mind gallops afar on the swift courses of fever. It has broken its halter and escaped."

Dr. Odic, who was himself finally imprisoned in Buchenwald, holds no place in the world of contemporary French literature. Although he has written a book, he cannot be said to belong to any of the recent schools of French expression and thought, which have been divided into "the literature of collaboration, the literature of occupation, and the literature of resistance." And yet how futile, when compared with his testimony of action and of faith, appear the rhetorical discussions of a "*littérature engagée*" and a "*littérature dégagée*"! How beggarly the cautious subtleties of a Gide written in the time of France's occupation! How utterly beyond debate the debatable roles that Guitry and Chevalier played! I believe that if no other book had been written in France during the years of its defeat, Odic's modest volume—revealing as it does the stature of its author—would alone serve as final answer and rebuke to the contemptuous doubts which have been advanced concerning the quality of French principles and French probity.

> The Jew is a myth [Dr. Odic concludes], the myth of German impotence. There is no more useful myth.
>
> The Jew exists because I have failed. Every time I fail, it is the fault of the Jew. Each of my failures shows the pattern of the Jew, and all these patterns make up "international Jewry."
>
> A German has a nightmare. On awakening it is the Jew that he accuses.
>
> "He wanted to ruin me, to soil me, to kill me."
>
> "Who?"
>
> "The Jew who hovered over my bed last night. That one, I recognize him."
>
> "That cannot be, he was elsewhere."
>
> "Then that one. All of them, for if it was not he, it was one of his."

Frankfurt in Our Blood

It was the half-bottles of wine that made them speak. Without them, the two women seated at a small table at the end of the dining car might have had nothing to say. Paris lay hardly twenty minutes behind them, but already the gently sloping green hills and the luxuriant fields of France were there, streaming swiftly past the windows; the villages, the feathery trees, the fluid country dimmed now to the quality of ancient murals by the veil of dusk which lay across the land. But inside the crowded diner of the Orient Express the illumination was as hard as brass, and the waiters swayed down the aisle between the tables, bearing their trays on high as if upon the current of a stream.

Behind the diner swung the nimble links of the long, racing train, the sleeping cars for Prague and Frankfurt coupled with those for Warsaw and Budapest, or with sleepers for

Bratislava, Vienna, Munich, Bucharest. By morning these cars, which roared through the pastoral stillness of the continent, would have taken their separate ways, shunted off at Bar-le-Duc while the travelers slept within them, and the people who shared tables for the evening meal would have forgotten the look of one another in a little while. The two women were strangers to each other, and the one who faced in the direction in which the train was going was young and soft-skinned, and she wore a blue-cotton short-sleeved dress, as simple as a schoolgirl's dress. She sat with her face turned toward the window and her chin held in the cushion of her ringless left hand. The small, stooped, aging woman who sat opposite had also turned her head to watch the deepening twilight, her flesh, hair, clothing, eyes, all of the same worn, faded grey. But there were the half-bottles of red wine before them, and it was the faded little woman who made the first move, and who leaned forward toward the girl.

"Perhaps we could divide a half-bottle between us?" she began, her diffidence coming meekly, patiently to speech. "We could share the expense of it," she said, her accent not quite English and not quite American.

The girl turned back from the window, her wide eyes startled, and looked at the woman as if waking from a dream.

"Yes, indeed. Yes," she said, and that might have been the end of it. It was the other woman who motioned the waiter to pull the cork of one of the two little bottles of red wine. Once he had done this, and wiped the bottle's dark mouth clean, it was her hand reaching, narrow and ivory-knuckled, from the suit's grey sleeve, which poured the wine carefully into their glasses. The girl had turned to the window again, her hands clasped on the table before her, her soft dark hair hanging long across the shoulders of her dress. "How I hate it," she said, and she looked out at the sight of the fleeing country as she spoke. "How I hate going back to Germany," she said, and she reached quickly and blindly out and took her glass up, and drank down the first swallow of red wine.

"Yes, going back," said the little woman, but she did not drink. Instead, she picked up her grey cotton gloves from where they lay beside her plate, and she laid the wrinkled fingers of them carefully together, and she smoothed them gently, reflectively, out upon her knees. "Yes, going back," she said.

When the woman began to eat the split-pea soup, the girl turned away from the window again, and she pushed the metal bowl of her own soup aside. It could be seen that her mouth was bright with lipstick and blemished by discontent, and that her glossy hair was cut in a fringe above the baleful eyes. The faded little woman watched her young hand, her bare arm, lift to fill their glasses with the strong good wine.

"Every time it's a little bit harder than it was the time before," the girl was saying quickly. She sat with her arms resting on the table, turning the glass of wine between her fingers. "You see, I go to Paris perhaps once a month, just for the weekend. And every time I have to go back it's like cutting my heart out and throwing it away."

"And you can't stay in Paris?" the woman said quietly.

"Well, I have a job," the girl said, still watching the glass turn on the cloth. "I'm a War Department civilian in Frankfurt." The waiter had carried the bowls away, the full one inside the empty one, and the girl took another swallow of the wine. "I took the job just to get over. Just to get on the same continent with France," she said and she lifted one hand to the side of her face as if to shield it, as though there might be tears in her eyes and she did not want a stranger to see them fall.

"Yes, Frankfurt," said the faded little woman. "It's been a long time, but I could tell you the name of almost every street still. You know, I went there as a bride once," she said, and she lifted her glass of wine again and drank a little, trying to make it sound, even after all the years that had passed, festive and jaunty and gay. "My husband taught in the university there," she said, with a sociable smile on her lips, but her hand as it set the glass down on the cloth was trembling like a leaf in the high wind of emotion that came sweeping through her heart. She looked at the ham in gravy which the waiter set before her, but she made no move to eat. "We lived there twenty-five years together," she said.

"You have memories. That's a certain kind of wealth," the girl said, seeming to begrudge them to her. "I have absolutely nothing except the things I want to be."

"Well, let's make this into a little celebration," said the woman, and she raised her glass as if they might drink a toast together, but the girl drank quickly, without acknowledging the woman's lifted glass or the tentative smile that hung upon her mouth.

"Six months ago I didn't believe that Germany would remain for me this alien, evil thing," the girl said, and across the table the woman looked meekly up at her young face. "I thought I would be able to get close to what it really is, or was," the girl said, speaking quickly, while outside the windows the lights of the villages and the rural stations of France were cast behind them in the dark. "But I see Germany like some isolated territory, like a lepers' colony, an infected island which free men conquered, and have, because of this, become ailing and evil and no longer free."

"Yes," said the woman, "but you know, there is a strange thing that can happen to people. Or perhaps, when people get older, this is the thing that always happens." The waiter bore the plates away, and the woman sat smiling, smiling almost in apology across the cloth. "I can only think of Germany now as it was when I was a child, and of Frankfurt as I knew it as a bride," she said. And now an unexpected look of audacity, an almost devilish look of mischief came into her worn, faded eyes. "You know, I have a little French money left, not much, but enough," she said, "and I would like to spend it on another half-bottle of wine."

The waiter uncorked the second half-bottle, and wiped its mouth clean, and then put the plates of lamb and peas before them. And now that the woman's voice had ceased to speak, the girl turned to the window again, and to the sight of the deepening darkness through which the country flowed swiftly, irretrievably past. Tomorrow there would be Frankfurt, and the bomb-gutted station in the early morning, and the houses laid open to the elements still bearing within their rubble outlandish bits and pieces of what had once been comfort and security. There would be the radiator hanging by its pipes through a floor that had capsized beneath it five years before, and the bathtub standing two stories high above the dead magnolia trees, its clawed feet resting on nothing, and the paneled door behind it still standing ajar.

"Or perhaps the place you began life as a bride is a place that can never change for you," the woman was saying now, and the girl turned abruptly from the window, and she poured their glasses full with wine. "There was my husband's work in the university, and there were other professors, and there were artists, too, writers, countless friends," said the little woman, smiling as she spoke. "There we had meetings, discussions, and not only among intellectuals, but among men of free crafts, the guilds, the unions. For Frankfurt was once the heart of liberal Germany. And then, in 1934, my husband died. He was very wise to choose that year to die in," she said, still smiling, but her hand was shaking as if with palsy as she took the glass of wine. "We are a Jewish family," she said, "so in one way or another we had to go."

"And you, where did you go?" the girl asked, and the turmoil, the protest, seemed to halt within her for a moment.

"We went to China. My sons and I left for China that year," said the woman. "We carried what we could of Frankfurt in our blood with us—its culture, its wisdom, its democratic history. Or perhaps the only thing we really took with us was the sound of Goethe's words saying many things to us who were also the German people, saying very clearly that wisdom's last decree is that freedom and life are deserved only by those who conquer them anew each day." The girl and the woman both finished the wine in their glasses, and the girl sat turning the glass in her fingers while opposite her the woman's voice went on speaking gently and patiently of a town that had been Frankfurt once, and a country that had been Germany. "That was a gift I had to give my children," the woman said, "a belief in free men that free men themselves had communicated to me."

And as the girl listened to the woman's voice going on with this, the city they traveled toward took on another aspect, and the sound of the familiar German voices perished, no longer saying, as they had said to her for six months now, "I lost everything in the bombings, everything—my house, my furniture, my business," for the woman was speaking of the Taunus hills, and of the walks they had taken there in the springtime, she and the others, the professors, the artists, the writers, the free men of Frankfurt who had seen freedom die.

"And now you are going back? After fifteen years, you are going back?" the girl said, looking at her, and forgetting to turn the wine glass on the cloth.

"Yes," said the little woman. "No choice was offered. The women and children of foreigners were being evacuated. I was flown out of China last week. I am going back to Frankfurt," she said, the smile hanging on her mouth again, "because there does not seem any other place for me to go."

"How many children did you have?" the girl asked, for it

was the members of this family which mattered, as the rest
of Germany had never mattered. It was what they had been,
and how they had spoken, and what answer they had given
when the questions had been asked.

"I had four sons," the woman said, and her hand had begun
to tremble again as she lifted her glass to drink. "Two of them
left Germany with me, the two younger ones. We went to
China together," she said, having wet her lips with the wine.
"The two others . . . ," she went on after a moment, but she
could not go on with it at once. "The two others," she began
again, and there was no hint of crying, nothing that even
resembled anguish in the words she said, "the two others died
with their countrymen and women in Dachau," was what she
was saying, but even the strength of the wine she drank was
not enough to lean on now, and her lips, her chin, her empty
hands, were trembling as if stricken with the plague.

"Now it is my turn to order another half-bottle," the girl
said quickly, and she made the sign to the waiter as he passed
with the *bombes glacées*. And then she reached across the table,
and she touched the woman's worn, aged hand that lay, like a
forgotten object, on the cloth.

"I am afraid to go back," the woman said, and her teeth bit
hard into her shaking lip. "I am not afraid of my memories.
I am afraid of hearing what the living now have to say."

"We can listen to other things," the girl said, and their
hands held to each other's as the waiter set the plates of crack-
ers and cheese before them and poured the fresh wine out.
And then the stooped little woman shouldered the burden of
patience and resignation again, and she smiled across the table at the girl.

"I shall make out very well," she said, and their hands drew
apart, and they lifted their glasses and drank. "I have a widow's pension accumulated at the university. It will be enough
to begin again on," she said, and an unsteady look of reck-

lessness or tipsiness came into her face. "It will be enough to pay my way into the Palm Garden in the afternoons, and there'll still be the orchid hothouse, with orchids as different as people, with wise faces, and foolish ones," she said, and she giggled as if she were a young and giddy woman now. "I don't remember how many species there were, but I knew them all by name once. And in the tropical conservatory there'll be the camellias flowering, reddish and white and waxy, as they flowered in China so profusely—" And then she stopped talking, "Unless," she said quickly, "I mean, was the Palm Garden bombed—are the greenhouses there still?"

"Yes, they are there," said the girl, and then the two women began to laugh across the table at each other.

"I must write to my sons at once, to my two boys in China," the woman said, wiping the tears of laughter away, "and tell them how tall the banana trees have grown."

Lucky Eyes
and a High Heart

William Butler Yeats wrote in his memoirs that when he was
twenty-three years old the "troubling" of his life began. "I
had heard from time to time . . . of a beautiful girl who had
left the society of the Viceregal Court for Dublin national-
ism," he went on. "In after years I persuaded myself that I
felt premonitory excitement at the first reading of her name.
Presently she drove up to our house . . . with an introduction
from John O'Leary to my father."

The year was 1889 and Maud Gonne, then twenty-two,
was on one of her countless peregrinations between France
and Ireland. From the day she presented her letter of introduction from the great Fenian leader O'Leary to the distinguished Irish portrait painter John Butler Yeats, the life of
the young Yeats was in turmoil. "Heavy red-gold hair and
large dark eyes set off her luminous complexion," Nancy
Cardozo writes of her in *Lucky Eyes and a High Heart: The*

Life of Maud Gonne. "Nearly six feet tall . . . confident, vital, dedicated to a single purpose—Ireland's freedom from England—Maud Gonne was an irresistible force" not only in Willie Yeats's life but also in a society in which women faced almost insurmountable obstacles if they sought to enter public life. At the age of twenty, stunningly dressed by Paris couturiers, she had already made a place for herself in the Irish nationalist movement, familiar with "princes and rebels, generals and conspirators, and with the intellectuals of Continental salons," at ease with Home-Rulers, separatists, and students from Trinity. Later she was to write, "I never willingly discouraged either a Dynamiter or a constitutionalist, a realist or a lyrical writer. My chief occupation was how their work could help forward the Irish Separatist movement."

Maud Gonne was born in England of a mother ill with consumption, who died when Maud was four and her sister two. The family came to Dublin when Captain Gonne, "the dashing soldier of the Queen," was transferred from Surrey to England's largest military base in Ireland. Maud was then two months old, and throughout her life she said that until that time she had not breathed the air of freedom. Thomas Gonne was not only affluent (grandson of an Irish importer in London of port and Madeira from Portugal) but he was also fluent in five foreign languages. After his wife's death, Gonne (now promoted to Brigade Major of the Cavalry of Ireland) decided to settle in the land of his forebears with his two little girls. Tommy Gonne was the first great love of Maud's life, and her son, Sean MacBride, the last.

Many Englishmen of independent means, Cardozo points out, found Ireland a congenial place to live. "The horse-raising country, the hunt, the relaxed social and garrison life" played their part in Major Gonne's decision, but Cardozo refers as well to the seduction of the ambivalent attitude these

Englishmen displayed toward their Irish peers, akin to "the feeling of affection and condescension of a legitimate son toward an attractive bastard brother." However much of this attitude was absorbed by Maud Gonne, it was tempered at an early age by the passion of her political convictions. Riding her horse across country, she saw piles of rubble, the houses of peasants destroyed by the battering rams of the agents of absentee British landlords. She saw destitute families wandering the roads, seeking shelter, carrying what they could of their miserable possessions with them, and she could not bear what she saw. In his poetry and plays, Yeats's women often spoke with the voice of Maud Gonne, and his Countess Cathleen expressed Maud's compassion, saying:

> I have heard
> A sound of wailing in unnumbered hovels
> And I must go down, down, I know not where.

The life story of Maud Gonne is inseparable from that of Yeats, and inseparable as well from the tragic history of Ireland in our century. The three well-documented records are skillfully interwoven by Cardozo. If there are occasional lapses into fancy prose and rhetorical questioning, such moments are easily overlooked in the fine achievement of the whole—an achievement which over and over makes credible the radiant presence and buoyant nature of Maud Gonne. John O'Leary, obsessed with Irish literature, saw it as a means of bringing about a nationally aware and united people, and he valued young Willie Yeats as his "most hopeful recruit." Yet despite the recommendation of a political leader she revered, and despite her response to Yeats's lyrical gift and his great love for Ireland, Maud Gonne could not bring herself to accept his continuously renewed proposal of marriage. Her lifelong need of him may well have been a part of her compulsive assembling about her of as many living creatures as possible who would be dependent on her for strength—the caged birds with which she traveled from country to country, the monkeys, the various breeds of dog, an occasional cat, and Yeats, the greatest captive of them all. Yeats writes in his autobiography that once, just before a demonstration, he found her surrounded by "many caged larks and finches which she was about to set free for the luck's sake."

Maud Gonne and Yeats "took hashish" together and recorded their heightened fantasies "in a notebook filled with sacred symbols," Cardozo tells us in as quiet a voice as the one she uses to report that there were many who called Maud Gonne "the most beautiful woman in Ireland," and others who hailed her as "the most beautiful woman in the world." Once they found that they could evoke the pagan gods, Willie transformed "the visions Maud saw in her trances into images of Druidic lore." Eventually Maud was to write of the Castle of Heroes they envisioned, "The land of Ireland, we both felt, was powerfully alive and invisibly peopled, and whenever we grew despondent over the weakness of the national movement, we went to it for comfort. If only we could make contact with the hidden forces of the land, it would give us strength for the freeing of Ireland."

But whatever her visions, Maud was above all a woman of action, as Cardozo makes abundantly clear. In one of her many articles in the *United Irishman*, Maud Gonne recalls an old prophecy "which says that Ireland will be saved by the women, and if Irish women will only realize the importance of this work of National education for the children I think this prophecy may come true." Aided by members of the Women's Franchise League she set up school canteens in the poorest sections of Dublin, and hot lunches were served to children close to starvation. By 1900, she had founded the Daughters of Erin, for and with "a new generation of women

[who] had grown up to find themselves still disenfranchised, still unrepresented by any member of their sex in government, except for the Queen." In April of that same year, she organized a peaceful demonstration of 30,000 schoolchildren who had refused to parade before the Queen. During her second imprisonment in Holloway, in company with such courageous women as Constance Markiewicz and Mary MacSwiney, she went on a twenty-day hunger strike to protest the crackdown on her Women's Prisoners' Defense League. The prison doctor, Cardozo records, told Maud she was "the most cheerful hunger striker he ever met, always laughing"; but at the end of the twenty days she had to be carried out on a stretcher.

A chain-smoker, addicted for a time to chloroform and sleeping drugs after the death of her first child, and to hashish during her "Spiritual Marriage" with Yeats, spitting blood into her handkerchief, warned by the doctors of several countries of what might be a fatal "weakness in the lungs," Maud Gonne radiated glowing health, except for those recurring instances when she collapsed with fatigue. She was a passionately devoted daughter to Tommy Gonne, who, motivated at least in part by her example, took the courageous decision to resign his commission and stand for Parliament as a Home Rule candidate; a surrogate mother to her sister Kathleen and to Tommy's illegitimate child, she took particular pride in her son, Sean MacBride, who set aside the gun of his early days in the IRA, became a lawyer of note, and was later to found Amnesty International and twice win the Nobel Peace Prize. James Joyce, tongue in cheek no doubt, referred to Maud as the Joan of Arc of Ireland, as did the ex-Secretary of the U.S. Navy, William McAdoo, in grave admiration of her during one of her lecture tours in the United States.

Oscar Wilde, A. E. Synge, Padriac Pearse, James Connolly, Lady Gregory, Roger Casement, Padriac Colum, Parnell, Oliver Gogarty, Mary and Terence MacSwiney, and at least a dozen other women and men of enduring achievement were among her acquaintances and friends, including the twenty-six-year-old Ezra Pound, who had become the humble secretary of Willie Yeats. But despite the unending political, literary, and social demands, there was still time for her to work tirelessly for the Amnesty Association, the forerunner of Amnesty International. She helped swell the membership of the Association to two hundred thousand in the British Isles alone, and she still had time to launch a campaign against the recruiting by the British of young Irishmen to fight the Boers in Africa, still time in 1914 to nurse the wounded "from eight in the morning to eight at night." When her own acting career on the stage of the Abbey Theatre had ended, she taught dramatics, and taught as well her own belief in the rising wave of women's power. To Emmeline Pankhurst's slogan, "Deeds not words," she added her own spirited admonition: "Men are destroying themselves, and we are looking on."

Nancy Cardozo has written the story of Maud Gonne's life in fascinating detail, and with enviable objectivity and deep respect (with the exception of her reference to the incident of the monkey gland transplant which Yeats insisted on undergoing in the hope of strengthening his virility). It is a life we need to be reminded of, and in Cardozo's telling of it emerges anew the full dignity of past and present Irish history.

Sisters of the Princess

On the fifth day of 1976, Princess Ashraf Pahlavi, sister of the Shah of Iran, published on the Op-Ed page of the *New York Times* an article, "And Thus Passeth International Women's Year," in which she stated that, despite the mournful passing of that year, some limited achievement was scored in publicizing and highlighting "the myriad problems of women throughout the world."

The Princess's point is well taken, and enlightened women must surely be in accord with her recommendations. It would perhaps be too much to expect of the Shah's sister that she deal in the specifics of her own country rather than in high-sounding generalities. The Princess referred, of course, to the International Women's Year World Conference which was held in Mexico City in June 1975. Representatives from 113 countries participated in that conference, and the Princess herself was chairperson of the United Nations preparatory committee. In her *Times* article, she hails "the widening feminists' culture-bound vision of 'sisterhood' " as one of the limited achievements of the conference, and she expresses her belief that the responsibility of women must now be to overcome by united action "the chronic apathy (i.e., concerning women) on the part of most governments."

It would have been of interest to many had she spoken of the plight of her imprisoned Iranian sisters who have been sentenced to death or to long prison terms without the benefit of other than military trials, defended (if such is the proper word) by lawyers appointed by the prosecution.

Protests and pleas from international organizations such as P.E.N., Amnesty International, and the New York-based Committee for Artistic and Intellectual Freedom in Iran, as well as from lawyers from the Western democracies, have invariably met with that government apathy which Princess Ashraf deplores. But Iranian women *have* been singled out for distinction in ways which the Princess perhaps did not have the space to report on in her article. As an example, Ms. Manijeh Ashrafzadeh was chosen in January to be the first woman in Iran to die, with eight of her male compatriots, before a firing squad.

The Committee for Artistic and Intellectual Freedom estimates at 4,000 the number of women political prisoners in Iran. Many of them are the wives, daughters, or other relatives of male political prisoners, CAIF reports, or are part of the growing number of Iranian women who are striving for liberation through activity in the political, social, economic and literary life of their country.

One of these is Atefeh Gorgin, who was imprisoned two years ago for having published an anthology of contemporary Iranian literature. Ms. Gorgin is the widow of the poet, Khosrow Golsorkhi, who was executed last year with the author Karamat Daneshian.

Another is Dr. Simin Salehi. She and her unborn child died in 1974 in Evin prison in Teheran as a result of torture. Chirine Moazed, arrested at the same time as Dr. Salehi, was reported in October 1974 in the European press to be "unconscious, in solitary confinement, with her chest and other parts of her body severely burned."

Vida Hadjebi Tabrizi, a twenty-six-year-old sociologist and researcher at the University of Teheran, was arrested as she drove home one evening in 1972. (The Stockholm daily, *Dagens Nyheter*, reported in August 1973 that Ms. Tabrizi's crime appears to be that she was writing a paper on the living conditions of the peasant population of Iran.) Ms. Tabrizi was sentenced at a closed military trial to seven years' imprisonment, and it is reported that as a result of the torture she has undergone she has developed heart trouble and lost all sense of feeling in her feet and hands.

Ms. Tahereh Sajjadi Teherani, arrested at the same time as Ms. Ashrafzadeh, has been sentenced in a secret trial to fifteen years' solitary confinement.

The lot of Iranian women, according to Betty Friedan, has been improved in recent years, thanks to the benevolence of the Shah's consort, Queen Farah Pahlavi, and her interest in women's rights. But surely the time has come to ask if these include an Iranian woman's right to freedom of speech, and her right to open civilian court proceedings in the event of her arrest, and her right to a defense lawyer of her own choosing. "What do these feminists want?" the Shah of Iran asked Oriana Fallaci during an interview (*The New Republic*, December 1, 1973). "You may be equal in the eyes of the law," he continued, "but not so in ability. You have never even produced a good cook . . . you have produced nothing great, nothing."

In her *Times* article Princess Ashraf writes with guarded hope of the United Nations designation of the decade 1976–

86 as "The Decade for Women." Can such a concept be anything but a mockery if the tragic situation of the women political prisoners of Iran is not immediately remedied by an
impartial investigation? The prisons of Evin, Ghast, Ghezel
Hessar, and Ghezel Ghalen are *our* prisons and *our* responsibility, just as were the political prisons of South Vietnam,
for we graciously placed the Shah of Shahs on his peacock
throne in the same manner, and for the same reasons, that we
placed political power in the hands of President Thieu.

Possibly it is because the voices of the women political
prisoners of Iran were not heard in Mexico City last June
that International Women's Year closed, as Princess Ashraf
put it, "without applause."

Seeing the Sights
in San Francisco

There are any number of unique spots of interest in this vicinity that are, unfortunately, not known to the majority of tourists who flock throughout the year to our beautiful and festive city. I have jotted down a few notes about two or three of these off-the-beaten-track places which vacationers should not fail to see.

Last year I frequently suggested to sojourners in these parts that Sunday was the best day of the week to make a tour of the fabulous Golden Gate Cemetery which lies in all its verdant beauty in the rolling countryside just beyond South San Francisco. On Sunday, one did not at that time run the weekday risk of being delayed an hour or more at the gates by half a dozen or so hearses bearing flag-draped coffins, and by the unavoidable accompanying press of the cars of families and friends.

Happily, this year the same problem does not exist on any

day of the week, for practically every well-tended inch of that vast, flowering expanse is now symmetrically covered with gleaming white headstones. As of late June, only the dependents of servicemen already resting there are being accepted, and this makes for a far more leisurely atmosphere. Thus a visit may be planned for any day that suits the sightseer's schedule. On one side, under the bluest of California skies, he will see the sparkling waters of the Pacific, and on the other, beyond the flowering area, he will see, rising in dramatic contrast, the wild, barren hills that the government hopes soon to be able to procure for further cultivation.

On arrival at this scenic wonderland, it will be well worth your while to leave your car or bus and stroll down the spacious, well-kept avenues that wind around and almost seem to embrace the grassy slopes. Thanks to the noted clemency of our winters, an endless profusion of gladioli, irises, roses in a variety of colors, and gold and white chrysanthemums presents a year-round breathtaking horticultural display.

Indeed, the abundance of flowers often makes it difficult to find the temporary markers which supply the names of those who lie under these freshly spread coverlets. But if you take a moment to kneel down and push aside some of the floral offerings you may read on neatly typed cards framed in metal and covered with sturdy transparent plastic, that Pfc. Stuart Hawkins, for instance, of the U.S. Infantry died on May 20, 1967, and was laid to rest here on May 26, 1967; or that Lt. David O'Hara of the U.S. Marines died on June 18, 1967, and was interred in this beautiful spot on June 23. It may cross your mind before you get up from your knees that just six weeks or so ago Pfc. Hawkins and Lt. O'Hara were walking around the streets of Saigon or Danang or somewhere like that, and this is quite an arresting thought. Indeed, after visiting this and other out-of-the-way sites, you will have an endless stream of unusual memories to take home with you.

Background to this particular offbeat outing is readily available to tourists who can spare the time for a brief visit to the mortuary home on Valencia, situated in the famous Mission District of the city. One of the interesting sights there is the arrival of Navy trucks from Travis Air Force Base several times a day. Each truck is equipped with tiers of shelves, or berths resembling those of a sleeping car, on which have been placed long aluminum containers, conveniently numbered and tagged. On each container, stenciled in black, are the words, DO NOT TIP. This is because the contents have been packed in ice at the Tan Son Nhut Air Base in Saigon, and, despite the high degree of refrigeration, there may be some loose water in the container by the time it reaches its destination. The Travis Mortuary Affairs office, however, is justifiably proud of the fact that never during the course of any previous war have erstwhile combatants been transported with such a short lapse of time from the battlefield to the embalmer's table. It is not at all unusual for the remains of returning servicemen to reach the base three or four days after demise in Vietnam.

Travis Air Force Base itself should not be overlooked as a site of truly exceptional interest. It has the distinction of being the one base to receive *all* the containers flown in from Southeast Asia. They travel on C-141-A jets, poetically known as Starlifters, and these giant military birds, carrying a mixed cargo, touch down on the runway at the rate of thirty or forty every twenty-four hours. The containers, speedily emptied of their contents at the Valencia funeral parlor, are then returned by truck to Travis, loaded on to Starlifters, and rushed back to Tan Son Nhut Air Base to serve again. Some of them—and this is reassuring confirmation of the rigid economy practiced by our military—have been in use since the Korean War.

Another example of the forethought with which this operation is handled may be noted in the fact that, the embalming completed, a one-man military escort accompanies each individual flag-draped coffin to its home destination. That destination may be as far from San Francisco as New Jersey or Rhode Island, or as close as Nevada or Washington State, but there is no doubt in the minds of the military authorities, or in that of the director of the funeral home, that wherever the young man's family may reside, this official gesture is highly valued. The military escort usually spends the night in the former serviceman's home, and it is customary for a brief notice to this effect to appear in the social column of the local paper. "It's a kind of status thing, and the family appreciates it very much," the director of the Valencia funeral parlor told me.

It is also fascinating to watch the sleek Navy limousines making their daily deliveries to this efficiently run funeral home. Each limousine, fitted with clothes-racks, brings as many as twelve or fifteen fine new uniforms to the mortuary. Dark blue and trimmed in scarlet and gold, they are carried with scrupulous care into the tastefully decorated interior of the funeral parlor. On one of my visits there, I learned that there is frequently not enough left of the young serviceman himself to fit into the uniform the army provides. The director, a personable young man with three young children and an attractive wife who live in the funeral home with him, was kind enough to invite me in to view some of the remains so that I might understand the problems with which he is faced. "It is far from being an enjoyable business," he confided.

If the interested visitor wishes to explore even further behind the scenes, he will learn that competitive bidding in the San Francisco funeral-services world has been brisk. But the director of the particular home on Valencia, who got the government contract in 1966, maintains that it is not as profitable a deal as the number of bodies processed every week might lead one to believe. "By the time they are ready to go home, they all look just as lifelike as the art we practice can make them," one of the embalming assistants told me. "We give the same care and attention to the preparation of servicemen as we would if they were on a retail basis. We feel we owe it to the boy's family that he goes home looking just as good as he did when he went away—and sometimes even better."

For a complete change of scene, I would suggest a day at Port Chicago on the other side of the bay. This sleepy little town is a pleasant hour-and-a-half drive from downtown San Francisco, and natives claim that it enjoys the best climate in the whole of Northern California. So as to take advantage of every moment of sunlit air and lively sea breezes, it is recommended that you take a box lunch with you. The seasoned traveler will not feel self-conscious about eating it quite openly, even though a number of hardy visitors who stand before the Naval Weapons Station may be observing a twenty-four-hour fast. Few signs are displayed by this handful of young people, and their presence can be easily overlooked. If questioned, they will be glad to tell you that nine percent of all the explosives sent to Vietnam, including napalm bombs, leave from this busy port.

The Naval Station is a leisurely ten-minute walk from the town of Port Chicago, and you will not, of course, be permitted to enter the confines of the station, which is designated as government property, but the distant masts and rigging of the docked munition ships silhouetted against the clear blue sky is the most picturesque of sights.

If taking your lunch with you presents a problem, a simple regional meal may be procured at modest cost in the little

restaurant in the heart of town. Lunching there also offers
the attraction of firsthand contact and conversation not only
with longtime residents of Port Chicago, but also with merchant seamen off cargo ships that have just returned from
Vietnam. Enter into the free and easy atmosphere that pre-
vails, and you will come away with a wealth of interesting
information. For instance, the property owners of the town
are wholly absorbed in a united effort to frustrate the navy's
plans to buy out the town so as to take over the entire area for
increased shipping facilities. As one store owner put it to me,
"I don't care what happens in Vietnam, but I'm not going to
sell my four lots to the navy for $700 each when each one of
them is worth $1,200." Another resident said he had no in-
tention of selling his $30,000 home for $11,000, which is
what the navy is offering.

The seamen, speaking in their quaint dialects (many come
from the Deep South), will tell you of the difficulties that are
encountered in getting crews together. Despite the high pay
and the generous bonuses, it is not an easy matter to man the
munition freighters. But now and then a note of true jubila-
tion is sounded by those seamen who have amassed small for-
tunes in war-zone pay. They will now be able to purchase
homes for their families, and even finance a son's or daughter's college education. For untrained, unskilled men, such
rewards were merely pipe dreams before. So even war has its
unexpected compensations. On one occasion a totally illiter-
ate seaman regaled me with a hilarious story of his attempts,
on the trip he had just returned from, to get transportation
from Saigon to Danang, through enemy lines, to see his GI
son who was in an army hospital there.

Among the many unusual visitors you will see standing
before the gates of the Naval Weapons Station, the most impressive is a blond young man of proud and distinctive bearing who is known to one and all as "Larry." Because he has

been seen standing there for over a year now, Larry Cooper has become a familiar landmark. The town sheriff, quite a personable young man himself, will stop his official car beside Larry and smile as he greets him, and Larry will lean in through the car window and have a pleasant five-minute chat with this officer of the law. Although Larry's hair is longish, it is neatly trimmed, and although he does have a bright blond Van Dyke beard, he is in no sense a hippie. Indeed, his dignified figure suggests that of an old-time, frontier preacher who has strayed for a moment from the Hollywood set where a Western is being filmed.

Larry describes himself as "a non-Christian minister of truth," and he says that his hope is to be "a point of light and truth for others to see the dignity of Man." It would be easy to picture him in his dark suit and white shirt, a soft-brimmed hat on his blond head, stepping out of an ambushed stagecoach in the wild and woolly days of the old West and persuading the shamefaced stickup men to lower their guns and let the stage continue on its way.

Other young people standing there before the gates, through which passes a constant stream of armored trucks marked EX-PLOSIVES, will tell you Larry is a graduate of a California ministerial school, and indeed there is a suggestion of benediction in the friendly hand he raises in greeting to all who pass. Larry will tell you that it was a merchant seaman he ran into in San Francisco in the spring of 1966 who told him about the shipments from Port Chicago. (The man had made two or three trips to Vietnam and his conscience was beginning to bother him.) And everyone, including the sheriff, knows that Larry stopped a running napalm truck last summer by standing before it, and that he still has a weekend or two to serve in jail to complete his fifteen-day sentence.

Everyone also knows that Larry has to come out from San Francisco by bus now, as in August of this year the two cars he used to bring visitors over for a day's outing were, one after another, destroyed by fire. The names of the young men from Port Chicago who destroyed the cars are known to Larry, and he raises his hand in greeting to them as well when they roar past in their jalopies, their spit often striking his face or the faces of other visitors standing before this vast expanse of government property.

Before setting out at the end of the day on the beautiful return drive to San Francisco, take a moment or two to pick up a memento from the debris of bright, discarded cans, flowering cactus, and broken bottles tossed by passing motorists. You will find bits and pieces of the shattered frames of what were placards in their time, charred syllables of words which once spelled "women" or "children" or "Vietnam." On my first visit to Port Chicago I had the good luck to find five words intact on a cardboard placard otherwise nearly destroyed by fire. They said, MEN ARE NOT OUR ENEMIES. . . . The partially burned and scattered lexicon you can salvage there will always make a fascinating conversation piece and may even prove one day a unique supplementary document to our current history.

If you feel so disposed before you go, do help Larry pick up the Pepsi-Cola and lemon-pop bottles that didn't break when they were thrown. He turns them in at the Port Chicago grocery store, and the refunded deposit money goes toward paying his bus fare back to town. "For the most part everyone's been very helpful," he will tell you. "Marines as well as the workers who load the ships came out and expressed their sympathy about the destruction of the cars. The men working here and the navy personnel know we aren't going to be frightened off, and they respect that. They know now that whatever happens, we're here to stay."

The Triumph of Principles

I think it should be cause for great rejoicing that there were a number of American writers among the hundreds of people who refused to take shelter in City Hall Park on the third of May of this year (1960). It is always good when the students of a country can rely on their writers not only to speak, but to act for them. For too many years I have felt that the writers of France—first André Malraux and Albert Camus—spoke and acted for the students of America and, in a sense, for the students of the world, and this is clearly not as things should be. I want to believe that the demonstrations in City Hall Park, in which so many college and high school students took part, and the demonstrations on the campuses of New York colleges, fervent and passive as they were, are a signal of the awakening of the young people of our country to the responsibility that is theirs.

No writers were arrested on the third of May, and this was certainly intentional, for writers are potentially explosive material. Thomas Mann once said that if the writers of Germany through their vision and their expression of that vision had made richer and more impelling promises than those Hitler made, it would have been Hitler, and not the writers of Germany, who would have been forced into exile. It is *always* the intellectuals, however we may shrink from the chilling sound of that word, and, above all, it is *always* the writers who must bear the full weight of moral responsibility. Frenchmen will tell you that the decision to speak out is the vocation and life-long peril by which the intellectual must live. I remember the days in Paris when we who were writers or painters or composers wrote pamphlets and distributed them in the streets and cafés. I remember when we signed manifestos and read them aloud on street corners, following without any humility whatsoever in the tradition of Pascal, Voltaire, Chateaubriand, Victor Hugo, Zola, so that the world would know exactly where we stood, for we considered ourselves a portion of the contemporary conscience, and we had no pity on the compromiser or the poor in spirit of our time. But now the pamphlet and the manifesto are practically nonexistent in American letters, although here in America they flourished with great vitality in prerevolutionary times. American intellectuals, indeed, prepared and oriented our revolution: the only revolution in history, one French critic has pointed out, which did not destroy the intellectuals who had prepared it, but which carried them to power. "By tradition," Raymond-Leopold Bruckberger said, "the European intellectual has a special character—a vocation beyond the limits of his own profession of writing or science or teaching. He believes himself called to a more universal responsibility than are other men, and that is to keep watch on the world, and to call the plays as he sees them, at whatever risk to himself. The dangers of his position are as real as poverty, exile, prison or death; and—unlike the soldier or the priest—he has no organized body to defend him."

No organized body defended the twenty-seven women and men who stood before a New York Youth Term magistrate in criminal court on the afternoon of May third. But they themselves, in a very humble way, were defenders of humanity. Earlier that day these twenty-seven women and men had remained in a park, with nearly a thousand others, and refused to take shelter during a civil-defense drill. That was their crime. They had carried placards explaining their action, and they had sung as they walked in the square. One of the songs was "We Shall Not Be Moved" and another was "The Battle Hymn of the Republic" and another "I Ain't Goin' To Study War No More." One of the placards said quite simply: "Let's Stop This Nonsense." Another bore the words of George Kennan, a man of whom America should be particularly proud, which said, in part: "Let us divest ourselves of this weapon altogether; let us stake our safety on God's grace and our own good consciences and on that measure of common sense and humanity which even our adversaries possess; but then let us at least walk like men, with our heads up, so long as we are permitted to walk at all." It is a good day when the writers speak out loudly and clearly. Read Stuart Chase's book *Live and Let Live* for a program of American action. Listen to him saying: "It is no longer a question of defending one's home by defending one's nation. Now it is only by defending all mankind that one can save his country." And listen to Adlai Stevenson crying out: "We need ways of motivating our young people to be creative individuals, to be daring and different. We must make America a center of intellectual vitality!" Because of voices like these, young people moved by high principle and deep moral conviction to protest know that they do not protest alone.

A MULTITUDE OF GHOSTS

The twenty-seven who were arraigned in criminal court on
May third stood there as representatives of all of us who
believe in the total futility of drills and shelters against nuclear attack, and who believe that the insistence on such pro-
cedures is the cruelest kind of deception, for it is a deception
that scales down to quiet human acceptance the ghastly finality
of nuclear warfare.

When the New York magistrate said to those twenty-seven
defendants that in America we have always expressed our
opinions by means of the ballot box, and not by public demonstration, not by defiance of the law, the laughter in the
courtroom was the laughter of many generations of Americans, for surely nothing more historically inaccurate could
have been said. Perhaps the magistrate realized this when he
flared into anger and offered the defendants Cuba, Korea, or
Turkey as alternative undemocratic homelands. But it was too
late then for him to take back his words. For a multitude of
ghosts—ragged ghosts, for the most part, but completely
American ghosts—made their way down the aisle of the
courtroom. They moved through the groups of college and
high school students who sat on the floor in that august building, doing their homework as they waited for sentence to be
pronounced on their fellow demonstrators and thus, in like
measure, on themselves.

JOHN BROWN'S SOUL

John Brown was in the crowd that moved toward the bar, and
he spoke first, saying slowly and distinctly in the courtroom:
"We shall never allow ourselves to be tempted by any consideration to acknowledge laws and institutions to exist if our
conscience and reason condemn them." Facing the magistrate
who had just offered other countries to the defendants, John

Brown said: "A minority convinced of its rights, based on moral principles will, under a republican government, sooner or later become the majority." And then Henry Thoreau, in his old grey trousers and his battered straw hat, spoke out from among the ghosts, saying: "The character inherent in the American people has done all that has been accomplished here. It would have done somewhat more if the government had not sometimes got in its way." That day in the New York criminal court Thoreau addressed all of us, directly, un-equivocally, saying: "Under a government which imprisons unjustly, the true place for a just man is also in prison." Be-cause the magistrate had not perceived these other Americans standing before him and because the guards had not heard these other voices speaking, Thoreau was able to go on saying that a government and its laws are merely a mode which the people have chosen to execute their will, and that when the laws fail to implement the people's will, then those laws and that government are inexpedient.

The ghost of a man called Emerson also stood at the bar, and he said: "It demands something godlike in him who has cast off the common motives of humanity and has ventured to trust himself as taskmaster. High be his heart, faithful his will, clear his sight, that he may in good earnest be doctrine, society, law, to himself . . . for nothing can bring peace to man or country but the triumph of principles!" In that group of fearless and indestructible ghosts were a number of men who had read our Constitution within hours after it was drafted and who had immediately cried out in protest: "Where is there any provision made in this document to prevent the government from interfering with the right of citizens to meet together peaceably? Where are the safeguards of our right to say what we think in public and to print our consid-ered opinions in newspapers?" Patrick Henry was in that group and because he and other men spoke out, we know that the Bill of Rights was forthwith drafted to assure those safe-guards.

But the spirit of the Bill of Rights was not in a place of authority in the New York criminal court on May third. Nor did it animate those who passed judgment on the fifty-three students of Brooklyn College who were temporarily suspended for their orderly protest against the civilian-defense drill. It had been forgotten, as well, by those who subjected the Hunter College and City College students to "college discipline" because of their refusal to take part in the sinister farce of seeking shelter from nuclear attack. "The Bill of Rights is our abiding testament of faith in democracy," Chester Bowles reminds us in his recent book, *New Principles for a New Age*, "but the Bill of Rights might not be voted today because too few of us understand the need to protect the freedoms of those with whom we disagree."

If the authorities in the courts and the authorities in the colleges and high schools failed to recognize the deeply happy meaning of the passive demonstrations of May third, there are others who place this protest of high-minded, nonconforming American citizens in true context in our history. To these others, Stuart Chase's words point out a direction for Americans to follow, a direction which even implies a new concept of law. "The nuclear age," Chase writes, "calls for a whole new system of values, habits and beliefs, and calls for them AT ONCE!"

Preface from
The Smoking Mountain

*Wretched German people, you built cities, built cathe-
drals, placed free tillers on a free soil, reached lofty heights
in art, in science, in law, in languages. You evolved the
Hansa, evolved guilds, evolved free crafts, found mani-
fold modes of expression for your nature. Your military
organization can only be considered as one aspect of your
complex social constitution. That department expanded,
grew all-powerful, swallowed up everything else. It broke
down all dikes and flooded over the boundaries of other
countries, and the tiller had to leave his soil, the workman
his work, the priest his parish, the teacher his pupils, the
youth his companions, the husband his wife; the people
ceased to exist as a people and became nothing but fuel for
the monstrous, smoking mountain, the individual became
nothing but wood, peat, fuel oil, and finally a black flake
spewed up out of the flames.*

THEODOR PLIEVIER

In the spring of 1948, I left France—a country I had made
my home in for nearly twenty years—and I came to live, and
write, in Germany. I came without eagerness, abhorring this
country's immediate past, knowing that those Germans who
had been free and fearless men had, in our time, been exterminated by their countrymen, or else that one had known
them as refugees on foreign soil. I had visited Germany during several summers as a child; and I had come briefly to
Germany in 1935, and 1936, and again in 1938, after the
Anschluss with Austria had taken place. The Germans I knew
were those who had fled, and fled not from an invader but
from their own people, and who still preferred to remain in
exile after the war was through. In early 1947, I returned to
visit Displaced Persons' camps in the American Zone, and in
that year I talked with many Germans, from street cleaners
to university professors, the residue of a police state; and, as
I listened to their stories of individual, if unwilling, acceptance of that state, I remembered the quality of French and
Spanish acceptance of the individual obligations to liberty.
And then, in 1948, I came to live here, and, by so doing,
committed myself to a painstaking and almost completely
loveless search for another face of Germany.

The mere act of entering this occupied country imposes
inexorable demands upon the heart and upon reason. If one
is, both as human being and recorder, to clear a way through
the complex and ignoble history of what took place, one is
not authorized for a single, hesitant instant to forget the
meaning of those issues which were so truly comprehended
during and after Germany's military defeat. Time or emotion
may not be permitted to deform by their insidious power the
perspective in which these issues were first seen. If it be asked
what force withholds this authorization, the answer is one's
belief that man is given a choice, and that the choice is not to
be evaded, but made. But, faced with the colossal ruins of

cities which have been seventy, or eighty, or ninety, or ninety-five, percent destroyed, the mind no longer recognizes cause and effect, and the explanation of why this had to take place is reduced to a monstrous absurdity. Thus, it is one's own reason which must set the limits as to what time and emotion may be permitted to accomplish, so that pity may be allowed its full measure of human tenderness, but nothing more. I believe there is an impulse far more compassionate than the act of experiencing compassion. After the first shock and sense of outrage at the sight of this monumental destruction, it is essential that the true computation be fervently made. For one comes to know, without pity, that the ruthless cause which produced these effects is still intact if only these walls, whose substance the hands can touch, have been destroyed.

As I attempt to set down my own evaluation of what I have found in my brief two years here, I am aware that all the analyses of this country, and the proclivities of its people, have been made. For decades, German philosophers and German poets and men of letters have wrung their disavowal of the German people from the depths of their commitment to that people. Among these were Goethe, Heine, Nietzsche, Mann, Plievier; and in their denunciation of, as in their dedication to, the German people they came by separate, even by antithetical, ways to the recognition of a single, fatal thing. Each came to his own separate vision of the duality of German identity, and, baffled, each sought to probe within that vision. "The Germans are more intangible, more ample, more contradictory, more unknown, more incalculable, more surprising, and even more terrifying than other people are to themselves . . . ," Nietzsche wrote nearly a century ago—Nietzsche who, in himself, has given us the perfect symbol of German man, of man divided within himself, unable to comprehend and judge himself because unable to see himself in his entirety. "German and Jew, patriot and Francophile,"

David Daiches has written of Heinrich Heine, "sentimen-
talist and ironist, radical and hater of the organized left,
Christian convert and passionate defender of Israel, charla-
tan and martyr, lyrical poet and journalist, lover of life and
perpetual self-torturer—his haunting figure looms out of the
mists of social and ideological conflict in early nineteenth-
century Europe to appear as the epitome of all the problems
that face sensitive man today." Was Germany then, one comes
to ask oneself as one lives here in its ruins, offered as warning,
and the people of Germany, Jews and Christians alike, sacrificed so that their drama might serve as admonition to the
modern world? Are the dual propensities of the German
identity to be taken, then, as symbols for the choice each man
is offered, and how much—or how tragically little—of the
drama have we officially understood?

I have heard Americans in official positions here say that
in the beginning of the Nazi regime, before the brutalities
became widespread, there was about as much difference between the Nazis and the non-Nazis as between Republicans
and Democrats at home. It might be possible to find something humorous in this definition did it not express the essence of our failure of comprehension here. We have never
wished to believe that the choice was not a political, but a
moral one, a choice between good and evil in the profoundest
sense, but there is ample evidence that the Germans themselves know this was true. A spokesman for a nationalistic
party stated recently that "had Hitler adhered to the traditional ideas of the *Rechtsstaat*, we would have had no war and
would be quite satisfied, except for the solution of the racial
question." Even more recently, West German Chancellor
Adenauer publicly declared that the time had come "for Germans to end the division of the people into sinners and innocents"; for *Germans*, he specified, know more bitterly and
more certainly than any foreigner can that the moral decision

each German made then is still, in 1950, burningly alive in the consciousness of every German; and know, too, that until the sinners and the innocents are merged into one there can be no hope for a united Germany.

Because this issue is not dead,* it was not only inevitable, it was essential, that the trial for murder of a man called Heinrich Baab should have begun in the city of Frankfurt in March of this year. It was a completely German trial, prepared and conducted by Germans, and it is significant that the man was brought to trial for murder although he was not accused of having, with his own hands, committed murder. It was as if the will of the German people were finally putting on trial in a German courtroom, before German judges and a German jury, the actual substance of German duality.

Heinrich Baab was indicted on a charge of participating in fifty-six cases of murder in Frankfurt in the years 1938 to 1943. Other charges included "aiding and abetting in murder, attempted murder, deprivation of liberty, use of coer-

---

*Although the preview performance of the Passion Play at Oberammergau on May 18, 1950, was attended by the President and the Chancellor and Cabinet Ministers of the West German Republic, and by the American and British High Commissioners, there has been much German criticism of the actor chosen to play the leading role. Anton Preisinger, who plays the part of Christus, is a former S.A. man, who participated in 1933 in the Nazi raid on the Ettal Monastery in Bavaria. The actor who plays Judas in the Passion Play claims to be the only male member of the cast who was not a Nazi Party member, and his protest against Preisinger being given the role of Christus has been the loudest and most eloquent. Cardinal Faulhaber of Munich was not present at the opening performance of the play, while Alois Hundhammer, the Bavarian Minister of Culture, and a devout Catholic, also failed to attend.

"Sources close to the [Bavarian] ministry," writes the *Neue Zeitung* (Frankfurt edition, May 19, 1950), "expressed the opinion that Dr. Hundhammer's trip to the United States was in the nature of a protest, and that he, as well as Cardinal Faulhaber, who was likewise conspicuous by his absence, were opposed to Preisinger having been cast in the role of Christus."

cion to obtain information, and assault and battery." It was reported that, before giving himself up to the authorities, Baab had confidently remarked that none of the people with whom he had had dealings during those five specified years could be expected to appear as witnesses against him, for they were all undoubtedly dead. The first sight I had of him, he was seated in the prisoner's dock, with only his large, balding head and his heavy shoulders visible above the panels of dark, varnished wood. He had a pallid, bloated face, this forty-one-year-old Frankfurt citizen, and he wore a khaki shirt, the collar of which seemed tight around his fleshy neck. His broad rayon tie, which had apparently been striped in yellow and brown in its time, was now faded, and his heavy head, with the front half of the skull naked of hair, hung sideways. For, despite the fact that he was on trial for the murder of fifty-six other Frankfurt citizens, he was concerned with some kind of tidbit, some kind of nut, which his fingers kept shelling out of sight below the panels of the dock. With his head inclined at this angle, the polished area of his broad, flat skull was mercilessly exposed, and his blunt-fingered, heavy hand could be seen only at those moments when he contrived to slip a nut into his mouth. As he prepared the next morsel of food for consumption, his sagging jowls went surreptitiously into motion, and his glance moved carefully around the courtroom as he chewed. His slightly bulging, heavily lidded eyes looked slowly and without expression over the occupants of the two benches which seated the press, and over the assemblage of spectators that packed the room, passing the two police officers at the double doors of the public entrance, and the green-uniformed guards at the door used by the press, seeming to seek not a face he knew there, but merely the confirmation that his furtive masticating was not being observed. Upon the entrance of the presiding judge, the two associate judges, and the eight members of the jury,

Heinrich Baab rose, as did all the others seated in the court-room, and one could then see the bull-like, nearly neckless torso in the cheap, shiny, striped wool jacket that could no longer be brought to close across his tightly belted paunch.

The hall in which the trial took place was small—un-fortunately, far too small to accommodate the crowds that pressed up the ancient stairs every Monday, Wednesday, and Friday of the four weeks the trial endured, and that waited, hour after hour, for word of the proceedings at the panelled doors. But those who came had no need to come, for they already knew the story well. No member of the local Ger-man-American Club, a social and essentially snobbish orga-nization introduced by Military Government for the purpose of improving German-American relations, with branches in every city and town of the zone, reached the courthouse at seven-thirty in the morning to wait at the closed doors for a seat, nor did any member of the Frankfurt Chamber of Com-merce; no handsome German cars, driven by chauffeurs in livery, waited outside the courthouse as they wait outside the Bad Homburg casino, or outside deluxe Frankfurt restau-rants where one may dine on trout in aspic and pressed duck and other delicacies, and where the German management re-serves the right to refuse service to American enlisted men. Had there been present one or two of those German busi-nessmen who are to be seen every day entering the former I. G. Farben building (now used by the American, British, and French occupation authorities, and known as the Head-quarters Building), in well-cut overcoats of imported wool, carrying leather briefcases in their smartly gloved hands, it would have given another meaning to the proceedings, and there might have been reason to believe that the German caste system had indeed begun to go. Not only was there no Amer-ican in that crowd, but no representative of the West German government in Bonn lent his presence to the chronicling of

this new chapter in German legal history. Those who were
the spectators at Baab's trial were, in the main, Baab's victims
as well. If they were not actually the murdered, they were
those whose annihilation had been attempted, or they were of
the flesh and blood of those who had died. They were poor,
and they were, in many cases, shockingly maimed. Their
jaws were askew, their teeth were gone, and, in some instances, the remnants of their shattered faces had been pieced
together so that they might once more bear some resemblance
to men. There were some without arms among them, and
others—and these not necessarily among the aged—whose
legs were so crippled that they walked with the aid of canes.
There was one young man who sat regularly in a spectator's
seat about whom it was later testified that not one thread of
his under or outer garments had retained its original color,
so drenched were they by his own blood after a visit to Heinrich Baab in 1942.

Of what, and of how many, was this man Baab a representative, this man who was, as were the greatest musicians, a
pure product of Germany? For how many had he acted, this
man with the heavily lidded eyes, the full cleft chin, and the
lips curved with a flourish of vanity and sensuality? For how
many did he speak in the years 1938 to 1945? When you put
this question to gently bred Germans, they will tell you that
Baab was no more representative of Germany than Al Capone
was representative of America; and it is possible to concede
that there is a resemblance between the two men in the flesh.
But there is one factor which must set them apart forever, and
that is that Baab functioned as an official, with official sanc-
tion, even after the population of Frankfurt knew, either
through experience or by rumor, the kind of man he was. For
Heinrich Baab was a Gestapo official, and an S.S. trooper,
who had been proud of his title, "The Terror of the Frankfurt Jews."

On November 21, 1945, in his opening statement at the

Nuremberg trials, Justice Robert H. Jackson, Chief of Counsel for the United States, said of the twenty-odd defendants there:

> These prisoners are living symbols of racial hatreds, of terrorism and violence, and of the arrogance and cruelty of power. . . . They took from the German people all those dignities and freedoms that we hold natural and inalienable rights in every human being. . . . Against their opponents, including Jews, Catholics, and free labor, the Nazis directed such a campaign of arrogance, brutality, and annihilation as the world has not witnessed since the pre-Christian ages. . . . If these men are the first war leaders of a defeated nation to be prosecuted in the name of the law, they are also the first to be given a chance to plead for their lives in the name of the law.

But Baab was a small criminal, and, as the prosecution was to point out in the course of the trial, he attained the status of a big criminal only because his quality was identical with those others whose names had come to be known throughout the world. Baab was not a war leader, and no such "hundreds of tons of official German documents" or captured film, as Mr. Justice Jackson referred to in his opening statement at the Palace of Justice in Nuremberg, existed in this man's case. The evidence against him had been collected almost entirely from the memories of living German women and men, but the proof was no less valid merely because it resided in nothing more ponderable than their anguished testimony.

A year after Germany's defeat, this S.S. trooper who had eventually achieved the rank of S.S.-*Untersturmführer*, had been released, because of ill health, from a French PW camp. He had then joined his family, who had been evacuated during the Allied bombings to the Eastern Zone. There he lived in Thuringia, in the mountains, unable to apply for work in fear of revealing his identity, for it was on record that he had, for a brief time in 1940, worked "in the interests

of the Gestapo" in Poland, and he had no desire to face trial
in a Communist-controlled court for the crimes he had committed there. It must be supposed that he, even more hun-
grily than other Germans, read the various reports in the East
Zone papers, and gave ear to the many rumors as to what was
taking place, in 1947, in the *Spruchkammer* (denazification)
courts of the West Zone. He, in company with even smaller
Nazis, must have welcomed the intelligence, so widespread
throughout Germany, that there had been since 1945 considerable change both in the viewpoint of the population and in
the viewpoint of the conquerors—at least in the American
Zone, the zone in which Heinrich Baab's interests lay. He
must have believed with great readiness, because he wished
so to believe, the report that to get employment in this zone
it sufficed to show your Nazi credentials to German business-
men. And he must have accepted without question the cynical
legend that, in 1947 in the American Zone, all worthy Germans looked upon German anti-Nazis as men who had betrayed their country in her hour of need. To accept all this
meant that Baab was secure in his knowledge that he had
never dishonored his Party, and he came to believe that only
in an East Zone court would there be any consequences to
fear. So, late in 1947, upon receiving a summons from the
Frankfurt *Spruchkammer* courts, he returned with his wife
and his two sons, confident that in submitting to denazification here he would be judged a "follower" (the five denazification categories are major offender, offender, minor offender, follower, and exonerated), would pay his fine, and
then go free. He had not counted on the mass grave opening,
and the halt, the blind, and the maimed, emerging from it,
for not one of those who had survived annihilation had forgotten either the syllables of Heinrich Baab's name or the
features of his face. In February 1948, before the *Spruchkammer* proceedings got under way, it became evident,
through the weight of evidence these many witnesses sub-

mitted, that this was not a case to be disposed of by a denazification court, but was indeed a criminal case. Baab was immediately placed under arrest on orders from the district attorney's office and was kept in prison during the two-year period required for the preparation of the case.

To those who read the stories in this book, it may be of service to point out that the courtroom scene described in the story entitled "Aufwiedersehen Abend" is that of a *Spruchkammer* trial, the whole basis and procedure of which differ from the established court procedure followed in the murder trial of Baab. In the *Spruchkammer* trial, there is no jury. The judges and prosecution officers for the *Spruchkammer* trials were originally appointed by the Denazification Branch of Military Government, and were chosen on the basis of their clean political record and not because they had previously had legal training. Whatever subsequent appointments have been made by the German Ministry of Justice, the onus of American protectorship remains in connection with these trials. Thus, in defying the legally untrained Germans who officiate at *Spruchkammer* trials, the defendants, and their experienced counsel, have the satisfaction of feeling that they are, by the same token, defying the authority of the occupying power. The particular session of the former newspaper editor's trial with which I deal in my story is largely factual. The anti-Nazi editor who testifies to his persecution under Hitler is based on the character of a Catholic journalist who, in company with a group of other liberal German newspapermen, recently spent three months as a guest of our government in the United States. The session described in my story was, unfortunately, the last to be held on this case. Inconclusive though it was, the high feeling of the townspeople against denazification proceedings and the defense tactics of ridicule rendered impossible any continuation of the case. The former Nazi editor, the defendant, has now begun publishing a newspaper in a town not far from the one where his paper flourished during the Nazi regime. He has circumvented occupation regulations by publishing it in his son's name.

With reference to German public sentiment concerning denazification, it is of interest to consider three of the points of a twelve-point program adopted in the autumn of 1949 by the three component groups of a leading right-wing extremist party, formerly known as the *Nationale Rechte*, and now known as the *Deutsche Reichspartei*. The formally adopted program of this party, which is now being organized on a national level, demands that the question of war guilt be decided only after all German documents have been investigated by a German committee, and an international commission has checked the records of all countries which participated in the war, in order to determine each country's share of the guilt. It further demands that all denazification activities be terminated, internment camps abolished, and compensation be made for unjustified imprisonment under denazification measures, and that the German government insist on the establishment, without delay, of an international court for crimes against humanity. Adherents to the principles set forth by the *Deutsche Reichspartei* have said to me that all official representatives and statesmen of countries which recognized, and had dealings with, Hitler in the postwar years should forthwith be brought to trial in the international court which this party has proposed.* It was perhaps the moment, then, when self-compurgation had reached such fanciful ex-

*Under dateline of May 10, U.P. reports that in Flensburg "a Rightist politician and ex-General Ernst Remer told an enthusiastic audience at Husum, in south Schleswig, that he could never accept the Nuremberg verdicts against German war criminals 'until the Allied war criminals are hanged beside the Germans.' His statement evoked thunderous applause from his four hundred German listeners. Remer, who got a jump promotion to major general because he smashed the July 20, 1944, plot against Hitler's life, said he did not regret his action against the plotters."

tremes, that the question of guilt should be settled in a smaller courtroom, among a handful of humble women and men, and that the case of Heinrich Baab should be accepted as a test case for them all. Like the twenty-odd defendants at Nuremberg, Baab was assigned experienced counsel, and was given the chance to plead in a court of law, not for his life, in this case, but for his liberty. For, except in West Berlin, the severest penalty permitted for any crime is hard labor for life, and this was the penalty the prosecution was to ask.

In the first days of Baab's trial, it was shown that the lives and the liberty of many hundreds of human beings had passed through this one man's hands. Had he not had the good fortune to be a policeman in a police state, it would be difficult to conceive of him as anything but a bored and belligerent taxi driver or café waiter, an unwilling servitor with a permanent chip on his shoulder, ready to dispute the amount of the tip one gave him as insolently as he had disputed the right of men and women to live. He could never have become a white-collar worker, for the signs of the requisite patience and industry were missing, and it is doubtful whether his vanity would have permitted him to labor with his hands. It was he who, as the head of Amt II B 2, the *Judenreferat* (the office for The Handling of the Jewish Question), from August 1942 to June 1943, had jurisdiction over the disposal of the Frankfurt Jews. (Baab's predecessor in this position, a man named Nellen, committed suicide in 1945.) "The once flourishing Jewish community of Germany," writes Jack Hain in his "Status of Jewish Workers and Employers in Post-War Germany" (Visiting Experts' Series, 1949), "which contributed so greatly to the German economy and its culture, has been reduced from more than 500,000 in 1933 to today's estimated population of 20,000. . . . In Frankfurt, for example, which city before the Nazi regime claimed the second largest Jewish community in Germany [over 30,000, according to official records], there are now only 365 German Jewish residents." But, in his foreword to this survey, Leo R. Werts, former Director of Manpower Division of Military Government, points out: "While the brunt of this inhuman attack was borne . . . by German citizens of the Jewish faith, it must be kept in mind that all social organizations, whether secular or religious in nature, were persecuted for holding firm to the ideals of equality and brotherhood." By February 1943, due to the fanatical zeal with which Baab, and his predecessor, performed their task, the last full-blooded Jew had been deported from Frankfurt. But, inasmuch as Baab's duties were not limited to the liquidation of one group of people only, the violated faces of those who watched him from the spectators' seats in the courtroom were not only the faces of Jewish women and men.

Among the one hundred and fifty-seven witnesses who were called to give evidence, there was, for instance, a tall, strongly built, stubborn-jawed young man, with a shock of thick, tan hair, who, neatly dressed in a gabardine raincoat, a grey suit, and well-polished shoes, took his place at the witness table which stood in the arena below the judicial bench. His brown hat lay on the table before him as he sat in the traditional manner, with his back to the spectators, and his stolid, florid, square-browed face raised toward the presiding judge. In accordance with German legal procedure, it was the judge who conducted the examination of the witnesses, but it was the prerogative of the defense counsel, the prosecutors, and also the members of the jury panel, to cross-examine the witness either during the judge's examination or after it had taken place. The sleeves of the witness's grey coat were pulled a little short as he leaned his arms forward on the table, and he posed them there with an awkwardness strange in one who appeared to have an impervious covering of phlegm or nerve beneath his healthy blond skin. But because that armor of phlegm or nerve had been shattered once, he used his strong arms in a singularly helpless, self-conscious manner, as if, for the rest of his life, it would be these arms alone of which he would be aware. For, from the height of the press bench, it could presently be seen that, on the inside of each wrist, the witness bore a deep, disfiguring scar. The story that he told in a low dogged voice was simple enough: in 1939 he had been denounced, possibly by neighbors, as an anti-Nazi who listened to foreign broadcasts. He had subsequently been arrested and taken to Gestapo headquarters at Lindenstrasse 27, a grey stone building that might better have served as library or museum, and that still stands, miraculously untouched by bombs, in the ruined heart of a residential section of the city. The building is now used for the offices of Frankfurt's *Oberbürgermeister*, and there the witness had first been questioned, and then beaten insensible by S.S.-*Oberscharführer* Heinrich Baab. The cellar of Lindenstrasse 27 was partitioned into cells, and the witness had lain in one of these cells for several days, during which time he could hear the screams of other prisoners in the cellar of the house. After several futile attempts, he had eventually managed to reach the light bulb which burned night and day in the ceiling of his cell, and, having broken it, he had sawed at his wrists in the darkness with one of the larger pieces of glass, but had not succeeded in reaching the arteries. When the witness had completed this much of his soberly given testimony, an elderly court physician was called upon to examine the mutilated wrists and to give a professional opinion on the possible consequences of the act which the witness next described. The day after the suicide attempt, the witness said, Baab had ordered him put in chains, and had then interviewed him again. In response to the presiding judge's attentive questioning, the witness admitted that he was at the time still suffering from the effects of the beating he had received and was, as well, weakened by the loss of blood. On the pretext of examining the wound, Baab had disarranged the medical dressing on the witness's right wrist, and then he had taken an indelible pencil from his jacket, and run the pointed end of the pencil under the bandage and into the open wound.

"Perhaps blood poisoning will accomplish what you didn't bring off," Baab's comment was when this was done.

The presiding judge, *Landgerichtsdirektor* Wirtzfeld, who had served for some time as a juvenile-court judge in Berlin, gave every evidence of being of a gentle and fastidious nature, a man of breeding and refinement, with a sharp, sad, patient face, and greying golden hair. Although almost consistently throughout the trial his features bore a look of alert forbearance, it was obvious that his heart and soul went sick within him as the details of this story, and the stories of others, were told by the men and women who were to sit at the little table below him in the darkly panelled room. It is to be supposed that he, and his two associate judges in their flowing black robes and crisp white ties, and the two women and six men of the jury, had examined the records of the evidence, for before each of them, as before the prosecutor and his associate, lay a copy of the forty-six-foolscap-page indictment (which was twice, during the trial, expanded by additional evidence). But Wirtzfeld and the ten other members of the Court listened with rapt attention, now and then making notes, now and then referring to the pages of the indictment, as the stories were given life by the voices of those who had, again by some miracle, not died. On one occasion, when a witness testified that he had called at Lindenstrasse 27 for his father, whom Baab had questioned, and had found him with blackened eyes and a broken jaw, one member of the panel, a plump, competent-looking man, with a bald head and a grey moustache, took off his glasses and spoke out clearly from the bench: "That is true! I saw him!" And there were those among the spectators who could not keep from groaning aloud in horror and protest either at the monstrosity of the thing that was described, or at the memory of what they themselves had once experienced or once seen done to others, which the words of the witness now recalled. On these occasions, Wirtzfeld would raise his hands in the most temperate of gestures, and ask that the spectators help, not hinder, the work the Court had undertaken to do. Mr. Justice Jackson has pointed out in his preface to "The Nuremberg Case" that "the German judges and the legal profession as a whole were among the last of the groups to stand out against the Nazi regime," and whatever proportion of that profession these men of the Court represented, it is certain that they were gravely concerned with the principles of justice and humanity.

It should not, however, be concluded that either the judges, who had been appointed to their positions by the Land Hesse Ministry of Justice, or the jury, whose members had been selected from a permanent jury panel of some several hundred names, had been chosen to sit at Baab's trial because of any expressed predisposition toward people of the Jewish faith or because of any active prejudice against former police agents of the National Socialist Party. The judges and the prosecution had simply been named to function at whatever criminal trials were scheduled for hearing on the calendar of the Frankfurt assizes during a specified period, and the men and women of the permanent panel are selected by a committee composed of representatives of the leading political parties and trade unions of Hesse. Panel members are chosen for their reliability and their standing in the community, and while the law bars only the first three categories of Nazis from serving on a jury, Dr. Riese, one of the associate judges, told me that he does not recall a former Nazi Party member having served on a Frankfurt jury, at least in the criminal

court. It is safe to say that they were, these two women and
six men, a valid cross section of the responsible citizenry not
only of Frankfurt, but of Germany, and although it would
be an error to see them as representative of the majority of
the German people, they are representative of a potential majority. The professions of the six men who sat on either side
of the three judges, and who were distinguishable from them
only because they wore no judicial robes, were given as: an
official in the bureau for the restitution of property to Nazi
victims, a messenger in the *Oberbürgermeister*'s office, two
clerks, a mechanic, and an employee of the Frankfurt streetcar company. One of the two women, a plump little woman
in her middle fifties, with grey, elaborately curled hair, owns
a tobacco shop in Frankfurt, while the other, a slender, dark,
worn-faced young woman, is a housewife, and the daughter
of Johanna Kirchner,* in whose memory a street in Frankfurt has been named.

With the exception of the chief prosecutor, *Oberstaatsanwalt* Dr. Kosterlitz, a man in his late forties and a Nazi-
classified "mongrel" from Berlin, it so happened that no one
of Jewish blood officiated in this trial which was one of a
number of criminal trials at which the same judges and same
panel would, as a body, preside. But the equity and patience
of even these diligent members of the Court seemed tried as
they listened to the physician explain at length, and in the
most tedious terms, and with endless reiteration, the various
kinds of blood poisoning which might prove fatal if the hy-
pothetical patient were not treated in time. The doctor was a
solid, pink-cheeked little man, with closely cut white hair,
and although he expended a great deal of valuable breath in
the effort, his voice was so asthmatic that it was not easy to

*Johanna Kirchner, a former secretary of the Social Democratic Party, was
in 1942 taken by the Nazis from France, where she had fled before the
outbreak of war, and was tried and executed in Frankfurt in 1944.

follow the laborious descriptions he insisted on giving of certain diseases which, while not in the remotest way connected with blood poisoning, might likewise, if neglected, produce symptoms of a suppurative nature and eventual death. It was perhaps not his lengthy monologue, but rather the sight of the cold-eyed defendant who did not cease chewing his surreptitious tidbits in the dock, which caused a young woman in the back of the crowded courtroom to slide, unconscious, from her chair. But the doctor's discourse was thereupon cut short by Wirtzfeld who leaned down from the bench to suggest that the doctor leave the examination of the witness for the moment and attend to the young woman who had been carried out by the court guards.

During the brief time the doctor was absent, another witness was called. This time it was an anxious, angular-boned, slight woman, wearing cheap patent-leather slippers with a strap across the bony instep, who took her place at the table below the judges' bench. She said she was a seamstress by trade, shifting uneasily on the chair as she said it, her voice so deprecatory that it was necessary to lean forward to catch her words. She wore a brown velvet hat on her knot of dark hair, and a beige suit that bore signs of having been cut and recut, lengthened and shortened, and pieced this way and that, time and again, by a seamstress's nimble fingers, in observance of the altering whim of fashion. A brown fur piece, composed of several tired, shabby little beasts, was fastened tightly around her agitated neck, and she spoke now and again with nervous belligerence, as if for a great many years she had been told (and perhaps even recently been warned again) that the things she was saying were not the proper things for a German woman worthy of the name to say. But still she testified that in 1942 Heinrich Baab had arrested her seventy-two-year-old Jewish mother-in-law, and, in the course of events, she had been permitted to go to the Frankfurt station to take the old lady some family photographs and a change of linen before she boarded a train. This train, the witness stated in response to Judge Wirtzfeld's gentle questioning, consisted of several sealed boxcars, in one of which her mother-in-law had left in company with "a great many other Jewish people." She said she believed there were four cars in the convoy, and she thought it possible, she added (as if hearing the far voices of neighbors speaking in rebuke and threat), that these Jewish people believed they were going to be "re-settled in the East." Then, two and a half months later, the witness had been notified that her mother-in-law had died in Auschwitz of "natural causes." That was all. It was for another witness to testify that Baab had frequently taken his young son to the Frankfurt station to watch these sealed trains leave.

When the doctor returned to the courtroom, the striking, grey-maned prosecutor, Dr. Kosterlitz, whose lively sense of drama was to add gusto to the theatrical quality of the trial, leaped to his feet in his flowing black robe, adjusted his white tie on his bold, opera-singer's throat, and asked Judge Wirtz-feld for permission to put a question to the medical man. It was granted, and as Kosterlitz drew one quick, strong hand back over his smoothly groomed, abundant hair, he could scarcely contain his impatience, scarcely temper the vehemence in his voice.

"For fifteen minutes," he cried out, "we have listened to your opinion on the effects of diphtheria on the mucous membrane, the effects of tuberculosis on the lungs, and the effects of cerebral meningitis on the brain! I believe you were asked by the Court to give a professional opinion as to the effects that might be produced by the insertion of the point of an indelible pencil into an open wound. Would you be so kind as to answer that question, please?"

In this outburst, it was evident that Kosterlitz was attacking far more than one pedagogue's inability to stick to a point. He was, there could be no doubt, assailing the rigid medieval mold of professional German thought, and the outrageous bombast of official German communication, and doing so out of long and enlightened conviction, knowing more literally than any stranger, who comes upon it only on occasion and can even find humor in it, how it can circumvent action, invalidate knowledge, and trouble the essence of truth. Once Kosterlitz had addressed this question to the elderly doctor, the latter murmured, "I was just coming to that, *Herr Oberstaatsanwalt.*" And there was a note of profound injury in his voice as he stated, in the space of half a minute, that an indelible pencil inserted into an open wound might, under certain circumstances, produce blood poisoning of a serious nature, and that it was probable Baab, as a layman, had believed it would cause the witness's death. Kosterlitz flung himself into his seat again with apparent gratification and made a written note of the physician's closing statement. Across the arena from him, the defense counsel, a lean, scholastic, Hamlet-visaged young man with horn-rimmed spectacles, sitting in his black robe in what appeared to be a chronic state of sour depression and distaste, also made a note of the physician's statement. The defense counsel had asked only one question of the witness with scarred wrists, and that was as to the width of the bandage and the degree of tightness with which it had been applied to the wrist, a question that contained the obvious implication that a pencil could not have been inserted into the wound if the bandage had been of normal width and had been properly affixed. But he made his note without any perceptible sign of satisfaction, as if aware that if the prosecution failed to prove the charge that the defendant had participated in murder, this evidence of the defendant's intent to kill at least one man might very well be the point on which the validity of the indictment would stand or fall.

It is not to be doubted that Dr. Lengsfeld was in bitter opposition to all that his client had stood for in Nazi Germany. While it is true that Baab had himself engaged Lengsfeld as counsel, he had done so because of his reputation for astuteness, and not for any known past political affiliations. A portion of Lengsfeld's obvious depression could perhaps be attributed to the fact that when Baab's money gave out early in 1950 and he could no longer pay counsel's fees, the Court had promptly reassigned the case to Lengsfeld, who had no choice but to carry on with it, no matter what his personal opinion may have been by that time, and no matter how small the Court stipend might be. During the pretrial selection of jury members from the panel, Lengsfeld insisted that no survivors of concentration camps should be permitted to serve on this particular jury, but it may be presumed that he made this stipulation in no other spirit than respect for the rules of equity. If he lacked the qualities of warmth and eloquence which would have drawn public sympathy to him in this role he had to play, it was evident that he had recourse to rich compensation in the way of fine points of law and in the complexity of legal interpretations and precedents that, to the mind of the average man and woman, could not but seem as dry as the dust of the ruins outside the courtroom windows. But Kosterlitz was made of other flesh and blood entirely.

Dr. Kosterlitz can perhaps best be described by the French word *fin*, which means that he is subtle and quick of mind, and exact and light of speech; although German, he had acquired, through intelligence, an almost exclusively Gallic fusion of shrewdness and lucidity. There were times when the others officiating in the Court seemed nothing more than effigies in wax, and he the one living man among them; for it could be seen that he was not only the appointed conscience of the state, but likewise the playwright and the producer of this drama in which he played. A man of mixed Jewish and

Christian blood, whose mother had died in Auschwitz, he must have known the lines by heart at least fifteen years before he had succeeded in getting the piece upon the boards and the words in the mouths of living players. He had studied law in Breslau and served as a judge in Upper Silesia before he was forced by the Nazis out of the legal profession in 1933. He then became a clerk in a charity organization in Berlin, but in November 1938, as the synagogues burned, Kosterlitz was removed from his white-collar job by the Gestapo and put to work with a road gang, carrying cement and breaking rock. He managed to procure a laborer's job in the Siemens factory in Berlin and worked there until 1943, when he was again arrested by the Gestapo and set to work laying railway ties. Arno Rudert, co-editor with Karl Gerold of the *Frankfurter Rundschau*, a liberal, nonparty daily, with the largest circulation of any newspaper in Hesse, said to me recently: "There will be no postponing and sabotaging of these trials as long as Kosterlitz is prosecutor here."

It is part of the record that Heinrich Baab came of honest people of the working class, a class into which, through pre-Hitler trade-union education, democratic ideology had been profoundly instilled. Baab's father was a tailor, and is said to have been a member of the Social Democratic Party (S.P.D.); Baab, while still in his teens, joined the *Reichsbanner*, a militant, uniformed branch of the S.P.D. The *Reichsbanner*, which functioned in violent opposition to the Nazi S.A., served principally as a bodyguard to S.P.D. speakers and kept order at party rallies. Its members derived prestige and satisfaction from dressing up in quasi-military outfits and throwing their weight around. This predilection for uniformed violence is not uncommon in the young of many countries and, in the ordinary development of children and events, it might have led to nothing. Had it not been for the temper that prevailed in Germany at that time, it is possible that Baab might have become the industrious locksmith his family had apprenticed him to be. But, in 1927, when his three-year apprenticeship was completed, the old urge for command, for uniformed prestige, possessed him again, and he withdrew from the trade-union influence and joined the Frankfurt police force instead of pursuing his trade. At one point during the trial, Kosterlitz brought up the question of Baab's choice, and it was shown that it had not been made for material gain. How much the traits of his character motivated his later decisions, and how much those traits were the result of the hideous pressures of that time, cannot be judged; but it can be said that his eight years of *Volksschule* education and his three years of apprenticeship had failed to produce a reasoning, responsible man. Baab and his early training must be of vital interest to us, for in the time that Baab functioned as an official he was not an exception to a rule of enlightened and sagacious men, but he, with other men who had received a like training, was of the calibre which an established government vested with greater and greater authority. That training must be of particular concern to us, for it is the same that young Germans receive today.

"The child of a German worker," Alice Hanson Cook wrote in 1947 of the still unimproved educational system in postwar Germany, "still goes to school until he is fourteen years old, and is then apprenticed at a few marks a month, usually for three years, during which time he receives one day's schooling a week in subjects closely related to his trade education. The chief educational influences which play upon him are those inherent in an apprentice relationship to a skilled workman—at best, a paternalism, at worst, three years of enslavement and exploitation." Thus, Mrs. Cook continues, the trade union and the labor party "historically became the educational agencies which influenced the further development of the worker as a rational and cultural being."

Whether Baab knew exploitation or paternalism during the years of his apprenticeship, it is certain that, at the termination of it, any further development for him as a "rational and cultural being" ceased. With panic and menace in the air about him, he made the ignorant and cowardly man's choice for the police side of the coming police state. Sometime within that interval, his belligerent fervor for democratic socialism had turned upon itself and become a belligerent fervor for National Socialism, and in 1932, on the eve of the ruthless Nazi annihilation of the German trade-union institution and the liquidation of its principal leaders in concentration camps, Baab joined the National Socialist Party "for idealistic reasons." By 1933, he had joined the S.A. and become a *Blockhelfer*, a *Blockwart*'s aide in the block-by-block Nazi supervision of the urban population, and in 1937, he offered his services to the Gestapo, not for any increase in authority, he is on record as saying, but because he had married in 1934 and now had a wife and child to support. As a Gestapo agent he received a fifty-mark monthly increase in pay. "Under the Nazis," Mr. Justice Jackson said in his opening statement at Nuremberg, "human life had been progressively devalued until it finally became worth less than a handful of tobacco—ersatz tobacco." The records of those days show that five Reichsmarks per execution were paid the inmates of concentration camps who were compelled to execute their fellow prisoners. Polish women were rewarded with a few cigarettes for inflicting corporal punishment on Russian women, and Russian women inmates were given the same remuneration when they were forced to inflict corporal punishment on Polish women. By 1937 the name "Gestapo" had become synonymous with "murder," and for fifty marks more a month Heinrich Baab chose it as the organization in which he wished to serve. In October of that year, he was put to work in the *Kirchendezernat*, the church specialist depart-

ment, with twenty-five agents working under him. "The Gestapo," Mr. Justice Jackson said in his closing address at Nuremberg, "appointed 'church specialists' who were instructed
that the ultimate aim was 'destruction of the confessional
churches.' The record is full of specific instances of the persecution of clergymen, the confiscation of church property,
interference with religious publications, disruption of religious education, and suppression of religious organizations."
In 1938, Baab was promoted to a position in the *Unterabteil-
ung* II A, the department for the persecution of Communists,
and by 1940 he was a member of the S.D., the hard core of
the S.S. organization.

Under examination on the first day of the trial, Baab
dropped his unseen bag of nuts long enough to stand up and
state that, in the years which the indictment covered, he had
always worked under the orders of the Frankfurt Gestapo
chief, Oswald Poche (who is believed to be in hiding in the
East Zone). The procedure for sending an offender to concentration camp or placing him in "protective custody" was
quite simple, Baab further testified as he stood with his two
hands spread heavily on the wood of the dock to support his
body's weight and his head thrust forward toward the judicial
bench in an attitude of craven anxiety. An oral or a written
denunciation sufficed for arrest, he said, and once an offender
had been questioned at Gestapo headquarters, his dossier was
drawn up and sent to Poche's office where the decision for
each individual case was made. The dossiers, initialled by
Poche, were then forwarded to the *Reichssicherheitshauptamt*
(R.S.H.A.—Supreme Headquarters of Security of the
Reich) in Berlin where the warrants for arrest were issued. It
was obvious, as Baab addressed the Court, that he had retained an unqualified respect for this man Poche, whom he
spoke of as being "unapproachable" to anyone as lowly placed
as himself; but it was likewise obvious that he had an un-

qualified respect for the authority of the black-gowned gentlemen who now sat in judgment on him. He gave his answers rapidly, but in an uncertain voice, his two hands holding him upright; for, inasmuch as all conscience and all capacity for distinguishing evil from good had long ago been eradicated from his cognizance by ten years or more of irresponsible action, there was as little coherence left in his mind as there was cohesion in his ailing flesh. One day, the apathy of his being clearly implied, you were told it was the right and proper thing to exterminate the Jews and other elements of menace to the German state, and the next day you were brought to trial for it. And it is possible that he was honest in his cold, sullen inability to understand how this change of superiors, this abrupt transforming of right into wrong, and wrong into right, had taken place. But if he was honest, then the spectacle of the man himself, and the general conclusion his attitude implies, become even more terrible to contemplate.

When he was questioned as to the methods employed to obtain information from those he had arrested, Baab said he had never administered any corporal punishment during the examinations other than "clouts on the ear." At this the entire courtroom, nearly to a man, rose to its feet and cried out its protest, and although he did not then or at any time during the proceedings turn his head to look at these people in the courtroom, his fingers could be seen to tighten on the wood of the dock, and in the soft flesh of his right jowl, a pulse began to beat, and his throat quivered for some minutes like the throat of a frog. Not until June 1942, he continued when the uproar in the courtroom had quieted, did the Berlin headquarters of the R.S.H.A. authorize "rigorous examination," and then it was permitted to bring pressure to bear on those detained. "Rigorous examination," he stated in answer to Judge Wirtzfeld's request for a definition of this term, con-

sisted of administering twenty-five blows with a stick, but
Baab added that he himself had taken no part in these beat-
ings. The "rigorous examination" had been conducted in
the cellar of Lindenstrasse 27 by two S.S. men who had
been "drafted into the service" for this operation. Following
this—sometimes as long as three days later, it was to be
shown, when those who had been beaten were able to walk
again—the detained were brought up to Baab's office for the
customary examination, and then, Baab stated, the report on
each case was sent to Poche for final disposition. In response
to further questions put by the Court, Baab explained that
Poche's initials marked in green crayon on the dossier of a
case were the authorization for "protective custody," a term
which, it developed, meant that the prisoner was placed in
concentration camp as well, but merely because it was "necessary to protect him from public violence." In general, those
entitled to "protective custody," Baab amplified, were Jews
or other undesirables who had World War I decorations or
who had lost sons at the front in World War II or other like
considerations. Such offenders were sent to Theresienstadt in
Czechoslovakia, which was "considered a great privilege for
Jews," Baab said. On March 17, however, a witness gave
evidence that prisoners paid Baab and Poche for this privilege. He himself had been a rich man, and he had "sacrificed
millions" to buy his and his family's way into this "old-age
ghetto" where one was temporarily spared the fate of entering
the gas chambers. But "millions" were not necessary, this
witness explained, the price for this privilege being, quite
simply, all the money one had.

As for those thousands who had been evacuated to Poland,
Baab stated that he had never known their fate, because such
information was top secret and would not have been divulged
to anyone in such a lowly position as his. He said, leaning on
the dock still, that he had been ordered by Sprenger (*Gauleit-
er* for Hesse, who also committed suicide in 1945) to see that

Hesse was "de-Jewed," and that he had, in the process of carrying out this order, organized twelve mass transportations of Frankfurt Jews. These journeys, he said in a low, hurried voice, were like any ordinary journey from one point to another, for the travelers paid their own fares to Poland and, before leaving, were asked merely to submit a written statement of their property to the authorities. In further self-vindication, Baab explained that when Poche demanded that Jewish offenders be sent off on twenty-four hours' notice, Baab had pointed out the impracticability of this, and Jews were thereafter usually accorded three days to wind up their affairs and were allowed to take fifty marks and fifty kilos of belongings per person with them. Apparently Baab considered this a very fair deal.

Before this spectacle of one element of a nation's people brought to trial by another element of that same people, the inevitable and unanswerable question arises as to how strong in Germany each of those elements now is. If this Germany for which Baab stands as symbol can be dismissed as a mere handful of madmen, then does it follow that the members of the Court and the spectators in it must likewise be dismissed as a mere handful of sane men who do not speak for the multitudes of Germany? Are the multitudes of Germany something quite different from either of these two groups of which I write? Are they the Germans with whom one talks in shops and in streetcars and on the streets every day and who still will not believe that mass annihilation took place? Whichever the true answer may be, it has been established that the handful of madmen for whom Baab spoke succeeded in exterminating six million people of the Jewish faith, while the handful of sane men and women sitting on the judicial bench speak for an element whose protest was never made audibly enough. In the spring of 1941 when the repercussions of this great madness swept across frontiers and into France, the Marseille police, under orders from Vichy, stood at every exit of the great railway terminus there. They had orders to check the papers of all those who arrived on the packed trains, and they were looking not only for foreigners of military age (survivors of Dunkirk or others seeking to get through to England) in order to hand them over to the German commission in Marseille, and not only for criminals, but for Jews of any nationality. The cars which the German Occupation authorities had left to defeated France were ancient and wooden, and the trains were slow-moving, and they ran irregularly for the main lines were kept open for the movement of goods trains carrying foodstuffs from the unoccupied to the occupied zone. People rode standing in the corridors of these crowded trains, packed even into the lavatories, or rode clinging to the outer steps of the cars. For down to this last rathole left in France came the refugees, the outcasts, seeking a way out—the professors, the lawyers, the doctors, the painters and authors and poets of Germany and Austria, with all they possessed in rucksacks on their shoulders, or contained in the suitcases they and their families carried. (And more than one of them bore in grief, in his belongings, a handful of the soil of Germany.) They were halted, these fleeing thousands, and those who were Jews were sent by the Marseille police in truckloads to detainment camps outside the city where they must wait until they had obtained visas for the countries where they hoped to go. It did not end there; in the night, in that year, the police would enter hotel bedrooms and ask for the papers of those who slept there, and those who were Jewish and who had no visa for another country must dress and pack their bags again and were escorted to where the other damned and hunted were held. It was said then that it was not members of the Marseille police force itself who were forced into this work, but special police brought from Vichy, and from the course of history and the sound of an entire people's protest, it can be said that they spoke for Fascist Vichy and for no elected French authority.

What, then, had happened to the German mind that it felt then, and has expressed since, so little revulsion for the known anti-Semitic laws as they were enacted and enforced? There is a woman I know, a professor of philology in a Hessian university, who was for a long time loath to talk with me about the fate of the German Jews. And then one night in 1948 she began abruptly to speak.

"It was a gradual process," she said, seeking to lead me to some understanding of it. "Fifteen years ago, the signs appeared at the entrances to towns, official signs saying *Juden unerwünscht* [Jews Not Wanted]. There was a sign like that on the bridge you can see down there and others placed at the streets which lead into the town. There was never any protest made about them, and, after a few months, not only we, but even the Jews who lived in the town, walked past without noticing anymore that they were there. Does it seem impossible to you that this could have happened to civilized people anywhere? I can only say that we, as you know, are a civilized, cultured people and that this did happen. And then one November night in 1938, the town synagogue was burned. It was burned by men in civilian clothes, but we never knew who they were. The next day, the Jewish people I knew remained in their houses, and there was no protest made, no delegations called on the *Oberbürgermeister* to speak out against it, and there was not a line about it in our newspaper. In fact, even among ourselves, there was very little said. I was on a streetcar the next day, and as we passed the smoldering ruins of the synagogue, someone in the streetcar said, 'I'm ashamed today that I'm a German,' and, it was a strange thing, but none of us turned to look at the person who had spoken, just as none of us turned to look at the smoking ruins after we had passed. There were certain things it was better not to hear or see. Two nights later the rounding up of the Jewish population began. One of our Jewish friends came to us after dark and asked to borrow a suitcase and the following morning many of us walked down to the station with them and helped them to carry their parcels and bags. There was one little girl who carried her doll, a very large, magnificent doll, and I've always thought it such a foolish thing for me to remember, but when we heard later that all the things the Jews had carried with them were taken away from them at the next station, which was Kassel, I could think of nothing but the little girl going on without her doll. None of them ever came back," she said. "In the first few months, there were one or two letters from them, sent through the Red Cross to their friends here, and that was all."

To the question as to whether there had been rumors about what had become of these people, she replied that there had been rumors.

"It was said they were put in work camps and that many died of privation there," she went on. "But we did not ask questions. It seemed better not to know. In 1938, I had some trouble myself, for it was reported that I did not have a picture of Hitler hanging in one of the rooms in my home where I conducted some of my classes. This room was considered university property, and it was required to have a picture of Hitler there. So I finally bought a picture of Hitler, but they had them at various prices, ranging from one Reichsmark and fifty pfennigs to twelve Reichsmarks. I bought one for one Reichsmark and fifty pfennigs," she said. "And then, in 1939, I was asked to take the oath of allegiance to Hitler, and twice I refused to do this. It was my students who persuaded me to do it in the end, for they argued that in taking this oath, which so many anti-Nazis had taken before me, I was committing myself to nothing and that I could exert more influence as a professor at the university than as an outcast in the town." For a little while she said nothing more, and then she finished the story. "In the place where Hitler's picture used to hang in my room, I now have the picture of a Jew, a Jew called Spinoza. Perhaps you will think that I did this ten years too late, and perhaps you are right in thinking this. Perhaps there was something else we could all of us have done, but we never seemed to find a way to do it, either as individuals or as a group, we never seemed to find a way."

It is the sound, then, of an entire people's protest for which one listens here. A Military Government Opinion Survey conducted in 1949 shows that, in some parts of Germany, anti-Semitism was stronger in 1948 than in 1946. "This survey discloses," writes Jack Hain in his "Status of Jewish Workers and Employers in Post-War Germany," "that young people between the ages of fifteen and nineteen show more anti-Semitism, while less is evinced by those in the age group from forty-two to forty-nine. Trade-union members show less than nonmembers. . . . In Bavaria, where anti-Semitism is most rampant, the Catholic Church has sought to foster friendly relations between Christian and Jewish communities, and the national conference of Christians and Jews working in Germany has made this its sole objective. In addition, there are German laws which seek to prevent discrimination,* although the good will to implement them at this time is often absent."

On the opening day of his trial, Baab divulged that in the

---

*An A.P. item, under date of May 7, Wiesbaden, reads: "Vigorous prosecution of all anti-Semitism has been ordered by the justice ministry of the West German State of Hesse. There have been numerous anti-Jewish incidents recently, including overturning of Jewish gravestones. Police have blamed all these graveyard incidents on small children, but Justice Minister Erwin Stein declared that parents must be held responsible for their children's acts. He ordered prosecution of parents for neglect of their parental responsibility." In a second A.P. item, dated May 20, Dr. James R. Newman, U.S. Land Commissioner for Hesse, is quoted as pointing out to the Minister-President of Hesse that "of five hundred Jewish cemeteries in Hesse, two hundred have been desecrated." Urging the Minister-President to "take every possible step to stamp out the remaining vestiges of racial prejudice," Newman said, "Nothing will do more damage to Germany's standing before the civilized nations of the world than the continued manifestation that racial prejudice and hatred are still alive and active and that these crimes continue to go unpunished."

case of Jews no denunciations or accusations were required. Frankfurt Gestapo agents, he said, were dispatched to the Jewish quarter of the city, and the residents were rounded up and taken to the marketplace. There, a functionary from the Ministry of Finance assisted while these people were searched, and their valuables removed from them. The functionary then made out an official receipt for the rings, brooches, watches, etc., that had been collected and gave this receipt to the head of each family. Everything, Baab said, was done in the most orderly way. At this Kosterlitz got to his feet and asked a question of him. Each time the prosecutor spoke, a sense of impatient and vigorous life seemed to waken in the courtroom, and now a high wind of emotion rose among the spectators as he asked Baab if it were true that when mothers herded in the marketplace had asked him in desperation what was to become of their children, he had answered: "Don't worry about those Jewish bastards. You'll soon be on your way up the chimney, and your troubles will be over."

"I was an idealist in my profession," Baab replied to this, his hands supporting the weight of his body still, his head thrust forward from his shoulders, his eyes bulging at the prosecutor from under their heavy lids. "If I used such expressions as 'Jewish bastard' or 'Jewish sow' it simply meant that this official language had become so much a part of my flesh and blood that I saw nothing unusual in it. I never used anything but spiritual weapons in dealing with offenders."

At the time when such expressions were an accepted part of the official language of Germany, the Jews of Frankfurt were liable to sentence of death if they walked in the public parks or entered a movie theatre or sat down in a streetcar. Those who had not been rounded up and disposed of must tread lightly, for to smoke in the street or present an identity card upside down to an official was sufficient for a Jew to be taken for examination to the building in Lindenstrasse which had come to be known as the House of Tears. One of these who had not trod lightly enough was a storekeeper who had been seventy percent disabled in World War I and whose offense was that he had either failed or refused to mark his military citation documents and his papers of honorable discharge from the German Army with the word "Israel." It was he who took his place at the witness table now. He was an emotional man, in his late fifties, rawboned, eagle-beaked, stoop-shouldered, and deaf, who appeared as outraged by the fact that Baab had not fought at the front as he was by the atrocities which Baab had committed at home, and who turned in the witness chair to fling his accusations at Baab not only in the name of humanity, but in the name of the beloved Fatherland as well.

And there were others. There was a tall, reticent, doe-eyed insurance salesman whose father had been the director of a Frankfurt insurance company. He sat nervously on the edge of the witness chair, his hat and briefcase on the table before him, swallowing the shyness and modesty in his lean throat as he said that his father had been subjected, on Baab's orders, to "rigorous examination" in the cellar of the House of Tears. His father had subsequently been sent to Auschwitz, he testified, and then he opened his briefcase with shaking fingers, and took out with care the last two letters his father had written him from there. They were dated 1942, and their edges were worn, and their folds had been reinforced with strips of transparent paper. The insurance salesman's hands did not cease shaking as he read to the Court, in a trembling but clear voice, these final paragraphs. In one letter his father had written:

"I have firm confidence in the justice and mercy of the German authorities."

One of the German authorities at that time was a small-boned, well-groomed little woman called Hannah Reitsch,

who had dinner with me on a summer evening in 1948. She
had been a test pilot for the Luftwaffe and had, in the final
phase of the war, specialized in testing jet-propelled planes.
As she drank a martini in the cool of the evening and looked
down across the river valley, she talked of these test flights,
giving a strange, an undefinable other meaning to the things
she had done, until it seemed in the end that it had been neither for country, nor leader, nor party, that she had so dar-
ingly and fearlessly flown, but for that love of the "obscure,
evolving, crepuscular, damp, and shrouded" which Nietzsche
speaks of as mirroring the German soul.* She had had a bad
crash in one of the jet-propelled planes, and her neat face
bore scars where the flesh had been expertly repaired. She
talked quickly, with efficiency and graciousness, of the
dreams she had dreamed all through the war of saving human
life.

"It was the young I cared about," she said. "I used to lie
awake at night, telling myself in desperation, 'Hannah,
Hannah, you must find the way! They must not die!' I believed that as a woman I had failed, and, above all, as a flying
woman I had failed, if I could not find the way for our planes
to cut through the cables of the London barrage balloons.
Every night our young pilots, our bomber crews, were dying,
dying uselessly, senselessly, because their planes would enter
the area of these balloons and fall. I was just completing an
invention, a system of knifelike blades in an advance position
on the planes which would be strong enough to sever the
cables, and then the jet-propelled missiles were perfected by

---

*"The German soul has passages and galleries in it, there are caves and
hiding places, and dungeons therein; its disorder has much of the charm
of the mysterious; the German is well-acquainted with the bypaths to chaos.
And as everything loves its symbol, so the German loves the clouds and all
that is obscure, evolving, crepuscular, damp, and shrouded; it seems to
him that everything uncertain, undeveloped, self-displacing, and growing
is 'deep.'" ("Beyond Good and Evil," Nietzsche)

our scientists! I think I began sleeping at night then when I knew those young men need no longer fly straight to their deaths," she said, and she looked at me with bright, transfigured eyes.

We had shrimps for dinner, and she called them "little crabs," and laughed about them. It was a long time since she had eaten "little crabs," she said. She was working with the expellees from the East Zone, and she said that those she knew were destitute and hungry.

"Now it has become my mission to work with them, to dedicate myself to these homeless people who will never, as long as they draw breath, relinquish their love for their soil and their homes," she said; and after drinking a glass of white wine with the shrimps, she spoke of April 20, 1945. "It was Hitler's last birthday," she said, "and I was in the last German plane to make a landing in Berlin." She had flown in with Field Marshal Greim, who was to take over command of the Luftwaffe, for Goering had by then turned traitor and begun negotiations with the Allies, and Greim had been summoned to Berlin to take his place. From the night of the twentieth until the twenty-seventh, she had remained in the Reich Chancellery bunker in company with Hitler, Eva Braun, Goebbels and his family, Bormann, S.S. General Fegelein, and a few others who had rallied to the Führer's side. "There were moving hours during those final days," Hannah Reitsch said, speaking quickly, softly. "Toward the end, Fegelein and Martin Bormann turned on their friends and left. But Fegelein was captured and, on Hitler's orders, was executed by his own men. On the twenty-seventh, Hitler ordered Greim and me to fly to the southeastern army and air command to rally all forces to the defense of Berlin. We accomplished the first part of our mission, that is, we managed to take off from the airfield, and we were the last German plane to take off from Berlin, and we got as far as Austria. There our gas ran out, and we made a crash landing. Greim committed suicide when the Americans seized us there."

She was eager to speak of these things, and she listened with interest to the things one said, but she did not wish to speak of, or hear of, the fate of the German Jews. She took a little drink of wine, and she said:

"You see, I was a flying woman, a birdwoman, I only knew what was taking place in the sky. I was not even a member of the Nazi Party, for I scarcely knew what the whole thing was about. If you belong to the air, you do not know what is taking place on earth. How can you know?" While she talked, her small hand dropped on my arm from time to time, and she spoke of love, of that tremendous love which women, above all, must possess to overflowing for humanity. "You have it, just as I have it," she said. "Love and pride. You will understand what I mean when I tell you that I could never work with the Americans, no matter how much love I might have for them, and no matter how much value my experience as a jet pilot might be to them. My pride tells me, 'no, Hannah, you cannot do this. You would be betraying those German flying men, those birdmen, who had faith in you.' But there are Americans who had faith in me, too—Americans in New York," she said, and she smiled as her fingers touched my arm. "I went there before the war, and it is indescribable, the ovation I had! On East Eighty-Sixth Street, near Third Avenue, I think it was, there is a fine big hall, and I still have the clippings describing my reception there. It was in a part of New York called Yorkville, where a great many fine Americans live, and the hall was decorated with German and American flags draped on the platform and hanging from the ceiling to the floor. It was one of the greatest nights of my life. Hundreds who had come to hear me speak had to be turned away at the doors, and when I came out on the platform, the crowds in the hall went mad! In one great voice they called my name out for a quarter of an hour without stopping for breath, and I tell you, the tears were streaming down my face when I began to speak. In fact," she said, and she gave an unsteady laugh, "I couldn't speak. I just had to stand there with my arms held open to them, to these people of your country who understood the great love I had for everyone and who gave me their love and their faith in return." She lifted her glass, and the tears were standing in her eyes now as she took another swallow of wine. "As things are now, I cannot set foot on an airfield, can't even touch the wingtip of a plane," she said. "This is not easy for one who belongs to the sky. But every time I see a plane going over, any plane, my heart goes with it, and I know that I shall fly again."

During the time that the various witnesses gave evidence in the courtroom, the restless vitality of Kosterlitz never knew surcease. He made rapid notes, ripped open letters which were borne across the arena to him by a green-and-black-uniformed court guard (a man with black waxed moustaches and a long shaved head topped by a narrow black brush of hair, who bore a startling resemblance to Kaiser Wilhelm II in his prime, but whose manner was as gentle with the shabbily dressed who constantly sought entry, as with the men who sat in their black judicial robes and whom he approached softly, on his toes). Once Kosterlitz had scribbled his answers in a firm hand across these letters, he would beckon the guard to take them for dispatch, or he would make notes on the foolscap pages of the indictment. At times he snapped his fingers for a glass of water which, his classical-featured operatic head flung back, he would down in a single draught. It was manifest in every gesture he made that he was impatient to play his role, but he was not idle as he waited in the wings. There were moments when he appeared to be working in restless fury on corrections of the original script,

for, indeed, nothing had been forgotten in the drama which
unfolded. Even humor was provided in the form of testimony of an ex-Gestapo *Kriminalrat* (a high official in the
criminal section) who, during those same years, had worked
under Poche in an office adjacent to Baab's.

The *Kriminalrat*, whose denazification proceedings are
still pending in the British Zone, was the perfect cartoon figure of the Teutonic man. He was poker-spined, his narrow
skull was shaved, and there were sabre scars across his cheeks.
Even seated in the witness chair, he did not remove the light-
colored, belted raincoat that, in common with knee-high
boots, is a predilection of the Nazi-minded and that, in his
case, was nearly identical to the raincoat Hitler habitually
wore. The *Kriminalrat* was obviously a man of better education than the prisoner in the dock, and to the questions put
him by Judge Wirtzfeld, he replied in a quiet, low-pitched
voice, and only after some moments of deliberation. In answer to one of these questions, he stated, with a certain wariness, that he had always believed that various courses in citizenship and other instructive subjects were given the inmates of concentration camps. In fact, he had been under the
impression, he said, that the initial purpose of these camps
was to instruct those who were lacking in an understanding
of their duties to the state, and he intimated that nothing that
had developed since had given him any reason to change his
mind. When the ensuing laughter of the spectators had sub-
sided, Kosterlitz, standing tall and statesmanlike in his black
robe, fixed the *Kriminalrat* from under his lively black brows
and asked him if he had at any time during the ten years from
1933 to 1943 heard rumors as to the extermination of human
beings being practiced in these camps.

The lapses of memory which the witness suffered were not
infrequent, and this was one of the occasions on which he
repeated the question slowly and carefully, as if striving to

get the sense of it, but in reality altering its outer shape and its inner essence so that no sense was left to it at all. "Extermination" was, in the end, the only word of the original question that remained, and as he said it, in slow puzzlement, he might have been using it with reference to vermin, but to what species of vermin he had not yet been able to make out. At this, Kosterlitz's voice sounded in warning:

"I must remind you that you are required to speak the truth here. Did you or did you not hear any rumors as to what disposition was being made of the inmates of these camps?" The *Kriminalrat* was then able to recall that "at a very late date" he had heard some sort of rumor. "At what date?" Kosterlitz asked.

"Oh, late. Some time toward the end of the war," the *Kriminalrat* answered after consideration, but Kosterlitz was not done.

"Would you say you heard that rumor before 1944, or later than that?" Kosterlitz asked, and, after a moment's reflection, the *Kriminalrat* ventured the guess that he had heard it some time in 1944. "And from whom did you hear the rumor?" Kosterlitz persisted. The *Kriminalrat* sought to avoid answering this question by referring, in measured words, to his concept of his legal rights. He did not see the necessity of answering this particular question, he said. "Indeed," said Kosterlitz, his voice light and clear, "you are required to answer any questions concerning this public matter that the state puts to you in this public courtroom, and you are required to answer such questions truthfully."

The *Kriminalrat* thereupon conceded that he believed it was a woman who had made mention of the rumor to him.

"And who was this woman?" asked Kosterlitz.

"A friend," said the *Kriminalrat*, speaking even these two words with the greatest care.

In reply to Kosterlitz's next questions, he said he did not

recall the woman's name or the name of the street or the number of the house in which she had made the remark to him.

"What rumor did she repeat to you?" Kosterlitz asked then, but the *Kriminalrat* said he had forgotten the details of the conversation and therefore could not say. "Did she speak of the Jews being sent to extermination centers?" Kosterlitz proceeded with it, and, after some moments of hesitation, the *Kriminalrat* said that he believed she had said something about Jews dying in the camps where they had been sent for reeducation. "Is it not possible that she, knowing your position, asked you if it were not true that Jews were being exterminated?" Kosterlitz suggested, and the *Kriminalrat* replied that he could not recall the exact words she had used, but it was possible that she had asked him in that way. "Did she use the word 'gassed'?" Kosterlitz said, his voice gone soft and winning, as if to charm the truth from him. But the *Kriminalrat* was being extremely wary. He said he did not recall that word being used. "What, at the time, was your reaction to what this friend repeated to you?" Kosterlitz asked.

"I told her not to mention such things again," said the *Kriminalrat*, choosing his words with care. "It was my duty to turn a person in who repeated stories of that kind, but, because of the circumstances, I did not do so. I was convinced that she had been misinformed. I myself," he added, "when I heard of the mass deportations to Lublin, was under the impression that the Jews were to be resettled there."

The testimony of this cautious man must have been of some comfort to the prisoner in the dock, and, as he listened, the mask of apathy seemed to shift a little on his features, but no richer, sweeter emotion was revealed beneath. He, who had protested that the witnesses had all been influenced in their testimony against him, sat motionless, unmunching, a faint wash of life seemingly restored to his face as he heard this witness state that the Gestapo had never been the all-powerful organization which everyone had been led to be-lieve it was. The Gestapo had been grossly misrepresented, the *Kriminalrat* said in his stolid, deliberate way. Gestapo agents had been merely members of a police force that had attempted to keep order. Kosterlitz then put the question lightly and gracefully to him as to why, then, everyone in Germany, if not in all of Western Europe, had stood in such dread of the Gestapo and had lived in fear of being sum-moned by the Gestapo for questioning. This, the witness re-plied, he was at a total loss to understand.

"The procedure was," he said, "that if it seemed advisable at any time to bring pressure to bear on an offender in order to obtain information essential to the safety of the state, an application for permission to bring pressure had first to be forwarded to the R.S.H.A. in Berlin. To my certain knowl-edge, on one occasion only was such permission requested by Frankfurt Gestapo headquarters, and it was not granted by the R.S.H.A." This was humor of so stark and uproarious a kind that the spectators rocked on their chairs with the vio-lence of their laughter, their mouths stretched open, their hands striking their thighs.

But it must have been smaller comfort to the prisoner when the *Kriminalrat* went on to say that Heinrich Baab had always shown great willingness in executing the orders of his supe-riors and had enjoyed the reputation of being particularly "strenuous" in his interrogation of offenders. And now word by word, the truth at which the *Kriminalrat* hinted became clearer, and it seemed plausible that, faced with the super-conscientious work of a subordinate whose zeal might even bring him to denounce his superiors, neither the *Kriminalrat* nor Poche had dared show themselves less violent than Baab in their persecution of the enemies of the state. (For instance, it was later shown that the witness who had cut his wrists after being examined by Baab had eventually been acquitted by the

district court of Kassel of the charge of having listened to the
foreign radio. And it was also shown that even after Baab's
transfer from the Frankfurt *Judenreferat* he had persecuted
"mongrels" although the official policy was to defer decision
on their status until after the war.) The *Kriminalrat* testified
that in 1943 he himself had seen that Baab was removed from
the *Judenreferat* and put to work in an anti-sabotage division—a piece of information which he volunteered, doubt-
less with his coming denazification trial in mind—apparently
in the belief that it made him appear the more benign agent
of the two. But he failed to add that by February of that year,
Baab had already accompanied the last convoy of full-
blooded Jews to the Frankfurt station and seen them into the
assembled boxcars, so that there was, in reality, no further
need for him in the *Judenreferat*.

There are those to whom fact is not fact unless it has been
transmuted by lyricism. This is just one facet of that genteel
and confused intelligence that judges persecution and extermination to be less grave matters when storekeepers and insurance salesmen are concerned than when the victims are
people of intellectual distinction. (A Nazi-classified "mongrel," a lady of breeding, said to me recently: "Of course, if
you had ever had anything to do with Polish Jews you would
understand how the Nazis felt. They were an uneducated,
grasping people, not at all like the cultivated German Jews.")
The protagonist for all those who made such distinctions
came to the witness chair in the gentle person of a Frankfurt
Jewish author, a man of seventy-two, whose wife had been an
Aryan. He sat at ease before the Court, with the light from
the high windows touching his olive-skinned face and his soft
white hair, not for an instant the long-haired artist out of
place in the company of common men, but a man whose voice
and manner, whose disciplined emotions and conservative
dress, gave him the air of being an academician, an honored

man of letters, who now addressed fellow members of honor in this judicial hall. He told the Court that in 1942 he had been arrested by the Gestapo and confined in a "Jewish home" in Frankfurt. This so-called home was, he explained in his quiet, cultivated voice, a mass quarters, or ghetto, where Jews were held pending final disposition of their cases. There he worked with the others at dyeing shoes, sorting potatoes, and similar tasks.

"I must speak first of the inner grandeur with which the people confined there accepted their fate, which was, almost without exception, death," he said. "They were the living figures in a frieze of such beauty and of such noble, heroic character that replicas of it should be painted upon the walls of every public building of the new Germany. There are no words in any language of the civilized world to describe the suffering the Jews endured at that time."

One of the first occasions on which this distinguished man of letters had seen Baab was when Baab paid a routine visit to the "home." While passing through a workshop, the witness's grave and precise testimony went, Baab had remarked in his presence: "When I put in an appearance, it means some corpses are due.

"After Baab's visit to the ghetto, a tide of terror and anguish seemed to sweep through the place," the witness said. "The weakest became panic-stricken and were submerged by it, while the strongest held their heads higher, as do the drowning, in an effort to outride the flood of fear." On the evening following the visit by Baab, an elderly woman hanged herself, the witness told the Court. She had been very musical, and in her luxurious home there had been two concert grand pianos, each placed so that the musician at the keyboard could look out upon the lawns and gardens as he played. She and her married daughter had spent three hours every day at one or both of these pianos, playing for each other, or playing duets, or playing arrangements for two pianos. During her confinement in the ghetto, the old lady had talked to the witness of reports made by students who had had themselves hanged by the neck for a certain period in the interest of research so that they might record the sensations experienced. And the reports, she had told him, were that, after the first deafening explosions, the ears of the hanging were filled with music of such incredible power and beauty that they were regretful, even resentful, when they were cut down and had to return to life again. "I like to believe that she died to the sound of that music," the witness said. "It had been arranged," he continued, "that her daughter and son-in-law should walk past her prison window every night at seven o'clock, so that she might know that all was well with them. This they had done with unfailing punctuality during the six months she was there. But on this particular evening she waited in the greatest agitation until twenty minutes past the hour, and when they did not come, she concluded that they too had been arrested by Baab and she took her life at the very moment that they passed." After an instant of silence, the witness proceeded: "My bed neighbor during those months was the former director of the Stuttgart Alliance Insurance Company, a gentleman of wealth and prominence who was then nearly seventy years old. On one of Baab's visits of inspection, he accused this eminent man of 'sabotaging the Führer's work' by not dyeing enough shoes per day, and he was forthwith removed to Auschwitz, where he died. I cannot tell you of the eternal loneliness which entered my soul the night he was taken from the home. It was not only that the bed beside mine was left temporarily empty of life, and in particular of the life of one I had known well, but for the first time I saw, wide and dimensional before me, the actual vista of each man's solitude, so vast, so terrible, so silent that I knew this window which had opened upon it was one I could never again close. Baab," said the witness, speaking without anger or bitterness, "knew that every person he sent to Auschwitz faced death. He was a mass murderer. When he summoned men and women to Lindenstrasse 27, the murder had already begun."

Witnesses came and went in a steady procession to and from the witness chair—witnesses who testified that they had been beaten by Baab and the teeth knocked from their mouths, witnesses who had been threatened by Baab with reprisals on their relatives if they did not inform, other witnesses who had survived the so-called ghetto who had heard Baab say to the guards: "The Jews will be taken to Auschwitz, where they will be gassed." There was one witness whose Jewish wife, after being interrogated by Baab, hanged herself in a cell in Lindenstrasse 27; another who had lost eighteen members of her family in the deportations from Frankfurt; others who had seen Baab knock down an old Jewish lady at the Frankfurt station; another who testified that Baab had sent the Jewish wife of a Frankfurt bank director to her death in Auschwitz because she had gone to an Aryan hairdresser; another, the mother of seven children, whose husband had been arrested by Baab with the words, "This is separation for life," and who testified that Baab had returned for the children on the pretext of letting them visit their father, and she had never seen any of them again. When one witness testified that he, and therefore presumably others in Germany, had known as early as 1941 that concentration camp inmates were being liquidated, even people outside the courtroom, could they have heard, must have stopped to listen. Postal orders sent to friends and relatives in the Lodz ghetto in Poland had been returned, he said, with the official notification stamped on them that the addressee had left without giving a forwarding address, and this was as final as if a death certificate had come. At the conclusion of each witness's testimony, Judge Wirtzfeld read out the name of the witness, his street address in Frankfurt, and the date on which he had come into contact with Baab. And each time this was done, Baab ceased chewing his surreptitious tidbits and got to his feet again and, with his hands gripping the wood of the dock, faced the two women and nine men of the Court. Each time his response to Judge Wirtzfeld's question was the same. With no inflection in his voice, and no apparent interest in his own words, Baab would repeat:

"The name is familiar, but I do not remember having seen the person before."

This obstinacy in denying that he had ever seen witnesses whose faces he had struck, or witnesses who had been to his office not once but half a dozen times to ask for news of relatives whom he had "detained," caused such outbursts of protest among the spectators that Baab, his face drained colorless and his bloated throat beating like that of a frog, asked, in accordance with Article 20 of the Hesse Constitution, for the protection of the Court. But the recitation and subsequent publication in the local press of the names and addresses of the witnesses had its effect upon the people of the city. Not from one source, but from many—from shop employees who served one from behind a counter, from taxi drivers, from postmen, or from the man or woman who happened to sit next to one on a park bench—came the incredible admission that for the first time, now that names and addresses had been given, statistics had ceased to be statistics and had been translated into flesh and blood. The Nuremberg trials were far removed, not only in time but in comprehension, for no little people had appeared as witnesses against those who had once been the great. For the first time, with the names and addresses of commonplace citizens crowding the scene, many in Frankfurt came finally to believe that vast numbers of other commonplace citizens, with names and addresses as

commonplace as theirs, had, in the Nazi years, been system-
atically and deliberately destroyed. The photographs of the
massed naked dead that were shown to the Germans in 1945
had been dismissed by most of them as propaganda photographs, for the general belief in Germany is that anything
may be resorted to in the dissemination of propaganda, inasmuch as propaganda is merely one means of putting over a
discreditable cause. "The Nazis did it for twelve years, and
now the Americans and the Russians are outdoing each other
at it," the Germans say with cynicism; but the sworn testimony of men and women who lived in the same streets in
which they lived, or just around the corner from them,
shocked and convinced them as no reports had done before.
Here a Herr Georg Wittmann, living at Laundhardtstrasse
1, in Frankfurt-am-Main, had told of things he had actually
seen done, and a Herr Peter Meister, Thorwaldsenstrasse 20,
had given similar testimony; and here was a Frau Grete Hoff-
man, a Jewess married to an Aryan, living as anyone else
might live at Wilhelm-Buschstrasse 24, who had endured
years of slave labor because she had omitted the Jewish name
Sarah from her ration card. Here, then, was the testimony of
simple, honest Germans like themselves, who had nothing to
gain by telling a lie.

The great majority of letters received at the *Frankfurter
Rundschau* offices on the subject of the Baab trial expressed
deep sympathy for the members of the victims' families, denounced Gestapo methods, and were violent in their condem-
nation of Heinrich Baab. Some correspondents even went so
far as to demand that special legislation be passed in order
that Baab might pay with his life for the crimes he had committed. Among these letters there was, however, a sprinkling
of anonymous communications, some scribbled in pencil on
postcards, expressing regret that Baab had not been the in-
strument for killing more Jews while he was about it, and

among them the editors of the *Frankfurter Rundschau* (who, incidentally, are not Jews). But these latter communications were in no way representative of the public's reaction to the trial. Fear was frequently voiced by irate citizens that the defendant might be acquitted on a legal technicality, for no member of the Gestapo had, in West Germany, been convicted of so much as participation in murder for the functions he had fulfilled.*

But, day after day, as the persecuted and the dead took on their separate identities, the man in the dock, in the same measure, became less and less man and more and more the detached inhuman symbol of the criminal organization he had served. So that the incident which took place in the courtroom on March 13 was startling to those who had long since ceased speculating on Baab's role as husband or father or son and who could hardly conceive of him in any surroundings more personalized or intimate than those in which they saw him now. On the morning of that day, one witness testified

---

*On March 16, 1950, at the height of the proceedings of the Baab trial a verdict of "not guilty" was returned in the trial of two former *Kriminalräte*, who had been tried in the Hamburg Criminal Court for having used "coercion to obtain statements" from prisoners during the Nazi regime. In his justification of the verdict, the presiding judge pointed out that "in every state means of coercion must be allowed the police," and that it had "not been proved that the defendants had abused the authorized means."

On March 23, 1950, in the Munich Criminal Court, the former S.S. Gestapo Chief of Munich and his deputy were both found "not guilty" of responsibility "in the execution without trial of at least twenty eastern slave laborers and Polish deportees," and of "aiding and abetting in manslaughter," and of "inflicting grave bodily injury" on the numerous prisoners who had been in their charge. Although the two defendants had admitted in Court that they had requested the R.S.H.A. for permission to hang ten slave laborers and that twenty-five to forty executions had taken place in the cellar of the Gestapo headquarters in Munich, the jury failed to find the defendants guilty on all counts.

In the latter instance, the prosecutor has appealed the verdict, and the case will come up for retrial.

as to the treatment which his mother had suffered at the hands of Baab in 1942. She was then over seventy, the witness told the Court, but despite her age and her delicate health, Baab, during his interrogation, had struck her so forcefully with his fist that she had been knocked the length of his office by the blow.

"I saw her only once after that," the witness said. "The following week she was deported to the East, and she died in the boxcar on the way. But this I did not know at the time. When I went to Lindenstrasse to beg Baab for news of her, I asked him, in the name of pity, if he did not have a mother of his own somewhere—"

"Yes!" a voice cried out from among the spectators. "And there she is!"

Immediately, two women dressed in black, one young and fresh-cheeked, the other old and squat and as bloated as the prisoner in the dock, rose quickly from their chairs at one side of the crowded room and, with lowered heads, hastened in panic toward the door. There the uniformed court guard, with his waxed moustaches and his black brush of hair, stepped forward on tiptoe to open it for them, and the men and women in the courtroom sat in shocked silence, watching Baab's mother and wife, who had so inexplicably and only for this brief instant taken shape before them, bow their heads and go.

On the sixth day of the trial, another former Nazi official took the witness chair.

Dr. Kurt Lindow, a man in his middle forties, had been director of the Criminal Section of R.S.H.A., in which position he had worked with Admiral Canaris. In contrast to the *Kriminalrat*, Dr. Lindow was obviously a man of superior intelligence and education, and he was not, it may be noted in passing, one of those of whom it might be said, as Mr. Benjamin Buttenweiser, Assistant United States High

Commissioner for Germany, said of the Germans in a recent address:* "Father, forgive them, for they know not what they do"; nor was Dr. Lindow one whom one might hope (to draw again on the text of Mr. Buttenweiser's speech) "to lead hand in hand along the pathways to a better life." Dr. Lindow's life had been, in fact, not a bad life at all. Both before and during the war, he had traveled widely abroad in a diplomatic capacity, representing Nazi interests at international conferences. His oval face was tanned, his dark hair immaculately groomed, and the grey felt hat he carried, his grey topcoat, his white shirt, his black shoes were impeccable. Since the war he had appeared as a witness in two of the Nuremberg war crime trials, and he had had his own *Spruchkammer* in Darmstadt in 1948. In his *Spruchkammer* trial, Dr. Lindow had been classified an "offender" (a member of the second category of Nazis), and sentenced to three and a half years at hard labor, a sentence that had been considered served because of his internment by the Americans since 1945. Dr. Lindow's manner was quiet and assured, for his experiences for the most part had been not disagreeable ones, and neither he nor anyone else in the courtroom, with the exception of Kosterlitz, anticipated for an instant the *coup de théâtre* which was about to alter the tenor of his life for an undetermined time to come.

Dr. Lindow had been summoned to appear in the Baab case in order to testify on the functioning of the R.S.H.A., but a detailed exposition such as was asked, he stated in response to Judge Wirtzfeld's questioning, he found extremely difficult to give. The implication was that he himself had

*This speech, scheduled to be delivered on May 14, 1950, in Chicago at the annual meeting of the Anti-Defamation League of the B'nai B'rith, was cancelled by a committee of the League because of the sentiments regarding denazification which Mr. Buttenweiser expressed. The speech was later given in New York before the Foreign Policy Association.

operated on such a high level that he scarcely knew what went on below, and he further reminded the Court that everything connected with the matter had taken place a good many years before, added to which, the duties of the bureau had been complex and multiple. When Lengsfeld asked him if, in the routine reports forwarded from subsidiary Gestapo bureaus to the R.S.H.A., it had been customary for the reporting Gestapo agent (Baab or whoever it might be) to make a specific suggestion about the disposition of the individual reported on, and, if so, whether the R.S.H.A. acted upon these suggestions, Dr. Lindow replied that matters of this nature had not come to his attention. He was, however, able and willing to explain the meaning of the term "protective custody." Protective custody, he said, was a measure which had been introduced "to protect from persecution individuals who had been under suspicion or arrest." For instance, if an individual had been tried and cleared by the People's Court, the Gestapo had the right to step in with a "staying order" on the ground that one who had been accused or suspected of an offense might be considered a "threat to the security of the state" and therefore required official "protection" (and one could only assume this meant protection from his neighbors and friends). On being asked what he had known of the means employed to dispose of the Jews, Dr. Lindow replied that when he saw no more people in the streets wearing the Star of David, he had concluded the Jews had all been resettled in Eastern ghettos and had given the matter no further thought. And now the high point of the session approached.

Dr. Lindow, as it happened, was the hundred and fifty-second witness to be heard, and his undramatic testimony was given not in the morning but in mid-afternoon, so that attention and emotion were temporarily depleted by the time he took the chair. It was therefore in keeping with the general spirit of exhaustion that Kosterlitz, when asked by Judge

Wirtzfeld if he wished to question the witness, waived this
right with a presumably fatigued motion of his hand. There
was nothing to indicate then that the records of Dr. Lindow's
Spruchkammer trial in Darmstadt were lying open on the table
underneath that hand. Judge Wirtzfeld requested Dr. Lindow to take a seat for the moment on the bench that stood at
all times before the spectators and which was reserved for the
overflow of the press and for witnesses who had already testified. Dr. Lindow waited courteously while Kosterlitz put
one question to Judge Wirtzfeld in an easy, conversational
tone. If the defense had no further interest in questioning the
witness, could not Dr. Lindow be immediately dismissed, he
asked. Judge Wirtzfeld turned toward the defense counsel
and put this question to him with his eyebrows, and, across
the arena, Lengsfeld nodded in sour agreement, not brooding over any objection, it may be supposed, but irked by the
life sentence he was himself condemned to serve, perhaps by
his digestive organs, in a solitary confinement of wormwood
and gall.

"Very well," said Judge Wirtzfeld, seemingly about to
yawn. "The witness is dismissed."

And then the three things happened simultaneously. The
faces of the spectators turned wearily toward the door, awaiting the entry of the next witness to be called; Dr. Lindow
rose from his chair and, immaculate grey felt hat in hand,
began his bow in the direction of the Court before taking
leave; and Kosterlitz jumped to his feet and called out in a
voice that roused the courtroom from its sleep:

"*Herr Wachtmeister*, place Herr Lindow under arrest! I
accuse him of defying all international and human law by
murdering Soviet PWs in his care!"

The police officer so addressed made his way to Dr. Lindow and requested him to follow him from the room. Dr.
Lindow completed his bow to the judicial bench with dignity,

and, with two men in plain clothes falling into step on either side of him, he walked toward the door. Some members of the press hastened from the courtroom and made their way down the hall beside him and his escort and followed up the stairs. And here, as he climbed, his composure left him. The color drained from his face, and, with each step he took and breath he drew, he sobbed like an aged man. When a member of the press speculated on his being extradited to Russia for trial, this one hundred and fifty-second witness covered his face with his hands, leaned against the soiled plaster wall for strength, and groaned aloud.

"Whether the [American] denazification program was handled intelligently and effectively or, as some believe, incapably and too complacently, I think it must be agreed that it is too late now to turn the clock back and reopen the entire question," Mr. Buttenweiser also stated in the address to which I have previously referred. "Any such move, I feel certain," he continued, "would produce chaos, which would render impossible the performance of the more constructive and far-reaching program of reorientation which lies before us and on which I fervently believe we are already successfully embarked." Kosterlitz, however, did not hesitate "to turn the clock back," needing no program of reorientation to tell him that it is a question that has never been closed. Dr. Lindow is at present in the city jail awaiting trial in the Frankfurt Criminal Court, a trial which may take six months to prepare.

On March 27, Heinrich Baab, accompanied by the members of the Court and representatives of the press, made a visit to the House of Tears. And here the fleshy, pouch-eyed, balding man could be seen in all his mediocrity. His apathy was dispelled, and he was visibly shaken as he passed through the doorway, stricken and trembling before his memories of the dead as he had not been before the living who had testified against him from the witness chair. He gave a cursory glance at the office which had once been his, not crossing the threshold of it; and he confirmed with a nod of his head that this one, adjacent to it, had been the *Kriminalrat*'s office, and this other had been the office of the Gestapo chief, Poche. Then he led the way to the cellar, showing his familiarity with the place in sullen pride. Letters had been produced in Court telling still more stories of the sufferings which those who had written them had once endured here—letters from Pittsburgh, Pennsylvania; Portland, Oregon; Cheyenne, Wyoming; letters from Amsterdam and Brussels, from those who had survived. And the walls of the cells bore further testimony, for the despairing had scratched words of appeal upon the stone. There were single words or phrases, in German, in Polish, in Hebrew, in Russian. "Mama!" "Papa!" had been scratched in desperation there, in several tongues, and the dates of various years recorded beneath them. The most recent message was written in French, and it was dated March 2, 1945.

"I have been freed," it said, "but I shall return for those who are still here."

There was the cell where a Jewish woman, a Swiss before her marriage to a Frankfurt Catholic, had hanged herself; in another, two men had taken their lives. And, like a surly museum guide who, despite long association with the wonders that he shows, has remained in total ignorance of their inestimable beauty and their inestimable worth, Babb conducted his visitors through dark winding corridors to a windowless cell, scarcely larger than a clothes closet, which was supplied with air by a small rusty pipe that pierced the outer wall. Here, he stated without emotion, the authorized "rigorous examinations" had taken place. Stooping in the doorway of this cell, Kosterlitz asked him in what position the prisoners had been beaten, and Baab replied that he had never assisted at an examination, and therefore did not know.

"I am not guilty of the death of these people," Baab said in the darkness of the crypt. "During my time of service with the Gestapo, my actions were all within legal bounds and were performed on the orders of my superiors."

From this place, Baab was returned to the Frankfurt jail where, ten years before, with Gestapo headquarters overflowing, he had conducted many of his interrogations. And there the group of men and women paused with him at the head of a flight of steep iron stairs and looked down the length of it in silence. Evidence had been produced in Court that Baab had once stood here with a Jewish woman he had finished questioning and, seeing the hysterical state to which despair had reduced her, said:

"Others have thrown themselves down here and put an end to it. There's nothing to keep you from doing the same."

The day following this trip to Lindenstrasse 27, Baab gave a *Frankfurter Rundschau* reporter a list of twenty-six names of Frankfurt citizens who, he declared, had worked as informers for the Gestapo during his service there. Two of the names on the list proved to be the names of two of the three members from Hesse of the present *Bundestag* at Bonn, while a third name was that of a Frankfurt city magistrate. Although the *Rundschau*'s publication of this fact—but not the names—aroused a degree of public interest and protest and incurred the expulsion from the Social Democratic Party of Karl Gerold, co-editor of the *Rundschau*, Baab's act of divulging the twenty-six names revealed more of the nature of the man himself than it did of the questionable character of those holding public office in Germany today. For it was easy enough to establish that many detained by the Gestapo had not infrequently been released on parole on a signed promise,

which they had no intention of keeping, that they would inform upon their neighbors and friends. At least one of the
Bundestag members from Hesse (all three of whom were
S.P.D.) stated publicly that this had been the consideration
on which he had been accorded amnesty by Baab.

On the twenty-ninth of March the prosecution presented
its summarizing argument, and the dusty stairs leading to the
courtroom were even more packed, the crowds who waited
outside the guarded doorways even greater, even more eager,
but no less patient, than before. The light of the spring day
came through a long window behind Kosterlitz as he stood
erect before his table, which was so close to the upper press
bench that those who sat there could have counted the stitches
of the neat patch in the back of his long gown. But this shabby
garment that he wore was expendable, for what endowed him
with dignity was his trenchant awareness that six million men
and women and children had had to die before he could be
given this role to play. As he spoke, he held a small black
automatic pencil in his right hand, and, when he did not
speak directly to the judicial bench or to the defendant in the
dock, his eyes would seek this pencil out and dwell on it, and
a portion of his exhortations was made to it, as if it were a
fragment of the actual charred flake of Plievier's individual
man. "How heavy is the guilt?" Plievier wrote in 1948 in
Germany. "Can guilt be weighed? How can it be weighed?
Children shot, women shot, old men, helpless prisoners
shot—according to orders, 'as the law provides.' What sort
of law? Is it a law of nature, of reason, of metaphysics, of
human intercourse? Is it a law dedicated to the preserving of
the interests of all? Is it the law of the German people, the
same people who brought forth a Gutenberg, a Matthias
Grünewald, a Martin Luther, a Beethoven, an Immanuel
Kant? Is it the law of a creative people living by the fruits of

its own creations? Did the German people have no other political face to show the world?"

It was this political face of which Kosterlitz defined the features in the first hour of his address. As he talked the defendant was forgotten, for it was clearly the principles and the acts of an entire society of men of which the prosecutor spoke. On the table before him, stacked one upon the other, were three unwieldy tomes of Nazi statutes, with markers set in various pages of them, and now and again he would seize one of these volumes and read aloud from the contemptible text. Here were expounded in legal terms the reasons why a certain portion of the population must wear the Star of David and must, according to sex, include the name "Sarah" or "Israel" on all identity documents or else be subject to arrest. Here was set forth the July 1938 Citizen Law, with its thirteen supplementary regulations, defining the nature as well as the civil status of a Jew and specifying the congenital moral and physical deficiencies that automatically excluded every Jew from the right to citizenship. And here were the paragraphs of the law, passed in July 1943, which brought the police courts of Germany under Gestapo jurisdiction, so that every avenue of appeal was closed. After Kosterlitz had read one of these passages out, he flung the volume from him, and then he spoke of the Gestapo regulations that had not been written into any law books, but that had been enforced as inexorably as those set forth in pompous official language for the eye of posterity. In accordance with these minor regulations, Jews had been permitted to go shopping once a week, but even on that one day the items they might buy had been rigidly controlled. They were permitted to buy one turnip a week, for instance, and any infringement of this regulation meant arrest. Germans whose ration cards bore the stamp of Israel were not allowed to buy white bread or eggs or butter or any other luxury items; nor were they permitted to read newspapers, have a telephone or a radio, or enter a theatre or any other place of entertainment, but, at the same time, they were required to pay a theatre and movie tax for productions they were not permitted to see.

"While it is true," said Kosterlitz, coming to the vital point of Baab's personal responsibility in the matter of his victims' deaths, "that the warrants for arrest were not signed by the defendant, but by Heydrich and Kaltenbrunner, it has been proved beyond any doubt that Baab could always be counted on to produce the evidence which the R.S.H.A. considered justified arrest." And then he spoke of two Frankfurt Jews whom Baab was reported to have saved. In this instance, "saved" meant merely that he had interrogated two Jews and, for some obscure reason, allowed them to go free. "This," Kosterlitz cried out, "this alone, is indisputable proof that the power of life and death resided in the hands of Heinrich Baab!"

In one of Carl Zuckmayer's plays, a Luftwaffe general is appealed to by his former mistress to intercede on behalf of a Jewish friend who faces extermination in a concentration camp. And, sitting there, well-groomed and handsome, on the stage, the general gazes bitterly out across the audience and, speaking some of the best lines in the play, voices a profound comment upon the unhappy people of Germany. "Now let us look into the mirror and dote on ourselves!" Zuckmayer makes him say. "What noble human beings we are! That's how we look! Each of us with a Jew or two to salvage his conscience so that we can sleep at night!" Can this, then, be taken as explanation of why Baab had allowed one Jew, of all the Jews who had been summoned to his office, to walk in the streets of Frankfurt with no Star of David on his coat and had allowed a second Jew to pack his bags and go? It would be too easy to answer that these two Jews had paid Baab for the favors he granted them, Kosterlitz cried out, for what of the other Jews who had paid Baab all the money they possessed, and still they and their families had died? One of the two whom Baab had spared had remained in Frankfurt, and he had told the Court that he was unable to explain why Baab had conceded him the "special favors" that he had. He denied, under oath, Baab's statement that he had informed Baab of a secret meeting hall where the Jews gathered for religious services after the demolishing of the synagogue.

"I could not have told him this, for I was incapable of uttering a word in his presence," this witness said. "Although he treated me with consideration, I always entered Lindenstrasse 27 in fear and trembling, my limbs shaking, my throat dry with terror, for the sound of his shouting filled the entire house."

If he had spared the lives of two, said Kosterlitz, then the power of decision had been his, and the Court had no choice but to find him guilty of the murders with which he was charged.

"This man," said Kosterlitz, concluding his five-hour address, "should be judged as a component part of the furious anti-Semitic program of those years. In passing judgment on him, you take upon yourselves the high honor of passing judgment upon an element and an epoch of Germany."

During Kosterlitz's argument, the defendant sat heavy and motionless in the dock, his eyes seemingly drugged, watching the prosecutor with the same lassitude with which he might, on a languid spring afternoon, have watched a voluble street vendor demonstrating a new kind of glue for mending broken crockery, or a new gadget for sharpening used razor blades, or a magical fluid for sealing together the fragments of a shattered looking glass. It was obviously a proceeding that he connected in no way with himself. Inasmuch as he possessed no broken crockery or used blades and would not

have recognized his own likeness in the glass even if it were
held before him, he would have preferred to saunter on down
the avenue and pick up another bag of peanuts somewhere
and stand looking at something else while he peeled the shells
mechanically away. Johanna Kirchner's daughter, who served
on the jury and who, being an S.P.D. member of long standing, had likewise been imprisoned in the Nazi days, had her
own explanation for Baab's air of nearly complete detachment
from the proceedings of his murder trial.

" 'Do whatever you wish with me' was his attitude," she
said to me some days after the verdict had been pronounced.
"He believed that any sentence passed on him would soon be
meaningless. With more and more Nazis being reinstated in
positions of authority every day, he knew he had nothing to
fear. He simply sat there thinking: 'Do your worst. I'll be
out in a short time anyway.' "

During the weeks of the trial, a young green-uniformed
court guard had sat at times at the end of the bench on which
the defense counsel sat below the prisoner in the dock and, at
other times, had stood at the doors of the press entrance, and,
because of the composed earnestness and intelligence of his
young face, one's eyes repeatedly sought him out. When one
glanced from the defendant's countenance to his, it was as if
one turned from darkness to light, from the opacity and
muteness of death to the clarity and eloquence of life. On the
day of the prosecutor's address, the young guard was not on
duty, but he sat, in civilian clothes, among the spectators,
and it was apparent that, on his day off, he had chosen to come
back and follow what was taking place.

On March 31 Dr. Lengsfeld made the defense summa-
tion, basing his argument with pained and scholarly conviction on the absence of conclusive proof. Standing with his
sour, sallow face raised, his great horn-rimmed spectacles
saddling his nose and his lean arms crossed within the folds

of his full black sleeves, he cited a verdict of the Nuremberg Tribunal that held that the Gestapo had had, as an organization, no connection with the operation of concentration camps. The prosecution had not only failed to produce a single arrest warrant bearing Baab's signature, he said, but it had failed to prove that the reports sent to the R.S.H.A. were in any way tantamount to verdicts. Neither had it been proved, Lengsfeld continued, that Baab himself had assaulted his prisoners; and, at this, the sound of protest and laughter rose in the Court.

"Quiet, please!" Judge Wirtzfeld called in admonishment from the bench. "Every man has the right to speak freely here!"

All the evidence produced during the trial showed, said Lengsfeld, that Baab had done no more than carry out to the letter the official regulations issued by the R.S.H.A. If justice were to be done, he said, Baab could not be held responsible for a system that others had set up. Baab had been in charge of one small section of a demogogic state that had been dedicated, in its entirety, to violence; he had been merely one link in an endless chain which had held captive many innocent men and women, he said. Was there, moreover, a legal precedent for the conviction the prosecution demanded, Lengsfeld asked; and he cited the Hamburg Criminal Court's acquittal verdict of March 16, a fortnight before, and the acquittal verdict returned by the Munich Criminal Court at an even more recent date.

"No *Kriminalsekretär* in the Western Zone has yet been convicted of murder," Lengsfeld said. "This fact cannot be lightly put aside. If Baab knew, as has been charged, of the ultimate fate of his victims, then he might be guilty of contributing to murder, but no evidence has been produced to uphold either this or the murder charge. One witness has stated that Baab would find no defense before a divine court, but it must be borne in mind that Baab is not being tried at this time before a divine court, nor is he being tried before a political court, but he is being tried before a criminal court, and it is neither divine law, nor political law, but criminal law which must, in all justice, be observed." As the defendant listened, his face seemed to alter, and the features of it appeared for a moment to be moved by a faint flicker of life, a life to which the name of hope might almost be allowed. "It is still to be proven," said Lengsfeld, the taste of the words seemingly as bitter as gall on his tongue, "that Baab himself raised his hand against any individual," and the protest of the spectators was roared aloud.

At the conclusion of his three-hour plea, Lengsfeld asked that the defendant be found morally but not legally guilty of the crimes with which he was charged. "No one," he said, "can, from the standpoint of morality, acquit him of his guilt. Deplorable as it may be that both the evidence and the proof that might establish a truer picture of events are lacking, Baab cannot be found guilty as a murderer." He concluded with an exhortation to the Court "to apply the law in its purest and strictest sense and not to be swayed by the pressure of public demand."

On the fifth of April, the day the verdict was to be returned, the young court guard with the steadfast face and the other, with the waxed moustaches and the black broom of hair, who patterned himself on Kaiser Wilhelm II, stood in their green uniforms at the press entrance, to keep the unauthorized from making their way in. It was a quarter past nine when Baab took his seat in the dock. Almost immediately after he had done so, a middle-aged woman carrying a black umbrella and wearing a black felt hat rose from among the spectators and walked across the Court arena to the vacant defense bench. With her umbrella lifted as a weapon, she flung herself at the defendant in the dock.

"You murderer! You murderer!" she cried, and her voice seemed to be pressed tight and small within her throat by grief.

As she sought to strike Baab's head, he retired quickly to the back of the dock, and the young guard sprang in between. He put one arm around the woman and led her back to her seat, and, when the umbrella slipped from her grasp, he picked it up from the boards and stood it carefully beside her chair and then left her crying into her hands. Just before Judge Wirtzfeld stood to read the verdict and the sentence, the two guards did a singular thing. They opened one half of the press door wide enough to let first one and then another and finally a total of six scrubwomen, hatless and wearing their soiled aprons, slip in and stand among the others who had waited since seven in the morning for the doors to open and who were packed into the courtroom now to hear the few words that were about to be said.

Although "guilty" was not the first word of the rendering of the verdict, it was the first word those present heard, and a sigh, scarcely more audible than that of water rising and falling along a shore, passed through the courtroom. "Guilty," said Judge Wirtzfeld, and as Baab stood with his hands supporting him on the dock, he seemed, for a moment, to lose control of the muscles of his eyes. It was as if an invisible, impersonal hand had without warning severed the rope of living fibre that held his eyeballs in their place, and, as he heard the sentence read, they drifted, unmoored and without destination, in his heavy skull.

Heinrich Baab was found guilty on fifty-five counts of murder, on twenty-one counts of attempted murder, on thirty counts of assault and battery while holding office, combined with six counts of employing coercion, on five separate counts of employing coercion, and on twenty-two counts of deprivation of liberty. He was sentenced to hard labor for life, the

loss of all civil rights, and the costs of the trial to be borne
by him, save for four charges (one of murder and three of
attempted murder) on which he had been acquitted for lack
of conclusive evidence. And, as Judge Wirtzfeld proceeded
to deliver a two-hour justification address in which he deplored the fact that the criminal in the dock should have been
of German nationality, the face of the young court guard
could be seen for an instant turned toward the press bench,
as clear as light with vindicated pride, before it was lost
among the faces of the crowd.

The stories in this book do not proceed from the sight of one
young man's face in a courtroom. They are, on the contrary,
the record of that painstaking search through time and emotion which led eventually to a court of justice. They are the
introduction to the trial. For here, in a trial which involved
in its essence every German whether he were in or out of
Germany, was defined in unmistakable terms the pattern for
a revolution which has not taken place, the outline for action
which might spring not from an outraged national honor, but
from the outrage of a deeper, wider honor. Here was offered
the vocabulary for that concerted protest which has through
history remained so alien, so repugnant even, to the people
of Germany—the protest which wells from a wronged and
broken but still wildly beating heart. Yet even Judge Wirtzfeld in his justification address expressed his regret that Baab
should have been not a foreigner but a citizen of Germany.
One of my great friends, a German writer, a refugee, wrote
me last week from New York: "The consequences of our failure as a nation are manifest in practically every individual.
We Germans have never fought on the barricades for freedom
. . . we have never tried and condemned one of our own
kings, or presidents, or leaders. We have never liberated ourselves." Here, in a criminal court, was the nucleus of revo-

lution offered, and the offer made not on foreign, but on German terms.

How many Germans are ready to accept the obligation of those "German terms"? An official in the Frankfurt city administration said to me a few days ago: "The Nuremberg trials were a highly proper proceeding in all except one respect: there should have been German judges as well on the bench." The stage to be prepared by others was his solution, then, as the union of Western nations is now being prepared by others, with German figures called in for the finale, although, until the last act of both productions, they had been outspoken critics of the plot, the libretto, and the score. How many who are not officials and who have neither realization of guilt nor knowledge of guilt (as those Germans of whom I write in the story "The Lovers of Gain") could be brought to accept a national responsibility? They dwell on their separate islands of pain, each waiting for a hand to reach out to him, for the word of explanation to be given, the inductive word of love to be pronounced in a language they can understand. For them there is no hope, no life, no self-liberation possible; they are the black flakes "spewed up out of the flames."

In this collection of stories there is one about a Wehrmacht soldier. On the basis of the evidence this story, "Cabaret," submits he might be taken for a self-liberated German, but "there are caves and hiding places and dungeons" within the German soul. Although he put on a skit which derided both Hitler and Goebbels with such vigor that it assuaged a portion of the German conscience by humor, in another program of this political cabaret, the Wehrmacht soldier played another part. He gave himself the role of an American Military Government officer, and when the curtain parted, he could be seen seated with his feet on his desk, chewing gum, and reading a copy of the *Stars and Stripes*, while his German secretary, wearing American nylons, her nails varnished blood red, handed out employment blanks to former high-ranking and now destitute Wehrmacht officers who sought employment tending furnaces or doing other menial tasks in the homes of American Occupation personnel. The situation was comprehensible, the repartee plausible, but the uproarious dénouement came when a former Wehrmacht general, standing in rags before the gum-chewing American, recognized this official as a former German citizen.

"Mein Gott, I knew you in Berlin!" the man in rags cried. "Your name is Blumenfeld, and you got out in 1933!"

"Wa-a-al, now it's 1948, and my name's Flowerfield, get it?" the American official answered, and the spectators at the *Weinstube* tables rocked with delight.

I discussed this skit with the Wehrmacht soldier, and he said if the use of a Jewish name seemed distasteful, he would change it to something else, but he could not see how anyone could object to it. Such humor was a far cry from the spirit that had destroyed the lives of men in gas chambers, he said to me one evening over wine. Five minutes of humor at the expense of a refugee could scarcely prepare the way for murder. But he changed the name of the American official to Hochstrasse, and then the audience saw nothing funny in the skit, and it was dropped from the program of the cabaret. And my friend in New York, who was once a German himself, would have answered: "Until there has been a national upheaval, a cleaning of our house by our own hands, the twilight will remain."

Design by David Bullen
Typeset in Mergenthaler Caslon Old Face #2
by Wilsted & Taylor
Printed by Maple-Vail
on acid-free paper